The Culture of the Second Cold War

The Culture of the Second Cold War

Richard Sakwa

ANTHEM PRESS

Anthem Press
An imprint of Wimbledon Publishing Company
www.anthempress.com

This edition first published in UK and USA 2025
by ANTHEM PRESS
75–76 Blackfriars Road, London SE1 8HA, UK
or PO Box 9779, London SW19 7ZG, UK
and
244 Madison Ave #116, New York, NY 10016, USA

© 2025 Richard Sakwa

The author asserts the moral right to be identified as the author of this work.

All rights reserved. Without limiting the rights under copyright reserved above,
no part of this publication may be reproduced, stored or introduced into
a retrieval system, or transmitted, in any form or by any means
(electronic, mechanical, photocopying, recording or otherwise),
without the prior written permission of both the copyright
owner and the above publisher of this book.

British Library Cataloguing-in-Publication Data
A catalogue record for this book is available from the British Library.

Library of Congress Cataloging-in-Publication Data: 2024946189
A catalog record for this book has been requested.

ISBN-13: 978-1-83999-297-1 (Pbk)
ISBN-10: 1-83999-297-2 (Pbk)

Cover Credit: © Adams / Telegraph Media Group Limited 2014; and the
Cartoon Centre of University of Kent

This title is also available as an e-book.

CONTENTS

Acknowledgements		ix
Introduction		1
1.	Back to cold war	7
2.	World orders	23
3.	The great split	45
4.	Fighting Cold War II	59
5.	Sanctions and moral economy	83
6.	Miscommunications	99
7.	Why this cold war is different	127
8.	Conclusion	151
Bibliography		161
Index		175

These are the only genuine ideas: the ideas of the shipwrecked. All the rest is rhetoric, posturing, farce. He who does not really feel himself lost, is lost without remission; that is to say, he never finds himself, never comes up against his own reality.

Ortega y Gasset, Revolt of the Masses, 1929

ACKNOWLEDGEMENTS

Enormous thanks go to the many people who have contributed to the development of this work. Balihar Sanghera provided many thoughtful comments, forcing me to rethink some issues, although it will take another full-scale work to do justice to his views. The anonymous reviewers have been exceptionally helpful, especially the one who provided many pages of detailed and substantive analysis. Some of the book's material was presented at the International Political Anthropology summer symposium in Santa Anna Pelago, Apennines, Italy, in July 2024, prompting much fruitful discussion. I am grateful to Agnese Horvath and Arpad Szakolczai for their hospitality and unlimited intellectual fecundity, and other members of the 'neo-Platonist' colloquium, including Bjorn Thomassen, as well as Giuliana Parotto and Harald Wydra in earlier years, with special thanks to Travis D. Smith, for his uniquely orthogonal view on international affairs and helpful comments. Many have been a source of inspiration and support, and above all friendship – too many to name but certainly not forgotten. Above all, I am grateful to Antonio Cerella, who originally suggested writing this book and who has been an unfailing source of support and ideas. Of course, none bears responsibility for anything stated in this work. Some of the virtues and all the vices are my own.

INTRODUCTION

This book began life as a talk at Nottingham Trent University in February 2023. The audience was appreciative and the discussion lively and engaged. However, I discovered later that complaints were raised about the event. The content of the talk was criticised, even though it was presented more in the form of an open-ended enquiry into the causes, course and consequences of the Russo-Ukrainian war than an *ex-cathedra* statement of dogma. The complaint carried threatening implications, not least for Dr Antonio Cerella, who had invited me. Fortunately, the audience feedback on the session was very favourable, and the matter was laid to rest without any serious consequences. The more positive outcome was that Antonio suggested that I write up the lecture to become the inaugural publication in his series on International Security and Sustainability for Anthem, which I was honoured and delighted to do, and the outcome is this book.

Unfortunately, the incident at Nottingham is far from the only instance in which the 'cancel culture' which accompanies and aggravates Cold War II has affected me. In 2016, I was invited to teach a course on European international relations at the College of Europe in Natolin, on the outskirts of Warsaw. Over the years I had taught the subject many times, accompanied always by lively and healthy debate. This time, from the outset I noticed something different, with a solid phalanx of Polish and Ukrainian students staring aggressively and refusing to participate in discussions. In the end, I asked one of the brightest students, from Germany, what was going on. She told me, glancing around to check that we were not being overheard, that 'we have been thoroughly brain-washed'. There could be no questioning of the righteousness of Western actions, the expansion of the North Atlantic Treaty Organization (NATO) was an unmitigated good, and the European Union (EU) was the repository of all the virtues. By contrast, Russia was the fount of all evil, and any questioning of these postulates was not only illegitimate but effectively prohibited. This does not make for a healthy scholarly environment. The line between education and indoctrination, analysis and advocacy, is dangerously blurred.

There have been other cases. In July 2023, I was invited to contribute an article on Russia and Europe to a special issue of the journal *Europe Now*. The invitation noted that 'essays in *Europe Now* are factually-based essays of opinions rather than scholarly articles', which seemed fine, but the enclosed sample article worried me. It represented the worst sort of closed thinking on Europe's future. Progress was unilinear, the future was 'European', although accompanied by an indissoluble tie with the United States. Any suggestion that history may hold plural outcomes and that the return of the scourge of war to the European continent was the result of folly on all sides was considered unacceptable. I was inclined to pull out, but I hesitated until the choice was made for me. The invitation stressed that 'All of us welcome debate, discussion, and dissent', but in September I received the message from the editors: 'We regret to inform you that we need to withdraw our invitation to you to contribute an essay to our special issue of *Europe Now*.' The given reason was a *Grayzone* interview with Aaron Maté, one of the most perceptive and well-informed analysts of contemporary international affairs, of April 2022. The note asserted that I took 'a strident position against one party in the conflict and for the other'. I do not believe that was the case and instead I sought to challenge extreme partisanship for a more balanced analysis. Either way, I was 'cancelled' and that was the end of the matter.

More disturbingly, the 'yellow press', as the right-wing popular newspapers were once called, took up the cause, questioning whether my intellectual agenda was the result of funding from the Kremlin. Here, two issues are conflated: the propriety of engagement with Russian politicians, academics and cultural organisations in wartime, which is an important and relevant issue on which views may differ (I respect the stance of those who defend a boycott, although I disagree with it); and the financial issue, the attempt to reduce a political stance to a venal one. Illicit sources of funding of course should be exposed, but the attempt to traduce a political position with the tawdry brush of corruption is a different matter. The gutter press, of course, makes its living by destroying lives, now amplified by the heaving tide of defamation on social media. Many years ago, that great doyenne of Russian language studies, Irina Kirillova, advised me to steer well clear of social media, and I am grateful to her for having spared me much (although not all) unpleasantness.

These incidents raise some disturbing questions. My fundamental view of international affairs has not changed over the decades, although of course responding to developments. I remain opposed to reductive and politicised approaches to the study of any nation or social system. Context and comparison are crucial. This does not mean relativism, since there is no fundamental incompatibility between commitment to a set of ethical norms and the dispassionate study of international affairs. Equally, I remain politically a committed European, but of the pan-European sort advocated by Charles de Gaulle, Mikhail Gorbachev and François Mitterrand, dedicated to the creation of some sort of inclusive security and political community from Lisbon to Vladivostok. This vision combines a strong sense of national sovereignty with substantive internationalism based on the norms and laws of the United Nations (UN)-based Charter International System established in 1945. However, the intellectual environment and scholarly culture have changed dramatically. What was once critical questioning and the interrogation of received wisdom has become suspect and renders one a pariah. Certain texts and sources, especially if they emanate from Russia or China, are considered suspect when not cancelled entirely. A Manichean vision of the world has become the staple of the Atlantic community.

What happened? Two trends have combined. First, at the international level, the world has sleepwalked into renewed cold war. The anticipation of some sort of positive peace at the end of the Cold War I, the subject of my book *The Lost Peace* (Yale, 2023), gave way to a quarter century of cold peace (1989–2014).[1] None of the fundamental questions of European security were resolved. The negative peace of those years nurtured conflicts that now define our era. In 2014, with the intensification of the crisis over Ukraine, this turned into renewed cold war. Cold War II is very different from the first conflict of that name, although it shares the characteristics of a cold war. This book discusses the origins and causes of the renewed conflict, but the focus is on the characteristics of the new era of confrontation. Second, at the domestic level, the way that Cold War I ended reshaped political and social relations. The triumphalism associated with 'end of history' ideologies, the false universalism and the enduring militarism and hegemonism of the leading power, the United States, and the isolation of elites and the rise of 'populist' forms of political engagement, generated antagonistic forms of political communication and exacerbated the crisis of representation that were long evident in Western societies. On the other side, countries like Russia, China and India have more forcefully asserted their distinctive paths, accompanied by a repudiation of the view that history is unidirectional and tends towards the world becoming a version of the 'advanced' West.

The end of World War II and the founding of the UN represented a moment when a positive peace order appeared in prospect – what can be

---

1 Richard Sakwa, *The Lost Peace: How the West Failed to Prevent a Second Cold War* (New Haven and London, Yale University Press, 2023).

called 'the spirit of 1945'.² The meeting of Soviet and American forces on the Elbe in April 1945 demonstrated the possibility of cooperation between the great powers to achieve common goals. The world was coming out of the most catastrophic war in its history, accompanied by genocide, the destruction of entire cities, and millions killed and maimed on the various fronts. In establishing the Charter International System, humanity vowed that it could do better. 'Never again' was the resounding anima of the time. In the event, within two years Cold War I was in full flood. In a cold war, the practices of a negative peace predominate, where the potential for war is ever-present but all parties strive to limit escalation under the shadow of the nuclear cloud. The spirit of 1945 was revived at the end of the Cold War in 1989. With the fall of the Berlin Wall in November and the ensuing dismantling of the iron curtain, the end of classical ideological confrontation and the reunification of the continent, the potential for a positive peace order was restored. Once again, the opportunity was squandered. The failure to build a European security order encompassing all of the states from Lisbon to Vladivostok generated tensions that ended in renewed cold war and worse. Today, even a negative peace would be an achievement. The constraints and guard rails of the earlier cold war have not only been dismantled but the culture that generated them has been lost.

It remains a puzzle to me as to many others why this is the case. As I give talks up and down the land and across the world, the most frequent question is why – why we have once again become embroiled in a cold war? Have we learned nothing from the past? I certainly do not have the definitive answer, but the following factors are involved. First, the generation who participated in and then lived in the shadow of the Second World War is dying out, and with it the visceral horror of war. War as the continuation of policy, now armed by the moral certitude of having history on your side, has once again become normalised. Second, the nuclear apocalypse seems to have lost some of its terror. I remember how during the Cuban missile crisis of October 1962 my father was glued to the radio, listening minute by minute if we would survive a day longer. I was just a boy, but I still recall the sheer panic of the time. Now, a certain irresponsible recklessness has overtaken society, as if the earlier red lines no longer matter, and that a nuclear war can be fought and won. We are living through a slow-motion Cuban missile crisis, and if we survived by extraordinary chance the first-time round, we may not be so lucky

---

2 On positive peace, see Johan Galtung, 'An Editorial', *Journal of Peace Research*, Vol. 1, No. 1, 1964, pp. 1–4; and idem, 'Violence, Peace, and Peace Research', *Journal of Peace Research*, Vol. 6, No. 3, 1969, pp. 167–91.

this time. Third, the new generation of Western leaders has been socialised into accepting and policing the hyper-normality into which they were born. Moral righteousness accompanied by ignorance and disdain for the abnormality outside of their garden of civilisation reinforces the recklessness and irresponsibility that their forebears would have considered contemptible. Fourth, elements of the missionary zeal of nineteenth-century liberal imperialism have been restored. This takes many forms, including a revival of the Russophobia that characterised that century, with a particular intensity during the Crimean War of 1853–56. It was also in these years (October 1860) that an Anglo-French force burned down the Summer Palace, the Garden of Eternal Brightness, in Beijing. Walking around the restored palace today, one can only wonder at the barbarism of the act and the arrogance that inspired it.

This book does not claim that Cold War II encompasses the entirety of international politics today. It is, nevertheless, a crucial element in the larger picture. In that composition, we are living through an epochal shift in the balance of economic power away from the West towards the rising and returning powers of the East and the Global South, the countries of the World Majority. This does not mean that the United States will not retain its economic and military preeminence for some time, but its relative position is declining. The economies of the EU have been dashed against the rocks of the Russo-Ukrainian war and are trapped in the intensifying Sino-US conflict, and may well be damaged beyond repair for at least a generation. Globalisation is also changing its forms, as supply chains are shortened and reshored following the shock of the Covid-19 pandemic and the Fourth Industrial Revolution takes hold, with Artificial Intelligence destined to play an ever-greater part in our lives. The weaponisation of the institutions of international economics stimulates the creation of alternative non-dollar payment systems and developmental bodies. Technological innovations and progress in the life sciences open up extraordinary vistas for social development and the all-round improvement in human dignity. Instead, we remain trapped in sterile, regressive and thoroughly avoidable conflicts.

This relatively short work focuses on the metapolitics – the profound structures – of Cold War II. The term 'culture' is used to describe the deeper processes, attitudes and perceptions of the participants. It explores the unseen and deep-seated structures that shape the decisions of individual politicians and is thus 'anthropological' in its approach. There is a distinctive culture of cold war, which pervades the entirety of a society, shaping morality, political culture, economies and the very nature of humanity.[3] As Raymond Williams

---

[3] See Terry Eagleton, 'Where Does Culture Come From?', *London Review of Books*, 25 April 2024, pp. 5–7.

wrote in his *Culture and Society* in 1958, culture is 'a whole way of life'. This is broader than the classical political science concept of political culture, the shared views and normative judgements held by a population, but encompasses the entirety of societal and elite behaviour and policy. It is on this basis that the extreme polarisation of this cold war, unprecedented outside of wartime, is examined. The criminalisation of the enemy is inherently dangerous and provokes a cycle of hatred and violence that ultimately threatens destabilisation on a global scale.

It does not have to be this way. This work calls for the supremacy of a renewed international legal framework for relations between rivals (at the normative level) and a revival of the spirit of 1945 (at the cultural level). The analysis is designed to prompt discussion and debate, and reflection on the current state of international affairs. The earlier cold war conflict between communism and capitalism has given way to a more amorphous but, paradoxically, more intense and pervasive struggle between representations of the political good. The book has some analysis of diplomatic history and processes in international politics, but the focus is on the underlying attitudes, ideologies and practices that have generated and sustained Cold War II. The very fact that an introduction of this sort has been written is indicative of the culture of this new cold war. By examining its features, a path towards a more positive peace can perhaps be found.

Canterbury, September 2024

Chapter 1

BACK TO COLD WAR

Cold War I ended in 1989, but the competitive logic that provoked the conflict was not transcended. The anticipated transformation in the conduct of international politics failed to be realised and instead cold war assumed new forms. This gave rise to the quarter century of the cold peace to 2014. The instruments that had fought the original cold war remained in place. On the Western side, this above all means NATO, which after some hesitation expanded from the 16 members when the Cold War ended to 32 by 2024. NATO is reinforced by the vast military–industrial and security–intelligence complex in the United States, as well as America's extensive network of bilateral security agreements spanning the globe, notably the security treaties with Japan and South Korea.

On the Russian side, the security apparatus inherited from the Soviet Union was reorganised but only partially reformed. The system as a whole remains largely in place. The Lubyanka building in central Moscow remains the headquarters of what is now called the Federal Security Service; the Foreign Intelligence Service inherited the buildings and networks of similarly profiled departments of the Soviet KGB, while military intelligence (the GRU) continues much as before. Destabilised by the Soviet collapse and the profound economic crisis of the 1990s, under Vladimir Putin's leadership the country regained confidence and coherence. The crunch issue between the two sides was NATO enlargement, but this was only symbolic of the larger failure to create an overarching security order encompassing the entire continent from Lisbon to Vladivostok. On assuming the presidency in 2000, Vladimir Putin sought to resolve the potential security dilemma by suggesting that Russia should join NATO. This was rejected by Washington, since it would threaten its undisputed leadership of the Atlantic alliance and change the character of the Political West in its entirety. More profoundly, if all the countries of Europe joined NATO, then against whom would the collective defence body defend? If all joined, then perhaps none needed to?

What Is a Cold War?

A cold war is qualitatively different from a traditional adversarial relationship. Based on analysis of Cold War I, Robert Legvold outlines five distinctive characteristics. First, ideological division, with starkly different representations of the desirable political and economic order. Second, each side holds the other responsible for the conflict, with no scope for introspection or reflection about how one's own actions contribute to stoking division. Third, both sides assume that the conflict is driven not out of the interaction of two countries but from the character of the other side: 'The essence of the problem [is] the essence of the adversary.' The struggle becomes one not over interests as over purpose and supposed values. Fourth, as a consequence, change can only come about if the other side somehow becomes something different, or at least is ready fundamentally to rethink its foreign policy. This is what happened at the end of the original Cold War in the late 1980s, when the last Soviet leader, Mikhail Gorbachev, reconfigured Soviet foreign policy in its entirety.

Finally, while cooperation is possible, it can only be 'limited and transactional, not cumulative and transformative'.[1] Thus, arms control negotiations between the superpowers following the brush with Armageddon in the Cuban missile crisis of October 1962 led to a number of agreements, including a telephone 'hotline' between Moscow and Washington and a partial test ban treaty, followed by a period of détente in the early 1970s. Nevertheless, the underlying logic of conflict was not transcended. This gave rise to various proxy wars (Vietnam, Angola, Mozambique, Ethiopia, Afghanistan and Nicaragua) in postcolonial borderlands accompanied by sustained ideological conflict. The main protagonists throughout avoided direct military confrontation. For Barry Buzan, the defining feature of a cold war is the presence of weapons of mass destruction, and thus cold wars by definition could not exist before the twentieth century. He stresses the centrality of cyberwar in Cold War II, as well as the shared-fate threat of climate change.[2]

In Cold War II, at least two conflicts run in parallel: the long-term shift in the balance of power away from the West towards the rising powers of Eurasia, Asia and the Global South and entrenched cold war practices, regenerated as a result of the failure to transform European international politics at the end of Cold War I. The collapse of the Soviet Union in 1991 left

---

1 Robert Legvold, 'Ending the Cold War with Russia', *The National Interest*, 2 February 2022, https://nationalinterest.org/feature/ending-new-cold-war-russia-199997. See also Robert Legvold, *Return to Cold War* (Cambridge, Polity, 2016).
2 Barry Buzan, 'A New Cold War? The Case for a General Concept', *International Politics*, Vol. 61, No. 2, 2024, pp. 239–57.

the United States with no rival to act as a check on its global ambitions, while domestically the cold war military–ideological complex faced little internal pushback as the 'democratic internationalist' bipartisan foreign policy consensus was consolidated in the era of unipolar globalisation. In Russia, the old Soviet elite and security apparatus was reconstituted, no longer driven by the ideology of Communist universalism but by geopolitical concerns about defending Russia's sovereignty and great power status. China came late to the Cold War II party, but following three decades of spectacular economic growth after the reforms launched by Deng Xiaoping in 1978, its leaders in the 2000s gradually came round to the view that the era of the country's 'peaceful rise' had come to an end.

The historic opportunity to build a just and sustainable peace, with shared prosperity and development for all, was squandered.[3] Instead, the world plunged into another cold war. The Russo-Ukrainian war from 2022, like the Korean and Vietnam wars earlier, marked an intense phase in the conflict, but as in those conflicts, the great powers sought to avoid direct confrontation. A cold war can play out in many different ways. Like a game of chess, the rules remain the same, but the outcome depends on the skill and experience of the players. Cold War I was static and defensive in Europe, with forces entrenched along the Iron Curtain, and the opposed 'sphere of interests' respected. The Western powers did not intervene when Soviet forces crushed reform movements in East Berlin in 1953, in Hungary in 1956 or in Czechoslovakia in 1968. The new cold war is more dynamic and therefore more dangerous. The dividing lines in the earlier conflicts were known and taken into account, but the easily understood struggle between communism and capitalism has now given way to an amorphous, and ultimately contingent, contest between great powers.[4] Couched in the vague language of a struggle between democracy and autocracy, the real *casus belli* remains uncertain. The antagonism is between contrasting models of development, modernity and ultimately civilisational perspectives, accompanied by a very specific contest for hegemony in international politics. It is also accompanied by physical and mental dividing lines across Europe. The iron curtain is back with a vengeance.[5]

---

[3] See, for example, Andrew Bacevich, *The Age of Illusions: How America Squandered Its Cold War Victory* (New York, Metropolitan Books, 2020).

[4] Of course, there were many types of capitalism and many communisms – Soviet, Chinese, Cuban, Vietnamese, Yugoslav and more – so Cold War I was never a simple binary conflict, although at the superpower level bipolarity was highly articulated.

[5] James Jackson, 'Poland Unveils New Iron Curtain to Defend Europe', *Daily Telegraph*, 27 May 2024, www.telegraph.co.uk/world-news/2024/05/27/poland-unveils-tusk-line

Russia's invasion of Ukraine in February 2022 seemed to offer greater moral clarity, but contrary to the general perspective of the Political West, the war was far from unprovoked. The conflict emerged out of a decades-long failure to create a genuinely pan-continental European security order, which then focused on the internationalisation of the internal contradictions of Ukrainian state development.[6] All participants share responsibility for the security dilemma that provoked the war.[7] In the more fragmented Cold War II, the line of confrontation at first ran between Moscow and Washington, reprising the fundamental axis of Cold War I. The issues that had provoked the first cold war had not been resolved and fed into the second. China played a relatively small part in Cold War I, and adroit US diplomacy exploited divisions between Beijing and Moscow to bring China into greater alignment with the West in the 1970s. This time, inept US diplomacy reinforced the Russo-Sino alignment that had been in the making since the demise of the Soviet Union in 1991. In January 2018, Washington launched a trade war with China that signalled an end to the deepening of the entanglement of the two economies, accompanied by recriminations, technological and trade 'decoupling', and political estrangement. Beijing and Washington pivoted against each other, and this ultimately became the main line of division in Cold War II. Whether they like it or not, other states are drawn into the gravitational field of resumed cold war. There is also renewed resistance to the malign effects of cold war. Like the Non-Aligned Movement of the earlier era and the Group of 77 (G-77), the Global South resists being drawn into a conflict not of its making.

Cold War II is very different from the first in both form and content. The contestants are far more integrated economically, although as the cold war intensifies a global 'sorting' is taking place. Russia is separating from Western economies, and China, along with Russia, adopts measures to insulate itself from technological, financial and other sanctions. Equally, this cold war is less binary than the first, with a reduced bipolar structure.[8] Instead of the stark Soviet–United States confrontation, there are at least four major powers

---

-defences-to-protect-europe/?utm_medium=email&utm_source=CampaignMonitor_Editorial&utm_campaig.n.

6 Richard Sakwa, 'Realism, Ethics and the Ukraine War', in Anton Leist and Rolf Zimmermann (eds), *After the War? How the Ukraine War Challenges Political Theories* (Berlin, De Gruyter, 2023), pp. 55–88.

7 For a sophisticated Ukrainian perspective, see Volodymyr Ishchenko, *Towards the Abyss: Ukraine from Maidan to War* (London, Verso, 2024).

8 A point made by Robin Niblett, *The New Cold War: How the Contest between the US and China Will Shape Our Century* (New York, Atlantic Books, 2024).

involved: China, India, Russia and the United States; and a range of significant middle powers: Iran, North Korea, South Africa, Turkey and many more. Nevertheless, some things remain the same. As Hal Brands notes, proxy wars were a constant in Cold War I, and today 'Two vast alliances are squaring off, albeit indirectly, on European battlegrounds. The fight in Ukraine has become the first global conflict of a new cold war.'[9] Cold wars by definition are permanently on a knife edge of potential escalation into outright military confrontation. Accidents and misjudgements can tip the balance. Christopher Clark, the author of a study of how the major powers 'sleepwalked' into war in 1914, notes that the bipolar stability of the Cold War 'made way for a more complex and unpredictable array of forces, including declining empires and rising powers – a condition that invites comparison with the Europe of 1914'.[10]

China explicitly repudiates bloc politics and military alliances, but the dynamic pattern of relationships between blocs, alignments and affiliations once again shapes international politics. Cold War II differs from the earlier conflict just as World War II differs from World War I, but in both cases the second conflict was provoked by unresolved contradictions in the ending of the first. Contrasting representations of the appropriate peace order precipitated a security dilemma and ultimately conflict. NATO's *Strategic Concept 2022* demonstrates just how far the global strategic environment has deteriorated. Adopted by the Madrid summit in June 2022, the Preface asserts that NATO remains a 'bulwark of the rules-based international order', while Russia's 'war of aggression against Ukraine has shattered peace and gravely altered our security environment'.[11] The gloves are off and Cold War II is in full flood. It is even argued that we have entered the long slide into World War III. As long as direct armed conflict between the major powers is avoided, it is best conceptually to think in terms of renewed cold war – but one conducted in the foothills of World War III.

---

9 Hal Brands, 'Ukraine Is Now a World War: and Putin Is Gaining Friends', *Bloomberg*, 12 May 2024, https://www.bloomberg.com/opinion/features/2024-05-12/china-russia-iran-have-made-ukraine-a-world-war-against-us-europe.

10 Christopher Clark, *The Sleepwalkers: How Europe Went to War in 1914* (London, Penguin, 2013), pp. xxv–xxvi.

11 *NATO 2022: Strategic Concept*, Adopted by the Madrid NATO Summit, 29 June 2022, https://www.nato.int/nato_static_fl2014/assets/pdf/2022/6/pdf/290622-strategic-concept.pdf.

The Persistence of Cold War

Cold War I ended in 1989 amid hopes that a new era of peace and development would ensue. This would be a positive peace, rather than the negative peace typical of a cold war. A negative peace is defined simply as the absence of war, whereas a positive peace order is characterised by a substantive cooperative, multilateral and developmental agenda.[12] In 1990, the United States and its allies worked with the Soviet Union to reverse the Iraqi leader Saddam Hussein's seizure of Kuwait. The military intervention in early 1991 was sanctioned by the UN. The combination of efforts seemed to herald an era when the UN-based Charter International System would finally work as its architects intended. Fundamental matters of war and peace would be adjudicated by the UN's Security Council, thus tempering the anarchy of international relations. It was not to be. Instead, the 25 years between 1989 and 2014 were marked by an ever-cooler cold peace between the United States and Russia, accompanied by chilling relations between the United States and China. The forced change of regime in Ukraine in February 2014, following prolonged protests in the central square in Kiev (the Maidan), brought to power a militantly nationalist administration. Russia considered the overthrow of the legitimately elected president, Viktor Yanukovych, a coup and responded in kind. It seized Crimea and, later, supported an anti-Maidan insurgency in Ukraine's Donbass region. The imposition of sanctions against Russia signalled the onset of Cold War II, which endures to this day.

With the benefit of hindsight, we can now see that Cold War I did not end in 1989 but simply changed its form. The cold peace was accompanied by numerous declarations of 'strategic partnership' and even friendship, but the fundamental structural issue – Russia's place in a world in which the United States would fight to maintain hegemony – was not resolved. In Europe, contradictions in Ukrainian state building were exploited by all sides.[13] Cold War containment of Russia resumed. This was marked by a consistent strategy to prevent Russia establishing anything like its own hegemony in Northern (post-Soviet) Eurasia, and in particular vis-à-vis Ukraine. Hegemony, it should be stressed, is not the same as an imposed dominance, but works best when based on consent. The neo-containment strategy was couched in terms of defending the sovereignty and independence of the post-Soviet states, a

---

12 In addition to earlier references, see also Johan Galtung, 'Social Cosmology and the Concept of Peace', *Journal of Peace Research*, Vol. 17, No. 2, 1981, pp. 183–99; idem, *Peace by Peaceful Means: Peace and Conflict, Development and Civilisation* (Oslo, PRIO, 1996).
13 Paul D'Anieri, *Ukraine and Russia: From Civilized Divorce to Uncivil War* (Cambridge, Cambridge University Press, 2019).

worthy goal but one that would have been better achieved without divisive external interference. The American strategy suited the nationalist agenda pursued by liberal and nationalist factions within Ukraine, who gratefully received Washington's support. The old Soviet temporal ideal of 'building communism' gave way to the spatial goal of joining 'Europe', presented as the solution to the country's developmental and political contradictions. Membership of the EU and NATO are represented as achieving the peak of civilisation, when in fact they constitute no more than joining a Political West that is in comparative decline.[14] Worse, this excluded the part of the population committed to maintaining cultural and economic ties with Russia and who defended a more traditional 'Soviet' plural representation of national identity.[15] The result was the exacerbation of intra-Ukrainian identity conflicts, entwined with regional and oligarch struggles. The contest between the United States and Russia was not as overt as military and ideological confrontation with the Soviet Union, but tempered by lingering aspirations for a more positive post-Cold War peace order. The final illusions about transcending the logic of cold war were shattered in 2014.

In an age when complexity is reduced to simple binaries – good vs evil, democracies vs autocracies and civilisation vs barbarism – Olga Baysha presents a healthy dose of sophistication. She gives voice to the 'other Ukraine', a society that is itself complex but which repudiates monolithic representations of Ukrainian identity. She notes how populist discourse was given a distinctive inflection. Instead of the usual contrast between the good populace against evil elites, the line was drawn between the civilisational (transnational) populism of the post-Maidan Ukrainian leadership and the allegedly regressive (Soviet) anti-Maidan forces. This civilisational conflict was not susceptible to resolution by traditional diplomatic means.[16] Any compromise in the struggle against tyranny and barbarism is considered worse than appeasement – it entails a betrayal of one's own values. This was accompanied by what she calls the 'uni-progressive' ideology that triumphed in the postcommunist era, the unidirectional view that progressive social change can only take the form of Westernization. As she notes:

---

14 See, for example, Glenn Diesen, *Europe as the Western Peninsula of Greater Eurasia: Geoeconomic Regions in a Multipolar World* (Lanham, Rowman & Littlefield, 2021).
15 Nicolai Petro, *The Tragedy of Ukraine: What Classical Greek Tragedy Can Teach Us about Conflict Resolution* (Berlin, De Gruyter, 2022).
16 Olga Baysha, *War, Peace and Populist Discourse in Ukraine* (London, Routledge, 2023), p. 5 and *passim*.

> [T]he 'progressive' imaginary, which envisages progress in the unidirectional terms of catching up with the 'more advanced' Western condition, is inherently anti-democratic and deeply antagonistic. Instead of fostering an inclusive democratic process in which all strata of populations holding different views are involved, it draws solid dividing frontiers between 'progressive' and 'retrograde' forces, deepening existing antagonisms and provoking new ones; it also naturalizes the hierarchies of the global neocolonial power of the West.[17]

This can also be described as the hyper-normalisation of a particular social order, which effectively subsumes alternatives and 'de-normalises' opposition and forces binary choices. In our case, the ambitions of the post-Cold War Political West expanded to the point that all alternatives were delegitimated, considered abnormal and deviant. The Political West claims to be the only rational world; others are not only irrational but also dangerous, hence need to be contained and constrained. This is a precise definition of a cold war.

The cold war logic of containment continues. Russian hegemony in post-Soviet Eurasia was stymied, while its ambitions elsewhere were constrained. Under the leadership of Boris Yeltsin in the 1990s this was not much of a problem, since Russia focused on an unprecedented social and economic transformation that created the rudiments of a market economy, although distorted by the overweening power of so-called oligarchs. Even then, despite elements of cooperation, there were conflicts in the former Yugoslavia in which clear policy differences emerged. This culminated in NATO's 78-day bombing campaign against the Federal Republic of Yugoslavia from March 1999, which rang all sorts of alarm bells in Moscow. On the 25th anniversary of the bombing, the Russian scholar Timofei Bordachev notes that

> The fundamental significance of NATO's aggression against Yugoslavia for international politics was that it was a collective attack, perpetrated by a large group of Western countries, against a sovereign state, and marked the watershed between a time when a peaceful world order could still be expected, and the resumption of the Cold War in a new form.[18]

---

17 Olga Baysha, *Miscommunicating Social Change: Lessons from Russia and Ukraine* (Lanham, Lexington Books, 2019), p. xi.
18 Timofei Bordachev, '25 Years of the New Cold War', *Valdai Discussion Club*, 27 March 2024, https://valdaiclub.com/a/highlights/25-years-of-the-new-cold-war/.

For Bordachev, Cold War II began in 1999, and his view is shared by many in Russia. What is not in doubt is that accumulating tensions in Russia's relations with the West finally boiled over into direct confrontation in 2014. How can we explain the failure of the post-Cold War peace to hold?

Clash of World Orders

A binary logic shapes international politics today, generating cold war Manicheanism. The Political West insists that it is upholding a consistent set of values, which are egregiously breached by illiberal states, while the latter point to the deleterious and immoral consequences of America's struggle to maintain its global supremacy. Liberal and illiberal states mimic the behaviour of the other, blurring their purported distinctiveness. There is no meeting of minds across this divide. Before analysing the bifurcation in international politics, we should define the international system in whose framework the distinctive representations of world order clash.

The UN-based international system was established in 1945, reinforced later by a growing body of declarations and protocols, as well as the corpus of international law. This is the normative order represented by the Charter system, establishing a framework for legitimate interventions and setting the standards and benchmark for relations between states. This is not world government, but the UN and its agencies, as well as the associated body of international public law, set the normative parameters for the conduct of international affairs. Those who transgress the rules are subject to censure, but there is no world police force to enforce appropriate behaviour. Intervention can and has been sanctioned by the UN Security Council, but in recent years joint action has been stymied by the veto power exercised by the five permanent members (China, France, Russia, the UK and the United States). The International Court of Justice (ICJ, the World Court), created originally by the League of Nations in 1921 but re-established in San Francisco in June 1945, lacks enforcement or policing powers, as demonstrated repeatedly in the Middle East. Since July 2002 and the adoption of the Rome Statutes, this is complemented by the International Criminal Court (ICC), a body condemned as susceptible to politicisation by the Western powers. The ICC has done little to deter impunity for grave crimes, due to the unwillingness, or inability, of the Security Council P5 to support the Court.

Within this international system are the various 'world orders' bringing together constellations of states, accompanied by associated military and ideological appurtenances.[19] The world order associated with the Soviet

---

19 Cf. G. John Ikenberry, 'Three Worlds: the West, East and South and the Competition to Shape Global Order', *International Affairs*, Vol. 100, No. 1, 2004, pp. 121–38.

Union collapsed in 1989–91, leaving only the one led by the United States, what in this book is called the Political West. There are two domains of the Political West.[20] The first is the 'commonwealth' aspect, cognate although not the same as the liberal international order (see below). Its roots lie in the free trade regime advanced by Britain, which fostered the 'first globalisation' between 1870 and 1914 based on the gold standard. In the post-war years, the United States assumed the role of champion of free trade, open markets, secure navigation, liberal values and competitive democracy. Its origins reach back further, to the Enlightenment and its views on progress, rationality, free trade and cooperation.[21] The post-1945 liberal international order assumed a community of liberal democracies based on the open trading and financial system created within the framework of the Bretton Woods Agreement of 1944, the International Monetary Fund (IMF) and the World Bank, as well as the use of the dollar as the primary reserve currency. The General Agreement on Trade and Tariffs of 1947 in 1995 became the World Trade Organization (WTO). Free trade, of course, favours the dominant economic power, and as US pre-eminence wanes it restores elements of the protectionist policy that fostered its spectacular growth in the nineteenth century. President Joseph Biden's Inflation Reduction Act included almost $400bn in subsidies to develop so-called 'cleantech' industries, accompanied by aggressive tariffs on Chinese imports.

The second domain is conventionally called 'empire'. The military arm of the Political West took shape as the Cold War intensified. The Central Intelligence Agency (CIA) was established in 1947, combining intelligence gathering and clandestine operations. The first phase culminated in the creation of NATO through the signing of the Washington Treaty on 4 April 1949. In the 1950s, a vast military–industrial complex was created, with deep links to Congress, the media, a dense mass of think tanks and military-funded research in universities and specialist institutions. Michael Glennon describes how a 'Trumanite' state was created, a security-centred 'deep state' that endures despite repeated changes of presidency and turnover in Congressional membership. The fundamentals of security policy remain the same, operating within the grand strategy shaped by cold war imperatives. The 'Madisonian state', the civil sector comprised of parties, elections

---

20 An issue explored by Samuel Moyn, who identifies a mismatch in Cold War I between cold war liberal theory and social democratic practices, *Liberalism against Itself: Cold War Intellectuals and the Making of our Times* (New Haven and London, Yale University Press, 2023).
21 G. John Ikenberry, *A World Safe for Democracy: Liberal Internationalism and the Crisis of Global Order* (New Haven and London, Yale University Press, 2020).

and the judiciary, is overshadowed by the Trumanite state. National security policy remains remarkably impervious to change.[22] Bipartisan policy convergence is shaped by defence sector lobbying and associated think tanks, which provide the intellectual rationale for high defence spending and a global network of US bases to defend US primacy. Most Congressional districts host defence sector enterprises, and any diminution in 'pork barrel' spending threatens jobs and thus votes for incumbents. Military Keynesianism was the industrial policy of Cold War I and remains the bedrock of the US economy. This does not mean that the money is well spent, and in fact the whole system increasingly promotes waste, duplication, corruption, cost over-runs and ultimately inappropriate weapons that are not fit for purpose in contemporary warfare.

These two domains, the commonwealth and the empire, and internally the Madisonian and the Trumanite states, reflect the two faces of the system. One is benign and from a liberal perspective advances global public goods. The neoliberal inflection of the commonwealth in recent years has seen excessive financialisation, provoking repeated crises, growing inequality within states and precarity among the labour force. Grace Blakeley notes that 'the neoliberal state is highly porous for capital but extremely impermeable for labour'.[23] The abuse of the instruments governing the liberal international order erodes its foundations.[24] The United States, for example, since 2017 has refused to appoint judges to the WTO's seven-member Appellate Court, rendering it inoperative, on the grounds of judicial activism and concerns over US sovereignty.[25] The commonwealth face of the Political West, with its political and economic freedoms, provided the normative framework to overcome the Soviet adversary, but it was always enmeshed in empire – 'all the many processes through the world's most powerful capitalist institutions [get]

---

22 Michael J. Glennon, *National Security and Double Government* (Oxford, Oxford University Press, 2015).
23 Grace Blakeley, *Vulture Capitalism: Corporate Crimes, Backdoor Bailouts and the Death of Freedom* (London, Bloomsbury, 2024), p. 179.
24 Cf. Gideon Rachman, 'America Breaks Global Rules as It Defends the Free World', *Financial Times*, 27 May 2024, https://www.ft.com/content/8249cd96-bda3-48c9-bf91-005df4125f9d?emailId=c172c52f-29f7-4044-9bd6-.
25 Tom Miles, 'US Blocks WTO Judge Reappointment as Dispute Settlement Crisis Looms', *Reuters*, 27 August 2018, https://www.reuters.com/article/idUSKCN-1LC19N/; Ravi Dutta Mishra, 'US Blocks Fresh Proposal to Restart Dispute Settlement Mechanism at WTO', *The Indian Express*, 28 January 2024, https://indianexpress.com/article/business/us-blocks-fresh-proposal-to-restart-dispute-settlement-mechanism-at-wto.

to plan who gets what at the level of the world economy'.²⁶ The interweaving of empire and commonwealth has become increasingly dysfunctional. The combination of geopolitical power and economic ambition generated a 'hegemonic' peace order dominated by the United States and its allies. Hegemony combines coercion and consent, with the most successful formula being the one in which coercion is invisible until overtly challenged, otherwise the liberal order manages narratives to ensure consent.²⁷ The creative tension between these facets of the Political West is now unravelling. As hegemony wanes, coercion increases.

The normative world of the international system is counterposed to the everyday practices of international politics. In the latter, states struggle for hegemony, if not outright dominance. When perceived as necessary, the norms of the international system are ignored or circumvented. The United States and its allies fought the Korean War under the aegis of the UN, since the Soviet delegation boycotted the relevant session, but the Vietnam and subsequent wars were mostly unilateral actions directed by Washington. Equally, Israel annexed the Golan heights and settled the West Bank in outright contravention of numerous UN resolutions, but justified its actions by security concerns. The United States and many other states recognised Kosovo's unilateral declaration of independence in February 2008, despite this running against the principle of the integrity of states. The decolonisation argument has been mobilised in defence of the action, but if it applies to Serbia, then almost no state is safe from secessionist movements. Kosovo is now home to Camp Bondsteel, an enormous NATO base. Russia's invasion of Ukraine in February 2022 was justified on the grounds of security, drawing on Article 51 of the UN Charter (the right of self-defence), but the absence of an immediate threat weakens the argument. In sum, there is a constant tension between norms and action, a gulf exacerbated by cold war conditions of confrontation. Not all conflicts today are generated by renewed cold war (notably in the Middle East, South and East Asia), but they are all intensified by cold war alignments and their resolution inhibited by cold war antagonism. The UN Security Council has become an arena for the conduct of hostilities rather than a forum for their resolution.

In sum, there are two ways in which the anarchy of international politics can be constrained, either by consensus or hegemony (although various combinations of the two are possible). The result today is the clash between two

---

26 Blakeley, *Vulture Capitalism*, p. 198.
27 As defined by Antonio Gramsci. See Perry Anderson, *The H-Word: The* Peripeteia *of Hegemony* (London, Verso, 2017) and James Martin, *Hegemony* (Cambridge, Polity, 2022).

models of world order, two representations of how international affairs should be managed to achieve a modicum of peace and development. The first is the consensual one, appealing to the rules represented by the Charter system and its associated body of international law, accompanied by an insistence on multipolarity, pluralism and sovereign internationalism. This is a universalism rooted in common principles separate from the immediate concerns of the power and status of any one state or power system. By contrast, hegemonic stability theory asserts that global anarchy can only be tempered by the dominance of a single power and its allies, representing the best hopes of humanity. As noted, hegemony works best when founded on the conviction that it represents the best approximation of global order. In our case, the combination of the imperial and the commonwealth aspects of the Political West makes it an attractive option. However, there is an iron fist in the velvet glove. Drawing on the well-known Kantian triptych of rationality, republicanism and economic interdependence, democratic internationalism recasts the world order of Charter internationalism. Instead of sovereign equality, there is 'Full sovereignty for the liberal West, and limited sovereignty for the rest'.[28]

International Order at Stake

The war in Ukraine from February 2022 represents a fundamental tipping point. The old era of integral globalisation is over, and the world is splitting into competing strategic alignments. Even before the war there was an emerging epochal clash between the relatively declining Political West and the rising power of China and a range of middle powers. Cold War I was marked by several proxy wars conducted in the Global South in pursuit of goals generated elsewhere, whereas in Cold War II the Global North has itself become the theatre for the struggle. The devastating conflict in Ukraine became a semi-proxy war, with one of the protagonists (Russia) locked in conflict with Ukrainian forces backed by the Political West. In East Asia, Taiwan became the focus of another proxy conflict, while various clashes in the South China Sea signal the breakdown of the regional peace order. In Africa, the old era of neocolonialism is giving way to renewed great power contestation over resources and influence.[29] Cold War II is extending into Africa, with Kenya designated a 'major non-NATO ally'. The intensification of the war

---

28 Glenn Diesen, *The Ukraine War & the Eurasian World Order* (Atlanta, Clarity Press, 2024), p. 3.
29 See Samuel Ramani, *Russia in Africa: Resurgent Great Power or Bellicose Pretender?* (London, Hurst, 2023).

in Palestine after the horror of the Hamas attack on settlements in southern Israel on 7 October 2023 generated a new pattern in international relations. The various regional wars are combining into a single mega-conflict.

These antagonisms not only mark the demise of old-style globalisation but also threaten the fundamental viability of the entire post-war Charter International System. International politics since 1945 were conducted in light of the perceived national interests of global actors, but the UN system and the framework of international law and its associated norms represented the essential baseline and framework which constrained the sub-orders, even when they acted in pursuit of their interests in contravention of Charter norms. The bipolar balance between the Soviet bloc and the Political West ensured that 'the other' was constantly reminded of the need to respect Charter principles. The balance was disrupted after 1989. In the unipolar era, the ideology of democratic internationalism subverted the autonomy of the Charter system and undermined its operative code – sovereign internationalism. Interventions not sanctioned by the UN became the norm, in pursuit of what were framed as higher goals, and justified by the perceived obstructionism of the anti-hegemonic powers (Russia and China) in the UN Security Council. Unlike Cold War I, the 'rules of the game' in this second contest are unknown, although both sides observe certain red lines, above all, avoidance of slipping into World War III. These informal constraints are flexible, and the level of confrontation is ratcheting up.

The predictable outcome is multiple deaths. First, of the imperfect and barely functioning post-Cold War European security order. In the 'cold peace' years, the promises given in 1990 about NATO enlargement were flouted by the Political West. A host of leading Western commentators predicted a harsh Russian response, yet when it came it took the world by surprise. Second, Gorbachevian dreams of a 'common European space', reinterpreted as 'greater Europe' in the Putin years, were finally and conclusively laid to rest. Europe will remain divided for our lifetimes and perhaps long after. Third, Russia's respect for the Political West, and vice versa, was destroyed, and along with it the trust essential for even a minimal diplomatic process. In the Soviet period, dissidents looked longingly at the West, but today the West has largely lost its allure and its representation as a model of the good life is tarnished. Fourth, the Russian and Chinese economies are necessarily decoupling from that of the Political West, forcing them towards self-reliance, import substitution and elements of autarchic development. Fifth, deglobalisation processes have accelerated as post-Western modes of economic integration thicken. There is a long-term shift away from the dollar for international payments and reserve holdings. Sixth, the United States-led 'rules-based order' has been exposed as setting its own rules and thus permanently generating double standards. Finally, the entire architecture of the post-1945 Charter International System is threatened. The Political West prides itself on its unity and solidarity during the Ukraine crisis, but this unity is characterised by overreach and blowback. The law of unintended consequences threatens to delegitimate and even possibly to destroy the Political West.

Chapter 2

WORLD ORDERS

The ideological clash between communism and capitalism gave way to a broader but no less entrenched confrontation. Manichean binaries are fostered, represented as a battle between 'good' and 'evil'. In his State of the Union address in March 2022, US president Joe Biden neatly divided the world into two camps: 'In the battle between democracy and autocracy, democracies are rising to the moment, and the world is clearly choosing the side of peace and security.'[1] Later that year, in a speech in Warsaw, Biden declared:

> We are engaged anew in the great battle for freedom; a battle between democracy and autocracy, between liberty and repression, between a rules-based order and one governed by brute force. [...] This battle will not be won in days or months either. We need to steel ourselves for the long fight ahead.[2]

This was a resounding statement of the liberal view of international affairs, dividing the world into progressive and regressive camps. It was also an implicit condemnation of the purported ethical nihilism of realist approaches, in which the focus is more on outcomes rather than the purity of intentions. Underlying the renewed dichotomous approach to international affairs is a profound 'epistemic' clash between contrasting visions of security, development and peace. The struggle is one between distinctive representations of universalism, the foundations of the good life within societies and the appropriate relations between states. The Political West advances democratic internationalism, the view that all societies must ultimately conform to a certain

---

[1] President Joe Biden, 'State of the Union Address', *The White House*, 1 March 2022, https://www.whitehouse.gov/state-of-the-union-2022/.
[2] 'Remarks by President Biden on the United Efforts of the Free World to Support the People of Ukraine', *White House*, 26 March 2022, https://www.whitehouse.gov/briefing-room/speeches-remarks/2022/03/26/remarks-by-president-biden-on-the-united-efforts-of-the-free-world-to-support-the-people-of-ukraine/.

model of modernity generated in the West, whereas Russia, China and many other states defend the Charter principle of sovereign internationalism – that the destiny of each state should be its own affair, as long as it remains broadly in conformity with Charter principles. Ultimately all states, including those in the democratic internationalist camp, insist on the right to defend their interests and therefore selectively apply Charter principles in the rough and tumble of international politics. This chapter explores the key developments and actors that shape the culture and politics of Cold War II.

The Expansion of the Political West

A Political West was created in the decades after World War II. Sometimes characterised as the 'historical West' or the 'collective West', the term describes the power system that took shape after the Allies' victory over Nazi Germany and Imperial Japan in 1945. It was then institutionalised in the context of the Cold War struggle against the Soviet Union. Forged in the Cold War, the alliance is characterised by military and ideological features that continue to shape its identity. The main military organisation is NATO, established in 1949, and the European Economic Community (now the EU), launched in 1957 through the Treaty of Rome. The Bretton Woods financial institutions, the World Bank and the IMF, regulate the global economy and provide development financing. On their establishment in December 1945, the goal was to prevent a relapse into the economic depression of the 1930s, which created the conditions for the Nazis to come to power. In other words, from the outset the Political West had the two faces identified earlier: the 'imperial', based on military force and the creation of a national security state within the United States, and a 'commonwealth' side, providing global public goods and domestic development. Within the Political West the United States exercises hegemonic leadership, shaping policy decisions mostly by consent, but applying coercion when necessary – as in blocking the rise of Communists to power in Italy in 1948 and 1976 and in Portugal following the democratic revolution of April 1974. By contrast, the Moscow-led Soviet bloc had a much greater quotient of coercion, and thus in the end proved more brittle. Nevertheless, it generated a degree of genuine loyalty that endures to this day.

As the world's most powerful state, US leadership is expected and appropriate, but only when exercised within the framework of Charter principles and norms. After 1989, there has been a growing gulf between the exceptionalist and universal ambitions of the 'imperial' aspect of the Political West (which it self-referentially describes as the 'rules-based order') and the norms of Charter system and international law in general. The rules-based order is untethered from the normative framework in whose name it acts, thus undermining not only the legitimacy but also the credibility of that order. It is drenched in imperial imperatives, provoking ill-fated expeditionary operations in Afghanistan, Iraq and Libya, to name just a few. Imperialism by definition is expansive and intolerant of outsiders. The commonwealth side of the Political West, also known as the 'liberal international order', is based on democracy, the rule of law, free trade, human rights and much more, but contrary to predominant interpretations, this aspect is inseparable from the geopolitics at the heart of the imperial side of the power system.[3]

The Political West was shaped by its global struggle against the Soviet Union, and later against China once the Communists came to power headed by Mao Zedong in October 1949. Two rival blocs, the US-led Political West and the Soviet-led communist system, dominated international affairs. It is at the level of international politics that competing 'world orders' are created – rival visions of how the world should be organised based on contrasting political systems. Their relative power depends on economic and ideological resources. World orders are subordinate to the larger system in which they operate. Since 1945, the UN-based Charter International System has been the operative one. The United States was its main sponsor, learning the lessons of the failure of the League of Nations and the country's interwar relative isolationism.[4] However, the contribution of the USSR in creating the Charter system should not be underestimated.[5] The enduring problem from the very beginning has been the tension between the autonomy of the international system and the tendency for the United States to adopt a tutelary relationship towards it – using the UN when it suits its purposes, but otherwise ignoring it. Later, after the end of Cold War I and the temporary absence of a major power to constrain its power, the problem of substitution became acute. The US-led Political West, now branded as the 'rules-based order', positioned itself as superior to the UN system. A sub-system, the rules-based world order, claims the prerogatives that properly belong to the international community as a whole.

It is precisely this logic that the theorists of the New Political Thinking (NPT) in the Soviet Union in the late 1980s sought to counter. The architects of Mikhail Gorbachev's *perestroika* (restructuring) envisaged a new era in international politics. They anticipated that once released from the bonds of cold

---

3 Cf. Ikenberry, *A World Safe for Democracy*.
4 Stephen Wertheim, *Tomorrow the World: The Birth of US Global Supremacy* (Harvard, Belknap Press, 2020).
5 Geoffrey Roberts, 'A League of Their Own: The Soviet Origins of the United Nations', *Journal of Contemporary History*, Vol. 54, No. 2, 2019, pp. 303–27.

war, the Charter International System would generate a positive peace order. By then it was clear that the USSR had failed to keep up with the economic and technological dynamism of the West, and in most respects had become its inferior, except in extended welfarism, military capacity and nuclear arms. When Gorbachev came to power in 1985, the USSR was still one of the two superpowers, and on this basis he appealed to Charter principles in putting an end to the Cold War. As far as Moscow was concerned, the end of the Cold War represented a common victory, and certainly not a capitulation to a superior rival.[6] This is why his visionary speech to the UN in December 1988 is so important, arguing that 'Further world progress is now possible only through the search for a consensus of all mankind towards a new world order'.[7] When the Berlin Wall came down in November 1989, the Soviet bloc countries went their own way and soon after the eastern equivalent of NATO, the Warsaw Treaty Organisation (Warsaw Pact) dissolved. The Political West took this as the signal not to achieve the transformation of international politics anticipated by the NPT but to adopt an expansionist agenda. In later years, the issue of NATO enlargement became the focus of controversy, in particular over what was promised at the time of German unification in 1990. Expansion beyond the united Germany was repeatedly and explicitly repudiated by leaders of the Political West.[8] The US position, however, was more ambivalent, and there remains a perception that Moscow's leaders were deceived.[9]

This sense of betrayal would echo through the years to foster mistrust and poison relations. The expansive and universal ambitions of the Political West certainly ran counter to the spirit of post-Cold War reconciliation. Despite the

---

6 As argued by an eyewitness to the events, the US ambassador to Moscow between 1987 and 1991, Jack F. Matlock, *Reagan and Gorbachev: How the Cold War Ended* (New York, Random House, 2004).

7 'Gorbachev's Speech to the UN', 7 December 1988, https://astro.temple.edu/~rimmerma/gorbachev_speech_to_UN.htm.

8 Svetlana Savranskaya and Tom Blanton, 'NATO Expansion: What Gorbachev Heard', National Security Archive, George Washington University, 12 December 2017, https://nsarchive.gwu.edu/briefing-book/russia-programs/2017-12-12/nato-expansion-what-gorbachev-heard-western-leaders-early. For an evaluation, see Mary Elise Sarotte, *Not One Inch: America, Russia and the Making of Post-Cold War Stalemate* (New Haven, Yale University Press, 2022).

9 Joshua R. Itzkowitz Shifrinson, 'Put It in Writing: How the West Broke Its Promises to Moscow', *Foreign Affairs*, 29 October 2014, https://www.foreignaffairs.com/articles/united-states/2014-10-29/put-it-writing; idem, 'Deal or No Deal?: The End of the Cold War and the U.S. Offer to Limit NATO Expansion', *International Security*, Vol. 40, No. 4, 2016, pp. 7–44.

disintegration of the Soviet bloc, NATO not only survived but set on the path to enlargement. When Boris Yeltsin understood that NATO's Partnership for Peace programme of 1994 was not the alternative but an adjunct to enlargement, he warned that 'the new Europe would be thrown back, if not to the Cold War, to a cold peace'.[10] All postcommunist Russian leaders and society opposed the advance of NATO to Russia's borders. Despite repeated warnings about the dangers, US leaders from Bill Clinton onwards proceeded, heedless to the consequences. As NATO prepared for its first postcommunist enlargement in 1999, the veteran US diplomat George Kennan wrote,

> I see nothing in it other than a new Cold War, probably ending in a hot one, and the end of the effort to achieve a workable democracy in Russia. I also see a total, tragic and unnecessary end to an acceptable relationship of that country to the remainder of Europe.[11]

There can be no more eloquent rebuttal of the view that the desire of the East European countries themselves to join NATO should take priority over larger questions of European security. Instead, the United States doubled down on what Kennan called a 'colossal blunder'.[12] Despite resistance from France and Germany, NATO's Bucharest summit in April 2008 resolved that 'NATO welcomes Ukraine's and Georgia's Euro-Atlantic aspirations for membership in NATO. We agreed today that these countries will become members of NATO'.[13] Russian remonstrances only proved the need for expansion. This was a trap of the West's own making, which in the end would blow back to destabilise the West itself.

Yeltsin was right about a cold peace. Palliative measures, such as the NATO-Russia Founding Act on Mutual Relations of May 1997, did little to resolve the dilemma. The NATO-Russia Council was established in May 2002 as 'a mechanism for consultation, consensus-building, cooperation, joint decision and joint action in which the individual NATO member states and Russia work as equal partners on a wide spectrum of security issues of common interest', but

---

10 The speech is summarised by Andrei Kozyrev, *The Firebird: A Memoir. The Elusive Fate of Russian Democracy* (Pittsburgh, University of Pittsburgh Press, 2019), p. 283. On cold peace, see Andrei Kozyrev, 'Partnership or Cold Peace?', *Foreign Policy*, No. 99, Summer 1995, pp. 3–14.
11 George F. Kennan, 'A Fateful Error', *New York Times*, 5 February 1997, p. A23.
12 Scott McConnell, 'George Kennan's Internal Exile', *Modern Age*, 17 July 2023, https://modernagejournal.com/george-kennans-internal-exile/218597/.
13 NATO, 'Bucharest Summit Declaration', 3 April 1998, https://www.nato.int/cps/en/natolive/official_texts_8443.htm.

the problem was not resolved.[14] At every crisis point, notably during the Russo-Georgian war of 2008 and the Ukraine crisis in 2014, the NRC proved redundant and was not even allowed to meet. Instead, a military alliance designed to counter Moscow threatened to advance to Russia's borders. Without a balancing counter-force and in conditions of unipolarity, the Political West broadened its claims and ambitions. Rather than dissolving and becoming part of a transformed post-Cold War peace order, the Cold War logic of the containment of Russia continued, generating the reaction in Moscow precisely as Kennan had predicted.

As a great European power undergoing a painful democratic transition, Russia anticipated joining the Political West, but not at the expense of its great power status. Unlike Germany and Japan at the end of World War II, postcommunist Russia certainly did not accept that it was a defeated power. In fact, it believed that it was vested with the laurels of the common victory at the end of Cold War I, hence enjoyed a privileged status. It would join the Political West as an equal, or not at all. This was certainly not how Washington saw it. Russia could join the West, but as a subaltern; it had to give up on the idea of classical sovereignty and its great power illusions. In the 1990s, Russia was broken and in chaos, with the economy wrenched out of the planning system and pitched into 'wild East' market relations, but even then it refused what was on offer: the bended knee or US hostility.[15] Moscow was faced with a Political West imbued with a sense of victory, making claims to a universality that properly belonged to the international system of which it was a subordinate part. As the impediments became clear, Russia's liberals and Atlanticists, who advocated rapprochement with the West, lost popular and elite support. In their place came reconstituted neo-Soviet factions, advancing various neo-traditionalist and Eurasianist ideas about re-asserting Russia as a sovereign great power.[16] International politics remained trapped in the logic of cold war, although now conducted with new ideas and new methods.

The Political West perpetuated the negative peace characteristic of the Cold War. The ideals and institutions of the Political West had indeed triumphed, but this was a temporary and conjunctural victory. The Warsaw Pact was dissolved in February 1991 and the Soviet Union itself disintegrated in

---

14 This is the description on NATO's website, http://www.nato.int/nrc-website/en/about/index.html. 'The Founding Act on Mutual Relations, Cooperation and Security between NATO and the Russian Federation' of 27 May 1997 can be found here, http://www.nato.int/cps/en/natohq/official_texts_25468.htm.

15 The strained quality of relations is vividly, and painfully, conveyed in Strobe Talbott's memoir, *The Russia Hand: A Memoir of Presidential Diplomacy* (New York, Random House, 2003).

16 Richard Sakwa, *The Putin Paradox* (London and New York, I. B. Tauris/Bloomsbury Publishing, 2020).

December of that year. Russia was recognised as the 'continuer' state, assuming the prerogatives, treaty responsibilities and debts of the Soviet Union, and entered a period of intense political and economic trauma. Despite its evident weakness, Moscow insisted that it would remain a 'co-creator' of post-Cold War international order. The only universalism that Moscow recognised was that of the Charter International System. Moscow insisted on the primacy of sovereign internationalism, the fundamental principle at the heart of the Charter system, whereas the United States advanced its own model of hegemonic internationalism, in which potential rivals would be deterred and contained.[17]

The confluence of neoconservative and liberal interventionist thinking radicalised the Political West itself, giving rise to 'democratic internationalism', at odds with the principles and norms of the sovereign internationalism at the heart of the Charter system. Democratic internationalism effectively questions the right of all non-democratic governments, or those so deemed by the Political West, to rule. As the scholar Elie Kedourie put it when describing the insurgent French armies storming across Europe to advance the revolution and French national power in the 1790s:

> [O]n the principle advocated by the revolutionaries, the title of all governments then existing was put into question: since they did not derive their sovereignty from the nation, they were usurpers with whom no agreement need be binding, and to whom subjects owed no allegiance. It is clear that such a doctrine would envenom international quarrels and render them quite recalcitrant to the methods of traditional statecraft; it would indeed subvert all international relations as hitherto known […] The ambitions of a state or the designs of a faction took on the purity of principle, compromise was treason, and a tone of exasperated intransigence became common between rivals and opponents.[18]

In claiming an exclusive victory at the end of Cold War I, the Political West in effect declared a permanent state of cold war. This explains the continuation of America's bloated military budget, neo-containment strategies against Russia and other potential rivals, and various military interventions without UN sanction. The transformative potential of the era was squandered. Russia's status concerns were reinforced, accompanied by a growing perception of

---

17 For analysis of the principles underlying hegemonic internationalism, see Stephen Wertheim, 'Iraq and the Pathologies of Primacy', *Foreign Affairs*, 17 March 2023, https://www.foreignaffairs.com/united-states/iraq-and-pathologies-primacy.
18 Elie Kedourie, *Nationalism* (London, Hutchinson, 1960), pp. 15, 18.

threat. As far as Russia's ruling class was concerned, the expansion of NATO and the other institutions of the Political West threatened the country's security. There was 'no place for Russia' in the new security system.[19]

The Rules-Based Order

The Political West is a particular and temporally bound version of the West in general. There is also a Civilisational West, the 500 years of imperial dominance accompanied by the Renaissance, Enlightenment and Industrial Revolution and a deeper Cultural Europe stretching back to the Axial Age. The cultural formation with which we are concerned is the Political West. It is not the same as the liberal international order (LIO), although it is close to its recent manifestation as the 'rules-based order'.[20] The LIO is a combination of international law, liberal democracy and open trading, with roots going back to the nineteenth century, although it came into its own after 1945 under the protection of US hegemony.[21] The rules-based order is a postcommunist manifestation of that order, having been radicalised by the collapse of the Soviet alternative in 1989–91. The Political West is a geopolitical project by its very essence, whereas the LIO is a broader category encompassing a civilisational and economic mode of development. Earlier, we described this as the tension between the imperial and commonwealth domains of the Atlantic power system. The Political West is a particular Cold War geopolitical instantiation of the LIO. Created in the Cold War, the Political West after 1989 sought to perpetuate unipolarity to ensure that no geopolitical, developmental or ideological alternative could challenge its dominance. It represents the hegemonic formulation of world order and thus repudiates multipolar or pluralist approaches.

After 1989, the Political West radicalised in five main ways. The first is Hegelian, with the old Marxist–Leninist version of historicism, in which the meaning and purpose of history is assumed to be known and thus realisable through purposive human action, replaced by a liberal version. This was expressed in terms of the 'end of history', with human destiny tending towards a universal

---

19 William H. Hill, *No Place for Russia: European Security Institutions since 1989* (New York, Columbia University Press, 2018).
20 John Dugard, 'The Choice Before Us: International Law or a "Rules-Based International Order"?', *Leiden Journal of International Law*, Vol. 36, 2023, pp. 223–32.
21 Ikenberry, *A World Safe for Democracy*. See also G. John Ikenberry, *Liberal Leviathan: The Origins, Crisis, and Transformation of the American World Order* (Princeton, Princeton University Press, 2011).

version of Western modernity.[22] Second, the Kantian imperative towards human rights and the Enlightenment vision of 'perpetual peace' generated by republican (democratic) forms of governance trumped sovereigntist approaches to the management of international affairs. Human rights in this period, became 'the last utopia', replacing concern for social and economic rights accompanied by a universalism that trumped traditional principles of non-interference.[23] Third, intensified militarism reflected a Hobbesian vision of order imposed by a mighty Leviathan, now projected into international affairs. US hegemony and leadership was presented as the only force holding back global anarchy while chastising recalcitrant states. The fourth radicalisation is the Hayekian one, with the neoliberal orthodoxy hollowing out the state while vesting the market with magical powers of self-correction and human liberation. The final form of radicalisation is the Straussian one, of particular importance for this work.

Leo Strauss has long been considered the inspirer of contemporary neoconservatism, but his influence is broader. It is associated with a certain ahistoricism, insisting on a corpus of immutable and unchangeable truths, described as an attempt to recover 'classical rationalism'. Strauss's idea of esoteric and exoteric knowledge suggests a fundamental continuity in a body of knowledge that only initiates can understand. This is akin to gnosticism, the rejection of reality's constraints by those to whom the promise of a realm of secret knowledge ('gnosis') has been vouchsafed, accessible only to its devotees. Straussians are notoriously unwilling to engage with critics and are intolerant of dissent. Neoconservatives in the United States are implacable and adamantine in their resolve to assert US primacy, as a condition for hegemonic world order, and are dismissive of critics at home and abroad. This has shaped a foreign policy inspired by theories of US exceptionalism as well as an expansive universalism inured to engagement with alternative viewpoints. Dogmatism and polarisation in domestic affairs is projected through Manichean inflexibility in foreign policy.[24]

Moscow repeatedly condemned the way that the Political West, self-designated as the 'rules-based order', usurped the rights and prerogatives that properly belong to the Charter system as a whole. The liberal international order that the United States sponsored after 1945, with its economic institutions based on the Bretton Woods institutions and the security structures

---

22 Francis Fukuyama, 'The End of History', *The National Interest*, No. 16, Summer 1989, pp. 3–17; idem, *The End of History and the Last Man* (New York, Free Press, 1992).
23 Samuel Moyn, *The Last Utopia: Human Rights in History* (Cambridge, Belknap Press, 2012).
24 There is a vast literature on Strauss, but a useful survey is Neil G. Robertson, *Leo Strauss: An Introduction* (Cambridge, Polity, 2021).

associated with the 'Trumanite' state', became liberal hegemony – the view that there could be no legitimate alternative and that the whole world would sooner or later become part of this system. US hegemony is presented not only as the *katechon*, holding back the tide of global anarchy, but also as the manifest destiny of humanity. The free trade regime, liberalisation of the international financial system from the 1970s, removal of restrictions on capital flows and much more was termed 'globalisation' and provided the framework for an unparalleled era of prosperity and global peace (although there were numerous regional wars). This was accompanied by universalism, the view that democracy, human rights and liberal freedoms were universal public goods, and should be applied everywhere and at the same time. Hegemonic practices gave rise to democratic internationalism, in which proclaimed ethical norms trumped national autonomy and sovereignty.

To the degree that these norms were vested in the Charter International System, the Political West was acting appropriately. In normative terms, the practices of democratic internationalism can be considered entirely justified. However, norm advancement is bound up with power considerations. The imperial aspect overshadows and distorts commonwealth policies, including their instrumentalisation as part of cold war struggles. This was certainly the case in Cold War I, when overseas development aid was typically instrumentalised to advance geopolitical goals. Above all, democratic internationalism undermines the fundamental international political norm of the Charter system, sovereign internationalism. This is a model based on Westphalia plus: the Westphalia treaties of 1648, which ended the Thirty Years War, introduced a world of sovereign states, but this is now accompanied by a substantive framework for multilateralism and the political representation of peoples within states. Sovereignty (including the principle of non-interference in the internal affairs of other states) combines with internationalism, a commitment to international law, human dignity and multilateral approaches to common challenges.

Instead, the Political West advances democratic internationalism through democracy promotion programmes, supporting NGOs and 'civil society' as agents of change. For critics, this amounts to nothing less than subversive and covert regime change operations. These are dubbed 'colour revolutions', of various stripes, beginning with the overthrow of Slobodan Milošević in Serbia in October 2000, taking in tulip and rose revolutions in Kyrgyzstan and Georgia, respectively, before the momentous Maidan 'coup' in Ukraine in February 2014, as well as later attempts in Georgia.[25] The sovereignty of

---

25 For a recent assessment, see Brian Berletic, 'Georgia Fight against US Subversion and Its Implications Worldwide', *New Eastern Outlook*, 22 April 2024, https://journal-neo .su/2024/04/22/georgia-fight-against-us-subversion-its-implications-worldwide/.

the target state is subjected to the weaponisation of democratic and human right norms, as and when the leaders of the Political West (acting typically in the guise of the rules-based order) decide is appropriate. This gives rise to 'democratism', the subordination of genuine democratic norms to geopolitical considerations – about which we will have more to say later.

Russian Neo-Revisionism

Russia's liberal democratic revolution ran into the sands in the 1990s, amid economic and political turmoil accompanied by social immiseration. Russia became a 'regime' system, in which the political elite escaped popular control, although the formal institutions of democracy remain. In a regime system, elections are not about a change of government but a change of system. With the stakes so high, elections have to be managed in case people vote the 'wrong way'. In the 1996 presidential election, Boris Yeltsin, the leader of the 'democratic' forces and president of Russia since 1991, was in danger of losing to the Communists led by Gennady Zyuganov. Russian oligarchs and Washington rallied to the 'democratic' cause with immeasurable financial support and advisors to ensure Yeltsin's victory. The so-called democrats won, but democracy lost. In retrospect, democracy in Russia would have probably fared better if the Communists had won. Instead, the 'dual state' was consolidated.

An 'administrative regime' stands over the institutions of the 'constitutional state', such as free and fair elections, an independent judiciary, a competitive party system and an open media.[26] This is analogous to the US system described by Glennon, but with the dualism greatly accentuated. Administrative principles were at work again in 1999–2000, when in a managed process Putin replaced Yeltsin. Putin perfected the administrative system, curbing the power of countervailing forces, above all regional bosses, independent business leaders and ultimately independent civic associations. He restored what he called the 'dictatorship of law' and 'normalised' administrative interventions in political life. Defence of regime power became the priority, although Putin also articulated a statist and technocratic model of national development. His stabilisation of political and economic life won him popular support. He also asserted a great power conception of the national interest that ultimately set Russia on a collision course with the Western powers.[27]

---

26 Richard Sakwa, 'The Regime System in Russia', *Contemporary Politics*, Vol. 3, No. 1, 1997, pp. 7–25; Richard Sakwa, 'The Dual State in Russia', *Post-Soviet Affairs*, Vol. 26, No. 3, July–September 2010, pp. 185–206.
27 For an overview, see Andrei P. Tsygankov, *Russia's Foreign Policy: Change and Continuity in National Identity*, 6th edn (Lanham, Rowman & Littlefield, 2019); Andrei P. Tsygankov,

The administrative system that took shape in the 1990s remains frozen in place. This has been described as Caesarean politics, based on patronage, state capture and identity politics. The patron controls an elaborate system of rewards and punishments, while the ruling party and administrative regime take control of core institutions, including the courts and the commanding heights of the economy.[28] As for identity politics, comparable systems in Poland and Hungary tap into nationalist and even xenophobic strains of public opinion.[29] In Russia, the focus has been on shaping memory politics and a narrative of resilience against foreign subversion and national development. In such a system, elections continue to be conducted in 'emergency' mode, as a plebiscite on the regime and not as a mechanism to renew governance. As long as the regime presents itself as the unique guardian of the national interest, then the emergency style of rule, in which constitution and the law are subordinated to regime preservation, will continue.

After a long period of deteriorating relations with the Political West, on his return to the presidency for a third term in 2012 Putin decided to make his stand on the ostensibly conservative but in fact right-wing communitarian hill of 'traditional values'.[30] There is no single comprehensive definition of what these entail, yet Putin was adamant that the new Russian ideology would be some form of conservatism. In his annual address to the Federal Assembly in December 2013, he outlined his vision:

> Today, many nations are revising their moral values and ethical norms, eroding ethnic traditions and differences between peoples and cultures. Society is now required not only to recognise everyone's right to the freedom of conscience, political views and privacy, but also to accept without question the equality of good and evil, strange as it seems, concepts that are opposite in meaning. This destruction of traditional values from above not only leads to negative consequences for society, but is also essentially anti-democratic, since it is carried out on the basis of abstract, speculative ideas, contrary to the will of the majority, which

---

The 'Russian Idea' in International Relations: Civilization and National Distinctiveness (London and New York, Routledge, 2023).

28 Henry E. Hale, *Patronal Politics: Eurasian Regime Dynamics in Comparative Perspective* (New York, Cambridge University Press, 2015).

29 Robert Sata and Ireneusz Pawel Karolewski, 'Caesarean Politics in Hungary and Poland', *East European Politics*, Vol. 6, No. 2, 2020, pp. 206–25.

30 Mikhail Suslov, *Putinism: Post-Soviet Russian Regime Ideology* (London and New York, Routledge, 2024), pp. 93–94.

does not accept the changes occurring or the proposed revision of values.[31]

Putin later appealed to an amorphous yet powerful representation of the 'Russian World' (*Russkii mir*), stretching across time and space, which he insisted

> embraces all generations of our predecessors and our descendants that will live after us. The Russian world means Ancient Rus, the Tsardom of Muscovy, the Russian Empire, the Soviet Union, and modern Russia that is reclaiming, consolidating, and augmenting its sovereignty as a global power. The Russian World unites all those who feel a spiritual affinity with our Motherland, who consider themselves Russian speakers, and carriers of Russian history and culture regardless of their ethnicity or religion.[32]

The Russian World represents a community of Russophone peoples across state borders, entailing an implicit threat to neighbours with large Russian-speaking communities such as Estonia, Latvia, Kazakhstan and Ukraine. The Russian Orthodox Church (ROC) is allotted an important role in this. Various think tanks and agencies have been created to advance the new ideology, including in 2009 the Russian Institute for Strategic Research and the Russkii Mir Foundation, and later the Rossotrudnichestvo organisation to promote Russian language and culture. A number of private foundations also play an important part in advancing the ideals of geopolitical and politico-theological Russophonia, including the TV channel (Tsargrad) funded by Konstantin Malofeev and Vladimir Yakunin's now defunct Dialogue of Civilisations annual forum held in Rhodes and later the Dialogue of Civilisations Research Institute in Berlin. The Izborsky Club brings together neo-traditionalists of various stripes, ranging from monarchists to national communists.

Putin argues that

> the Russian world and Russia itself do not and cannot exist without Russians as an ethnicity, without the Russian people. This statement does not contain any claim to superiority, exclusivity or chosenness. This is simply a fact just like our Constitution's clear definition of the

---

31 Vladimir Putin, 'Presidential Address to the Federal Assembly', *Kremlin.ru*, 12 December 2013, http://eng.kremlin.ru/news/6402.
32 Vladimir Putin, 'Plenary Session of the World Russian People's Council', *Kremlin.ru*, 28 November 2023, https://en.kremlin.ru/events/president/transcripts/72863.

status of the Russian language as the language of the state-forming nation.[33]

The July 2020 constitutional amendments indeed introduced the controversial assertion of Russian as 'the language of the state-forming people' (Article 68.1), although Russian nationalists had pressed for the statement to go further to assert that (ethnic) Russians were the state-forming people, which was a step too far for Putin. The amendments eroded the liberal spirit of the 1993 constitution, in which individual rights were the highest value, in favour of the communitarian view that collective rights are supreme. The changes also allowed Putin to run for a fifth term in 2024 and potentially a sixth in 2030. Russia placed itself at the head of a putative Fifth International, bringing together communitarian, traditionalist, illiberal and authoritarian states opposed to the hegemony of liberal ideology. This is couched in the language of civilisational autonomy and ideological pluralism, accompanied by geopolitical resistance to American primacy. Critics argue that Moscow once again, as in the days of the Third (Communist) International (Comintern), funds subversion, places sleeper agents across the territory of adversaries, interferes in elections and conducts propaganda campaigns to divide the Political West. Russia is condemned for 'sowing discord' and confusing populations with disinformation and misinformation.

The result is the intensification of cold war contestation, fought on a different terrain to that of Cold War I but with similar instruments and practices. The Charter system has itself become an object of controversy. In Cold War I, although honoured more in the breach than in practice, both sides claimed to operate within the Charter system's framework. However, in Cold War II, one of the world orders, the US-led Political West, effectively claims to be synonymous with the Charter system as a whole, subordinating the UN, its agencies and norms to imperatives defined by the rules-based order. Gorbachev's NPT had tried to do the opposite: subordinating contesting world orders to Charter norms, and postcommunist Russia operated within this intellectual framework. Thus, Russia became a neo-revisionist power: condemning the perceived usurpation of universal principles by a particular power system while asserting continued loyalty to the Charter system itself.[34] Russia's neo-revisionism seeks to change how international politics operates, rather than attempting to change the international system itself. From this perspective, it is Russia that is a conservative status quo power, resisting the perceived revisionist character of the

---

33 Putin, 'Plenary Session'.
34 Richard Sakwa, 'Russian Neo-Revisionism', *Russian Politics*, Vol. 4, No. 1, 2019, pp. 1–21.

Political West. The West's attempt to mould the world in its image is considered revolutionary, against which an axis of resistance is gradually taking shape.

The ideological conflicts of Cold War I moved to the cultural, even civilisational, terrain. Traditionalism is counterposed to the regressive decadence of the West. The transnational alignment of conservatives represents the globalisation of culture wars. This adds another layer to the putative security threat. By the time of NATO's Madrid summit, cited above, the cold peace had decisively given way to cold war:

> The Russian Federation is the most significant and direct threat to Allies' security and to peace and stability in the Euro-Atlantic area. It seeks to establish spheres of influence and direct control through coercion, subversion, aggression and annexation. It uses conventional, cyber and hybrid means against us and our partners. Its coercive military posture, rhetoric and proven willingness to use force to pursue its political goals undermine the rules-based international order.[35]

This was an undeclared war over 'spheres of influence', defined in both territorial and ideational terms. Spheres of interest are 'framed by appeals to absolutes and fixed certainties that are moralising and irrefutable'.[36] When defined in this way, the term has been delegitimated. The door is closed to more flexible approaches that recognise multiple and overlapping forms of 'neo-medieval' governance.[37] Ukraine fell into the 'grey zone' between the encroaching ambitions of its neighbours. However, the notion of a 'sphere of influence' is more than a geopolitical term but also denotes the grey area of ideological contestation. At the end of Cold War I such nuance was lost. The Reagan-era designation of the Soviet Union as an 'evil empire' gave way to Russia being characterised as an 'evil civilisation', with an inherent propensity to violate rules and to degrade all that it touches.[38] There can be no negotiation with such an evil force. The only remedy is containment, confrontation and even war.[39] Once trapped in this wormhole, common pol-

---

35 *NATO 2022*, Paragraph 8, p. 4.
36 Iain Ferguson and Susanna Hast, 'Introduction: The Return of Spheres of Influence', *Geopolitics*, Vol. 23, No. 2, 2018, p. 280.
37 Iain Ferguson, 'Between New Spheres of Influence: Ukraine's Geopolitical Misfortune', *Geopolitics*, Vol. 23, No. 2, 2018, pp. 285–306.
38 For example, Keir Giles, *Russia's War on Everybody: And What It Means for You* (London, Bloomsbury Academic, 2023).
39 For example, although stopping short of advocating war, Keir Giles, *Moscow Rules: What Drives Russia to Confront the West* (Washington, DC, Brookings Institution Press, Chatham House, 2019).

icy concerns such as non-proliferation and climate change can no longer be resolved through diplomacy. If Russia is such an evil polity, can its presumed security concerns ever be considered legitimate?

China's Reframing

Chinese foreign policy seeks to avoid falling into the cold war trap.[40] Instead, China proposes an agenda for a positive peace. This is the substance of the various formulations that adorn its documentation: 'win-win situation', 'community of common destiny' and many more. The goal is to reframe the terms of foreign policy discourse, and in reshaping the narrative, to restore China to its accustomed centrality in international affairs. China has moved beyond the 'quiet rise' stage in its development, masterminded by Deng Xiaoping after he launched market-oriented reforms in 1978, although the underlying rhetoric remains focused on modernization. This means, in the words of Fu Ying, a former deputy foreign minister and chair of the foreign affairs committee of the National People's Congress, not following 'the old debate on geopolitics. China's development and its growing international status cannot be ascribed to geopolitical gaming. The kind of zero-sum-game geopolitics derived from the era of imperialism and colonialism can no longer explain today's world'. Instead, she stresses international cooperation 'without getting caught up in geographical restrictions and competition'.[41]

This has not prevented China from being accused of being a spoiler and even an outright disruptor. In the 2010s, US strategic documents and Western commentary asserted that China had become a revisionist power, intent on challenging the foundations of international order.[42] This is to misconstrue the challenge. China, along with Russia and some other rising powers, look to change the conduct of international politics but not to destroy the Charter system, the neo-revisionism defined earlier. In fact, the basis of the challenge is rooted in defence of that system. The two powers are dissatisfied with the way international politics is conducted, questioning the privileged claim to

---

40 This section draws from my *The Lost Peace*, pp. 136–66, and 'Is China Revisionist? China, The Political West, and the International System', in Nenad Stekić and Aleksandar Mitić (eds), *New Chinese Initiatives for a Changing Global Security*, The 3rd 'Dialogues on China' International Academic Conference, Belgrade, 9–10 November 2023, Conference Proceedings (Belgrade, Institute of International Politics and Economics, 2023), pp. 33–46.

41 Fu Ying, *Facing You Is Me* (Beijing, ACA Publishing, 2023), p. 218.

42 John M. Owen, 'Two Emerging International Orders? China and the United States', *International Affairs*, Vol. 97, No. 5, 2021, pp. 1415–31.

manage global affairs asserted by the United States and its allies. US primacy is rejected on the grounds that the world is becoming increasingly multipolar, although elements of US hegemonic leadership are accepted if conducted within the framework of Charter multilateralism and in pursuit of commonwealth goals. The usurpation of international law and Charter principles by the Political West, in the guise of the rules-based order, is unequivocally condemned. Thus China, like Russia, is a neo-revisionist state. Analysed in these terms, China is a conservative status quo power, and it is the United States and its allies that have become revisionist. China positions itself as the defender of the established system and challenges only the intrusive and hegemonic practices of the liberal powers.

This is the tenor of a range of documents issued by Beijing in recent years. They all affirm the pre-eminence of the Charter system, but challenge the conduct of the United States and its allies at the level of international politics. China presented the *Global Development Initiative* (2021), the *Global Security Initiative* (2022) and the *Global Civilization Initiative* (2023). These are flanked by the *Joint Statement* with Russia of 4 February 2022, just weeks before Russia launched its 'Special Military Operation' (SMO) in Ukraine on 24 February. In September 2023, the document *A Global Community of Shared Future: China's Proposals and Actions* was issued, followed in October by *The Belt and Road Initiative: A Key Pillar of the Global Community of Shared Future*. This was accompanied by an increasingly strident condemnation of the United States. The document *US Hegemony and its Perils* of February 2023 catalogued US misdemeanours since its foundation and the abuse of its hegemonic position, characterised by a pattern of regime subversion, double standards and interventions.[43] In the *Joint Statement* of May 2024, issued in Beijing during Putin's first visit after being re-elected for a fifth term in March 2024, the two countries called for an international order free of 'neo-colonialism and hegemonism' and condemned countries that 'attempt to replace and subvert the universally recognised international order based on international law with a "rules-based order"'.[44] The challenge throughout is not to Charter principles but to the practices of liberal hegemony.

---

43 PRC Ministry of Foreign Affairs, *US Hegemony and Its Perils*, 20 February 2023, https://www.fmprc.gov.cn/mfa_eng/wjbxw/202302/t20230220_11027664.html.

44 'Joint Statement of the People's Republic of China and the Russian Federation on Deepening the Comprehensive Strategic Partnership of Coordination in the New Era on the Occasion of the 75th Anniversary of the Establishment of Diplomatic Relations between the People's Republic of China and the Russian Federation', *Xinhua*, 17 May 2024, News.china.com.cn/2024-05/17/content_117193497.shtml.

In light of this, the question posed by John Ikenberry: 'Will China overthrow the existing order or become part of it?' is fundamentally misleading.[45] China considers itself a founding member of the international system and now its defender, hence there can be no question of 'joining' anything else. What Ikenberry had in mind, of course, was whether China would join the world order associated with the Political West. This proved impossible for Russia, and even more so for China. It would mean accepting US dominance, and that is something both states refuse to do. They can accept US leadership, as appropriate to one of the world's leading states, and can even tolerate the commonwealth aspects of hegemony, but primacy (implying domination and empire) is beyond the pale. Since the 1980s, the United States and Chinese economies have become deeply entwined, but in the end this was not enough to overcome growing contradictions at the level of international politics. US dominance of global political economy institutions, such as the IMF and World Bank, and perceived abuse of the WTO, also alienates the two powers. Equally, China stands accused, above all by the United States and the EU, of violating the rules of globalised political economy. These infractions include the poor defence of intellectual property rights, unfair access to the Chinese domestic market, the dominance and distorting effect of state-owned enterprises (SOEs), of militarising the South China Sea and intimidating countries in which it has invested to prevent criticism of China.

The more assertive China of President Xi Jinping amounts to what Elizabeth Economy calls a 'third revolution', a new phase in communist China's development following the revolutionary élan of Mao Zedong and the 'quiet rise' masterminded by Deng Xiaoping. She notes that on becoming leader in late 2012, Xi talked about the rejuvenation of the 'Chinese Dream', which was defined not as political reform or constitutionalism but 'a call for a CCP [Chinese Communist Party]-led China to reclaim the country's greatness'.[46] Economy argues that Beijing seeks a radical change in international politics whereby the United States is essentially pushed out of the Pacific and becomes merely an Atlantic power.[47] Given the economic weight of the Asia-Pacific region, this would turn China into the new global hegemon.[48] The goal is no longer simply to exercise China's increased economic muscle but

---

[45] G. John Ikenberry, 'The Rise of China and the Future of the West: Can the Liberal System Survive?', *Foreign Affairs*, Vol. 87, No. 1, January/February 2008, p. 23.

[46] Elizabeth C. Economy, *The Third Revolution: Xi Jinping and the New Chinese State* (New York, Oxford University Press, 2018), p. 4.

[47] Elizabeth C. Economy, *The World According to China* (Cambridge, Polity, 2021).

[48] As argued by Rush Doshi, *The Long Game: China's Grand Strategy to Replace American Order* (New York, Oxford University Press, 2021).

Xi's vision of the centrality of China 'connotes a radically transformed international order'.[49] The failure to distinguish between system and order renders the argument confused and confusing.

The structural factors that prevented Russia becoming part of the Political West after 1989 apply with greater force to China. As a European power, Russia assumed after 1991 that its commitment to Charter rules would act as the ticket to join the historical West. However, joining the Political West would have entailed a degree of subordination, and Russia's self-image as a sovereign great power prevented this. Ikenberry called for the liberal order to become 'so expansive and so institutionalized that China has no choice but to become a full-fledged member of it'.[50] The conditions of entrance into 'liberal order' were problematic for Russia, but prohibitive for China. Beijing will not enter into a hierarchical relationship with Washington, let alone become a subaltern like the post-war European legacy states and Japan.

China's sheer scale, power, sense of purpose and historical grounding renders the country a far more formidable adversary than the Soviet Union ever was. China is potentially the centre of its own model of world order, incorporating a modified version of sovereign internationalism into some sort of recreated tributary system. In such a system, power is exercised through informal suzerainty rather than sovereign domination. This China-centred order will subtly but corrosively subvert the norms and principles of the Charter International System, although not formally repudiating it. This is the fundamental charge advanced by China's critics in the West. China's return to global pre-eminence is undoubtedly a paradigm-shattering process, but while China like all great powers may strain at the limits of the Charter system, it remains within it. Beijing defends globalisation and international law to enjoy the privileges, status and protections they afford. The United States–China clash so far is between interpretations of order *within* the international system, but the conflict erodes the viability of that system.

China is now caught in the same spiral of deteriorating relations with the Political West that Russia found itself trapped. The United States repeated with China the pattern of relations that had so disastrously failed with Russia. Many of the same factors are at work. The relationship had been based on two key principles. First, that China's development would also benefit the

---

49 Elizabeth Economy, 'Xi Jinping's New World Order: Can China Remake the International System?', *Foreign Affairs*, Vol. 101, No. 1, January–February 2022, pp. 52–67.
50 Ikenberry, 'Rise of China', p. 37.

West. For many years this was indeed the case, with China the locomotive for a sustained period of global economic growth in the 2000s, including pulling the world out of recession after the 2008 financial crash.[51] China's rise lifted millions out of poverty, but it also benefitted the broader international community. However, common economic self-interest is not enough on its own to overcome divergent political and strategic imperatives. The second postulate is that engagement would lead to system transformation, along the lines of Germany's *Ostpolitik* 'change through trade' strategy with the Soviet Union from the 1960s. The limitations of such an approach were exposed when Xi changed China's grand strategy from an essentially defensive posture to one actively advancing China's global interests. China will not become a pale imitation of the historic West, let alone the Political West as constituted during the Cold War.

An epochal shift is underway. The Chinese and American economies are entwined and even interdependent, but a divorce is underway. A comprehensive programme of technological decoupling is envisaged. In the sphere of communications, Huawei has been excluded from 5G development, and Chinese media and chat platforms, such as TikTok (on the grounds that it poses a threat to children and US national security), constrained. China is excluded from United States-centred cloud-based storage systems, undersea cables and even from US mobile app stores.[52] Washington banned the supply of advanced microprocessor technology, forcing China to develop a more self-sufficient technological base. Biden's CHIPS Act in 2022 committed $50bn to 'reshore' microchip manufacturing from Asia. Four decades of engagement based on cooperation and mutual benefit came to a shuddering end. The United States and China slid into open-ended confrontation, with the Political West as a whole gradually aligning with Washington. On the other side, a Political East began to emerge. A group of states aligned with post-Western associations such as the Shanghai Cooperation Organisation (SCO), the Brazil, Russia, India, China and South Africa (BRICS)+ association, as well as alternative financial institutions and trading arrangements.

---

51 For the long-term effects, see Adam Tooze, *Crashed: How a Decade of Financial Crises Changed the World* (London, Penguin, 2019).
52 Michael R. Pompeo, 'Announcing the Expansion of the Clean Network to Safeguard America's Assets', press statement, *State Department*, 5 August 2020, https://www.state.gov/announcing-the-expansion-of-the-clean-network-to-safeguard-americas-assets/.

For the Political West this represents a threat to 'global order', but for the post-Western states it is the opposite: a reversion to the operation of the international system as originally intended in 1945. The 'democratisation' of international politics reflects the maturing of the postwar order, to which we now turn.

Chapter 3
THE GREAT SPLIT

The Political West usurps the rights and prerogatives of the international system. The rules-based order set itself up as an alternative to international law. This in effect means that the Political West has become revisionist, although it is a revision of a system that it had itself earlier established, generating what has been called 'internal revisionism'.[1] This self-defeating revisionism undermines the foundations of the system that allowed the Political West to exercise its hegemony in a flexible and multidimensional manner. Hegemony is becoming the assertion of a divisive and militaristic dominance. In response, resistance not only challenges US primacy but also more broadly the hegemony of the Political West in its entirety. A global anti-hegemonic world order is emerging. Russia, China and other countries insist that they are not challenging the UN-based international system, and hence are status quo, even conservative, powers. However, their challenge to the rules-based sub-order means that in the sphere of international politics they are indeed revisionist – resisting the primacy of the Political West and its presumed usurpation of the privileges and prerogatives of the UN-based international system. This hybrid form of anti-hegemonism is neo-revisionism: opposing the claims of the Political West at the level of international politics, but supporting the institutions and norms of the international system in which international politics is embedded.

The Political East

The Eurasian powers of Russia and China are at the core of the challenge, and the two increasingly aligned as Cold War II intensified. Both fear the defeat of the other at the hands of the United States and its allies. Unless they stand together, they are liable to be hanged separately. The two Eurasian powers are part of what can be called the Political East, the counterpart of

---

1 Philip Cunliffe, *Cosmopolitan Dystopia: International Intervention and the Failure of the West* (Manchester, Manchester University Press, 2020).

the Political West but operating according to very different principles. The characteristics of the Political West include militarism, hermeticism and ontological closure, issues that will be explored in more detail later. By contrast, the rhetorical focus of the Political East is on development and peace. It is anti-hegemonic, repudiating the logic of hegemonism in international politics, rather than simply counter-hegemonic, challenging the specific form of hegemonism represented by the US and its allies. However, in the intensely competitive culture of Cold War II, the nascent Poltical East generates hegemonic strategies of its own.

The Political East represents an asymmetrical set of post-Western institutions and processes.[2] It operates according to a very different logic. Instead of militarism, for example, the emphasis is on peace and development. While the Political West is defined by the logic of cold war and bloc politics, the Political East relies more on a network doxa. China explicitly repudiates the creation of a cold war-style alliance system, with all of the accompanying inflexibility of bloc politics. This provides the framework for more malleable and contingent relationships within the Global South. The Political East is an open set of alignments whose overall goal is to become part of a modernity that is free from the hegemony of the Political West and thus allows pluralism and multipolarity to flourish. This is a positive agenda, driven by the view that hegemonic practices are antithetical to their interests as sovereign nation states. This, for example, was always the view of the Association of Southeast Asian Nations (ASEAN), which since its foundation in 1967 has proclaimed its ethos to be in conformity with the spirit of 1945 and the Charter system. The emphasis is on sovereign internationalism and the associated rejection of democratic internationalism, with its damaging interventions and systemic double standards. In the ASEAN region, a multiplicity of political systems coexist peacefully, in part because the organization works on the basis of consensus.

Deeper civilisational patterns associated with the legacy of colonialism and imperialism continue to shape geopolitical concerns. The outcome is a 'multiplex' world rather than one dominated by the hegemonic West.[3] Chinese views of world order modify traditional interpretations of hegemony and international legitimacy.[4] Russia now positions itself as an anti-colonial

---

2 Fareed Zakaria, *The Post-American World* (New York, Norton, 2009).
3 Amitav Acharya, 'After Liberal Hegemony: The Advent of a Multiplex World Order', *Ethics & International Affairs*, Vol. 31, No. 3, 2017, pp. 271–85; Idem, *The End of American World Order*, 2nd edn (Cambridge, Polity, 2018).
4 Carlo J. V. Caro, 'Is "The Chinese World" the Future? Confucianism and Xi Jinping', *The National Interest*, 19 March 2023, https://nationalinterest.org/feature/%E2%80%9C-chinese-world%E2%80%9D-future-confucianism-and-xi-jinping-206327.

power, a stance that is ambiguous and contradictory, given its own imperial past. For China, overcoming the 'century of humiliation' remains a potent political resource, buttressing the CCP's developmental and political agenda. Recognition of distinctive cultures and traditions, tempered by the normative demands of the Charter system, establishes a normative framework for a positive peace system. India, too, chafes against the West's assumption of moral pre-eminence, perceived as an imperial legacy, as well as its attempt to mobilise the world against Russia. The former Indian foreign minister, Shivshankar Menon, writes: 'Alienated and resentful, many developing countries see the war in Ukraine and the West's rivalry with China as distracting from urgent issues such as debt, climate change, and the effects of the pandemic.'[5]

The Political East brings together the Eurasian powers and the Global South. Its key features include:

1. Defence of the priority of the UN-based international system, thus repudiating the perceived usurpation by the rules-based order.
2. The complex alignment of the Eurasian powers with the Global South. This creates what Russian commentators call the 'World Majority'. There is no homogeneity of views across the Global South, but like the Non-Aligned Movement earlier, they seek to avoid having to choose sides, and they reject having the choice foisted on them. A diverse set of nations rally behind a common programme: 'to amplify the voice and agency of countries in historically subordinate positions by pooling their economic and political strength to force a rebalancing of global power'.[6]
3. Active non-alignment. The Global South refuses to be drawn into the endemic civil wars fought in the Global North. Thousands of Indian, Moroccan and other 'colonial' forces fought on the side of the Allies on the Western Front in World War I and once again in World War II. No longer.
4. The post-colonial state system has matured. There are 206 sovereign states and entities in the world today, with 193 of them members of the UN. Only five powers have permanent representation in the UN Security Council (China, France, Russia, the UK and the United States),

---

5 Cite by Anatol Lieven, 'Austria Should Buck the West and Welcome Russia to Key Security Meeting', *Responsible Statecraft*, 14 February 2023, https://responsiblestatecraft.org/2023/02/14/austria-should-buck-the-west-and-welcome-russia-to-key-security-meeting/.

6 Erica Hogan and Stewart Patrick, 'A Closer Look at the Global South', *Carnegie Endowment for International Peace*, 20 May 2024, https://carnegieeurope.eu/research/2024/05/global-south-colonialism-imperialism.

reflecting the balance of power in 1945. Another 10 are lesser members, each elected for two-year terms. All the rest, including an increasingly confident band of middle powers, now insist on their voice being heard in international affairs.
5. Functionalist rather than spatial integration is the original impetus behind the creation of the EU and now motivates the Political East. The focus is on certain functions, such as developmental institutions, including the BRICS+ New Development Bank based in Shanghai, and the Asian Infrastructure Investment Bank (AIIB). China has sponsored its own global development project, the Belt and Road Initiative (BRI).
6. The Political East, like the Political West, can be disaggregated into its cultural, civilisational and political components. The Political East is a more nebulous formation, drawing on widely disparate cultures. There are numerous civilisations, notably the Sino-centric ones and those based in the Indus Valley. There is considerable cross-fertilisation between the two, but they pursue divergent political trajectories.
7. The key feature of the nascent Political East is opposition to the hegemony of the Political West. This has spawned a range of anti-hegemonic alignments, complemented by a growing network of post-Western economic associations and processes, which we will examine below.

The valorisation of a post-Western world is generated as much by ethical as power considerations. The critique of US hegemony as harmful and destructive may well be appropriate, but the ethical basis of resistance remains undeveloped. If resistance simply means the replacement of one power system by another, which may not necessarily be able to deliver the entirety of the public goods promised (although too often not delivered) by the Political West's commonwealth dimension (including individual freedoms, a free press and a competitive political process open to the agonistic diversity of democratic opinion), then there is not much to choose between them. Commitment to Charter principles and procedures is important, but given the endemic problem of double standards in a competitive system of international politics, there has to be a substantive ethical dimension to anti-hegemonic resistance. To date, this has been largely derived from anti-colonial and non-alignment principles, drawing on repudiation of the West's historical dominance over the rest of the world, but there has to be more to it than that. Socialism provides part of the answer, but it too requires intellectual work to ensure that it can deliver more than it negates. The ethical dimension of anti-hegemonic resistance requires something qualitatively superior to the system that it challenges. Elements of that are in place, including the declared commitment to peace and development rather than militarism and exploitation, but the ethics of a post-hegemonic world order require more articulation.

Rise of the Political East

There is a growing range of 'post-Western' organizational developments.[7] Russia and China are closely aligned and work with a growing list of institutional partners. The original SCO members (China, Russia, Kazakhstan, Kyrgyzstan, Tajikistan and Uzbekistan) in 2017 were joined by India and Pakistan, and then Iran in 2023 and Belarus in 2024. The BRICS bloc in 2015 established the New Development Bank, based in Shanghai, as well as a Contingency Reserve Authorisation pool. The 15th BRICS summit in South Africa in August 2023 invited six states to join: Argentina, Egypt, Ethiopia, Iran, Saudi Arabia and the UAE, although in the end Argentina declined and Saudi Arabia deferred. Over 30 other states including Algeria and Indonesia have expressed an interest, while NATO-member Turkey in summer 2024 submitted a formal application. The 16th summit in Kazan, Russia, in October 2024 invited 13 countries to become BRICS+ 'Partner-States'. The BRI is a multi-billion-dollar project encompassing over 150 countries for investment in transport infrastructure, networks and ports. It reflects China's more assertive stance in international politics. Beijing also created the AIIB, which already invests more in developmental projects than the World Bank.

Cold War II reflects the larger shift in the centre of economic gravity to the East. The BRICS+ countries encompass 45 per cent of the world's population and 37 per cent of global economic output. The comparative decline of the EU is striking. With only 5.5 per cent of the world's population and 14.5 per cent of global GDP, the EU ultimately is no 'position to emancipate itself from the USA'.[8] The battle over Ukraine was a way of asserting the EU's global relevance, but the war only confirmed its growing divergence from its origins as a peace project. Unrestrained militarism on the Eastern front discredited the EU in the Global South. The demographer Emmanuel Todd argues that the West is locked in a doomed attempt to prop up Ukraine in its war with

---

7 Oliver Stuenkel, *The BRICS and the Future of Global Order* (London and Lanham, Lexington Books, 2015); Oliver Stuenkel, *Post-Western World: How Emerging Powers are Remaking Global Order* (Cambridge, Polity, 2016).

8 Michael von der Schulenberg and Ruth Firmenich, 'The EU Must Change Course on Ukraine, or Risk Breaking Itself Apart', *Brave New Europe*, 3 September 2024, https://braveneweurope.com/michael-von-der-schulenburg-ruth-firmenich-the-eu-must-change-course-on-ukraine-or-risk-breaking-itself-apart.

Russia, a struggle that could end in the destruction of the West itself.[9] The war also confirmed Russia as one of the main proponents of the Political East. Putin drove through economic integration in post-Soviet Eurasia before turning his attention to larger integrative projects. The result in the first instance was the creation of the Eurasian Economic Union (EEU) in January 2015, bringing together Armenia, Belarus, Kazakhstan, Kyrgyzstan and Russia.[10] Putin first publicly talked of a 'Greater Eurasia Partnership' in his annual address to parliament on 3 December 2015, calling for the creation of an economic association between the EEU, ASEAN and the SCO. His speech drew on the ideas outlined in a Valdai Club report of June 2015 on how to link the EEU and Silk Road Economic Belt (a component of BRI) within a larger Eurasian framework. The aim was to maintain stability in Central Asia and to avoid Russo-Chinese rivalry.[11] At the St Petersburg International Economic Forum in June 2016, Putin outlined grandiose plans for 'greater Eurasia'. Russia promoted the 'integration of integrations' across a range of institutions encompassing Eurasia. Its geographical limits were unclear, at the minimum encompassing just North Eurasia, Central Asia and China while in others it ranged from Shannon to Shanghai, including the entirety of the ASEAN region.[12]

The goal is to render Eurasia an autonomous subject of international politics, to prevent it once again becoming the playground for external powers. The language of the 'great game' is repudiated as both demeaning and inaccurate. This is accompanied by condemnation of the perceived usurpation by the Political West of the prerogatives that should properly belong to the Charter system as a whole. The Political East challenges the Political West's hegemonic claims, but above all defends the autonomy of the Charter system. The principle was asserted in the *Joint Statement* of Russia and China on 4 February 2022, on the eve of the Ukraine war. The *Statement* condemned the attempt by 'certain states' to impose their 'democratic standards', opposed 'further NATO enlargement' and called on the alliance to 'abandon its ideologised Cold War approaches'. This was accompanied by the reaffirmation of the centrality of the UN Charter and the Universal Declaration of Human Rights as 'fundamental principles, which all states must comply with and

---

9 Emmanuel Todd, *La Défaite de l'Occident* (Paris, Gallimard, 2023).
10 Alexander Libman and Evgeny Vinokurov (eds), *The Elgar Companion to the Eurasian Economic Union* (Cheltenham and Northampton, Edward Elgar, 2024).
11 Valdai Discussion Club, *Towards the Great Ocean – 3: Creating Central Eurasia*, Valdai Report No. 3, June 2015.
12 David G. Lewis, 'Geopolitical Imaginaries in Russian Foreign Policy: The Evolution of "Greater Eurasia"', *Europe-Asia Studies*, Vol. 70, No. 10, 2018, pp. 1612–37.

observe in deeds'.[13] This is the core of the final statements and communiqués of the SCO, BRICS, ASEAN and many more.

The creeping advance of the Political West into the Asia-Pacific region, in the form of the Quadrilateral Security Dialogue (the Quad, comprising Australia, India, Japan and the United States), AUKUS (Australia, the UK and the United States, and potentially Japan) and the increased activism of NATO, is perceived as introducing destructive European-style cold war practices into the region. There is considerable reluctance to reproduce the fissures and tensions as part of Cold War II. This would once again impose a Eurocentrism on a region that is trying to free itself of colonial legacies. The globalisation of the last three decades is giving way to a world dominated by two contending economic blocs. The US-led one is intent on maintaining its dominance. To achieve this, it is engaging in various forms of economic warfare. Harsh sanctions regimes imposed on Russia and Iran are accompanied by a technological blockade of China. The ban on the transfer of advanced microchip technologies indicates widening economic divisions, superseding the integral globalisation of the past. Countries in the Global South are wary of aligning with China, and Russia if only out of fear of being hit by secondary US sanctions, yet an alternative global financial and economic architecture is emerging. The Bretton Woods institutions are gradually being bypassed. Together, organisations and associations give substance to the emerging Political East.

The era when the West could teach the rest of the world how to live has passed, and respectful mutual interactions are now demanded. The age of empire is over, and the Political West is facing the legacies of the earlier era, accompanied by deepening internal contradictions. The fundamental principle is that modernity is multiple and that international politics should be multipolar and plural. Liberal pluralism is defended against the claims of liberal anti-pluralism.[14] An increasingly formalised Political East is taking shape, countering the expansive claims of the Political West and offering alternative models of social and political development. Rather than suppressing systemic diversity, pluralism is welcomed. This is apparent in the way that ASEAN+ states accept a considerable range of social systems and political orders and do not interfere in the internal affairs of other members. Relations are based on genuine sovereign internationalism, devoid of the teleological implications

---

13 'Joint Statement of the Russian Federation and the People's Republic of China on the International Relations Entering a New Era and the Global Sustainable Development', *Kremlin.ru*, 4 February 2022, http://en.kremlin.ru/supplement/5770.

14 Gerry Simpson, 'Two Liberalisms', *European Journal of International Law*, Vol. 12, No. 3, 2001, pp. 537–71.

of democratic internationalism. The Political East defends the autonomy of the Charter international system and stands in opposition to any usurpation of the universal norms of the Charter system by the 'rules-based order'.

This division is crucial to understanding international relations in Cold War II. The tension between sovereign internationalism, in which respect for sovereignty is tempered by commitment to Charter values, and democratic internationalism, the expansive and liberal anti-pluralist view of international politics, shapes international politics. This is the metapolitics of our era. There is not only a clash between world orders, in particular the US-led rules-based order, and the alignment of Russia, China and some other states, but also ontological contestation at the level of the international system. This was not the case in Cold War I and explains why Cold War II is so much deeper and more intractable. The palpable ideological differences of Cold War I, with capitalist democracies pitted against the legacy powers of revolutionary socialism, in this light appear as relatively superficial. Cold War I was conducted *within* the framework of the Charter International System (however much observed in the breach), whereas Cold War II is *about* the system itself. This double conflict, operating simultaneously at the level of system and orders, imbues the conflict with unprecedented depth, while at the same time remaining amorphous and protean.

Epistemic Contestation

The influential international relations scholar Hans Morgenthau put it well:

> The moral code of one nation flings the challenge of its universal claim into the face of another. [...] Compromise, the virtue of the old diplomacy, becomes the treason of the new; for the mutual accommodation of conflicting claims [...] to surrender when the moral standards themselves are the stakes of the conflict. Thus the stage is set for a contest among nations whose stakes are no longer their relative positions within a political and moral system accepted by all, but the ability to impose upon the other contestants a new, universal, political and moral system recreated in the image of a victorious nation's political and moral convictions.[15]

The clash of universalisms adds a dimension to great power politics that is certainly not new, since powers perennially present their national interests in the language of some higher purpose and greater good. However, since

---

15 Hans Morgenthau, *Politics among Nations*, 1st edn (New York, Knopf, 1948), p. 193.

at least the Westphalian settlement of 1648, there has been an attempt to separate ideology from interests. A cold war by definition repudiates this logic and restores the crusading mentality to international politics. Over a third of the population of the Germanic lands perished in the struggle of faiths in the Thirty Years War. Cold War II has become a struggle between pre-Westphalian conceptions of uncompromising absolutes and Westphalian plus approaches to international politics.

The category of 'evil' has returned to the political vocabulary: the unmediated assertion of identity and 'moral clarity' in international affairs. As the French scholar Todd notes, this distinctive inflection gained currency after the Al Qaeda attack of 11 September 2001 (9/11). As he puts it:

> The American rhetoric about an 'evil empire', an 'axis of evil', or any other earthly manifestations of the devil's handiwork is so grossly inept that one has to smile and shake one's head or else scream in outrage depending on the moment and one's personal temperament. However, it ought to be taken seriously in its decoded form. This rhetoric truthfully expresses an American obsession with evil that is identified accusingly as emanating from outside the country when in fact it originates from inside the United States. The menace of evil in the United States is truly everywhere if one thinks of the renunciation of the principle of equality, the rise of an irresponsible plutocracy, the overdrawn credit card existence of millions of consumers and the country as a whole, the increasing use of the death penalty, and the return with a vengeance of obsessions about race.[16]

In a postscript he adds:

> This talk of evil by American politicians is explicable if they are aware at some level that they are turning America into a monster but cannot accept the alternative – a world without a permanent war in which America is one nation among others.[17]

The judgement is harsh, but raises the cardinal issue about the source of the remoralisation of international politics in cold war forms.

This tempers all associated questions. How can security be defined and achieved, what is the appropriate model of development in condition of postcolonial state development and climate change, and is an alternative peace

---

16 Emmanuel Todd, *After the Empire: The Breakdown of the American Order* (London, Constable, 2003), p. 120.
17 Todd, *After the Empire*, p. 209.

order a realistic option? These are fundamental questions, and the parties to Cold War II have come up with radically divergent answers. This renders discussion and dialogue elementally problematical. The meaning attached to words and concepts diverge. The way of looking at and interpreting the world belong to different mental universes. This is string theory applied to international politics, with a multiplicity of universes inhabiting the same space. Truth and falsehood are blurred. Nevertheless, while the known laws of physics may be challenged by string theory, a set of physical laws cannot ultimately be denied. So, too, in international affairs facts remain facts, however much open to selection bias and interpretation.

International affairs in Cold War II is like a Rubin's vase, in which the picture can be interpreted either as two profiles in black facing each other, or as a white vase, but not both. Perceptions shape interpretations. In such a system, by definition, there can be no centre. This bifurcation creates a void and negates consensus between the great powers. While they all claim allegiance to Charter principles, interpretations of when and how its norms should be applied differ and provoke further alienation. This is a topsy-turvy world in which traditionalists accuse the Political West of having become the new Soviet Union, applying neo-communist forms of repressive governance, while liberal states condemn their adversary for parroting anti-hegemonic, anti-colonial and Charter slogans as a cover for illiberal and authoritarian practices. The net result is a diminution of tolerance, pluralism and above all understanding across the board.

Double Standards

Double standards are a systemic feature of Cold War II.[18] Hypocrisy is the tribute that vice pays to virtue, and double standards are always garbed in moral righteousness. This is nothing new, but the systemic character of double standards in Cold War II is unprecedented. A leaked State Department memorandum of 17 May 2017 made this explicit. The brief sought to instruct the incoming secretary of state, Rex Tillerson, in the ways of the world. The document drafted by Tillerson's policy aide, Brian Hook, warned him that 'Allies should be treated differently – and better – than adversaries. Otherwise, we end up with more adversaries, and fewer allies'. As the commentary on the text noted, this is 'a starkly realist vision: that the U.S. should use human rights as a club against its adversaries, like Iran, China and North Korea,

---

18 See, for example, Rachman, 'America Breaks Global Rules as It Defends the Free World'.

while giving a pass to repressive allies like the Philippines, Egypt and Saudi Arabia'.[19] The inconsistency in condemning US adversaries while retaining a discreet silence about the criminality of allies is in fact 'a standing policy within the inner workings of the US government'.[20] Human rights and democratic inadequacies of allies of the Political West are routinely ignored while the failings of adversaries are the target of criticism and, *in extremis*, regime change operations.[21] It is not just a question of hypocrisy, with the West setting 'lofty goals' and then failing to live up to them. 'It's that Western governments, by insisting on the primacy of their own rules-based order, are actively undermining multilateralism and the existing system of international law.'[22] The Political West considers itself to be so hyper-normal that the conventions of international politics do not apply and thus it can ignore the security and developmental concerns of others. It also means that its proclaimed rules do not apply to itself. As the British diplomat Robert Cooper famously put it, 'The challenge to the post-modern world is to get used to double standards'.[23] The rules that pertain to the 'civilised' world do not apply to the 'jungle' beyond. This view is said to have influenced Tony Blair's foreign policy.

A classic case is that of Julian Assange, the founder of WikiLeaks in 2006, who was held without trial in the Belmarsh maximum-security prison for nearly five years. The 'globalist' elite was strangely silent about his human rights. A UN report condemned his incarceration since 2019 as 'prolonged psychological torture'.[24] His 'crime' was to expose the secret workings of the Trumanite state, hence the US extradition demand. WikiLeaks released

---

19 Nahal Toosi, 'Leaked Memo Schooled Tillerson on Human Rights', *Politico*, 19 December 2017, https://www.politico.com/story/2017/12/19/tillerson-state-human-rights-304118.
20 Caitlin Johnstone, 'The US Has a Standing Policy of Ignoring the Human Rights Violations of its Allies', *Medium*, 15 November 2023, https://caityjohnstone.medium.com/the-us-has-a-standing-policy-of-ignoring-the-human-rights-violations-of-its-allies-a2f90b851b76.
21 Cf. James Headley, 'Challenging the EU's Claim to Moral Authority: Russian Talk of "Double Standards"', *Asia Europe Journal*, Vol. 13, 2015, pp. 297–307.
22 Jerome Roos, 'Rewriting the Global Rulebook', *New Statesman*, 14–20 June 2024, p. 29.
23 Robert Cooper, 'The Post-Modern State', in Mark Leonard (ed.), *Re-Ordering the World: The Long-Term Implications of 11 September* (London, Foreign Policy Centre, 2002), https://www.esiweb.org/pdf/esi_europeanraj_debate_id_2.pdf. See also his *The Breaking of Nations: Order and Chaos in the Twenty-First Century* (New York, Atlantic Press, 2003).
24 For a good account, see Thomas Fazi, 'Why Even Julian Assange's Critics Should Defend Him: The WikiLeaks Founder Must Not be Extradited', *UnHerd*, 20 February 2024, https://unherd.com/2024/02/why-even-julian-assanges-critics-should-defend-

thousands of confidential Pentagon, CIA and NSA documents exposing civilian massacres in Iraq and Afghanistan, illegal rendition programmes, mass surveillance and diplomatic cables. The Pentagon acknowledged that the Chelsea Manning leaks, for which Assange was persecuted, had no strategic impact on US war efforts and did not lead to any deaths. The case demonstrated that 'nominally democratic states are willing to bend and even break the law to silence those who threaten the status quo, including journalists'.[25] WikiLeaks itself came under sustained financial and political pressure, with PayPal freezing donations at the purported request of the State Department. 'External stakeholders', including the White House and even Ukrainian intelligence,[26] sought to shape the media environment.[27] The mainstream media (MSM), including the *Guardian*, which had initially collaborated with Wikileaks in publishing the revelations, has also been charged with complicity in keeping Assange confined for so long.[28]

The contrasting approaches to atrocities in Ukraine and Gaza brought this home. According to a critic of Israel's military assault in Gaza in autumn 2023, when analysing 'the heaviest bombing campaign since the Second World War', it is

> misguided to view any of this as a failing of the American-led liberal order: it *is* the American-led liberal order, working as it was always intended to work. Morality is only cited to punish America's enemies: when it's America's allies whose actions disgust the world, nuances and diplomatic cover can always be found.[29]

---

him/#:~:text=If%20the%20British%20state%20allows,co%2Dauthored%20with%20Toby%20Green.
25 Fazi, 'Why Even Julian Assange's Critics Should Defend Him'.
26 Aaron Maté, 'FBI Helps Ukraine Censor Twitter', *Substack*, 7 June 2023, https://www.aaronmate.net/p/fbi-helps-ukraine-c.ensor-twitter.
27 Matt Taibbi, 'The Most Embarrassing "Facebook Files" Revelations? The Press, Exposed as Censors', *Racket News*, 28 July 2023, https://www.racket.news/p/the-most-embarrassing-facebook-files. See also Michael Shellenberger, 'The Censorship-Industrial Complex, Part 2: Testimony to the House Select Subcommittee on the Weaponization of the Federal Government', 30 November 2023, https://judiciary.house.gov/sites/evo-subsites/republicans-judiciary.house.gov/files/evo-media-document/shellenberger_testimony.pdf.
28 Jonathan Cook, 'It Was the Media, Led by the Guardian, that Kept Julian Assange Behind Bars', 28 June 2024, https://www.jonathan-cook.net/2024-06-26/media-guardian-julian-assange/.
29 Aris Roussinos, 'The Post-America War Has Begun', *UnHerd*, 10 November 2023, https://unherd.com/2023/11/israel-could-collapse-the-american-empire/.

The Brazilian president, Luiz Inácio Lula da Silva, condemned the International Criminal Court as putting developing countries at a disadvantage, since the United States had not ratified the Rome Statute, the court's founding document. The ICC in February 2023 indicted Putin and an associate for alleged mass child abduction in Ukraine, and in May 2024 it brought charges against the perpetrators of mass murder in Gaza. The Political West condemned Russia's actions in Ukraine, yet proved remarkably indulgent when it came to Israel's violation of international humanitarian law in Palestine. 'In the global south, this perceived inconsistency may prove to be particularly damaging to Western claims of a "rules-based order" – the central refrain leaders from Europe and the United States invoke to rally support for Ukraine's fight against Russia'. Rules and norms were applied selectively, 'according to geopolitical interests rather than in a universal fashion'.[30] As Rashid Khalidi notes,

> This blatantly biased approach is a double-edged sword: while it may serve Israel in the short run by shoring up the diminishing core audience for its skewed portrayal of reality in Palestine, the inherent double standards are transparent to the rest of the world.[31]

This dualism in the conduct of international affairs undermines the legitimacy of the UN Security Council and the Charter system as a whole.

Josep Borrell, the head of the EU's External Action Service, argued that 'Diplomacy is the art of managing double standards'.[32] The erosion of the supremacy of Charter internationalism, based on diplomacy and dialogue within the framework of sovereign internationalism and multipolarity, allows a set of states to claim certain exclusive privileges in the determination of when and how Charter norms should be applied. The unipolarity that predominated in the 1990s has evidently eroded, yet the practices of hegemonic internationalism remain. Double standards attest not only to a political

---

30 Oliver Stuenkel, 'Why the Global South Is Accusing America of Hypocrisy', *Foreign Policy*, 2 November 2023, https://foreignpolicy.com/2023/11/02/israel-palestine-hamas-gaza-war-russia-ukraine-occupation-west-hypocrisy/.
31 Rashid Khalidi, '"A New Abyss": Gaza and the Hundred Years' War on Palestine', *The Guardian*, The Long Read, 11 April 2024, https://www.theguardian.com/world/2024/apr/11/a-new-abyss-gaza-and-the-hundred-years-war-on-palestine. See also Ronen Bergman and Mark Mazzetti, 'The Unpunished: How Extremists Took Over Israel', *New York Times Magazine*, 16 May 2024, https://www.nytimes.com/2024/05/16/magazine/israel-west-bank-settler-violence-impunity.html.
32 Cited by Wolfgang Münchau, 'What a Netanyahu Arrest Warrant Means for the EU', *New Statesman*, 24 May–6 June 2024, p. 9.

failing, but by normalising cynical practices of denial and distortion, the very possibility of an alternative mode of conducting international affairs is negated. Sovereign internationalism is a rather 'thin' form of solidarity, to use English School terminology, but at least it provides a platform for the development of a more substantive positive peace and development order.[33] Instead, hegemonic practices subvert the very foundations on which pluralist and progressive social orders can be built.

---

33 As argued for so eloquently by Jeffrey D. Sachs, 'Achieving Peace in the New Multipolar Age', 9 August 2024, https://www.jeffsachs.org/newspaper-articles/asfymsw3wydpfjlx4pbfz92mmcr4j5.

Chapter 4

FIGHTING COLD WAR II

After 1989, NATO became a politico-military organisation and ultimately transformed the Political West in its image. Neo-realists assumed that having completed its primary task, the containment of the Soviet Union, NATO would disband. Instead, it launched various expeditionary wars while remaining the cornerstone of the collective defence of Western Europe. It thereby became an obstacle to the transformation of the European security order. A collective defence body is very different from a system of collective security. It applies a logic of inclusion and exclusion and imposes hierarchy into alliance relationships. Russia was stuck on the outside of an expanding system centred on Washington. Transatlantic ties took priority over a re-envisioning of European continentalism. From this failure stemmed incalculable consequences. Instead of indivisible security on a continental scale, Washington enlarged NATO to bring the former Soviet and some other states under its defence umbrella. This was the free choice of the countries concerned, but their choice was structured by the options on offer.

It is not hard to imagine an alternative pan-European security structure encompassing all states in some sort of continental security confederation. In the early 1990s, the Organisation for Security and Cooperation in Europe (OSCE) was touted as the framework for such an entity, while NATO's Partnership for Peace programme was welcomed by Moscow. The idea of some sort of OSCE security council, analogous to the UN Security Council, was also advanced as a way of regulating great power relations in the region. A major security role for the EU was also proposed. In the end, the paucity of institutional and intellectual innovation at the end of Cold War I is striking. NATO enlargement became the only game in town. Any short-term gain was balanced by the long-term degradation of the European security environment, as well as the profound internal transformation of the Political West itself. In the absence of a security order that included Moscow, the security dilemma intensified. European security became defined against Russia, rather than with Russia. In May 2024, Russian foreign minister Sergei Lavrov noted that an acute foreign policy confrontation between Russia and the West was 'in full swing', with the Western powers seeking to impose a 'strategic defeat' on Russia and the very existence of the country under threat.[1]

Militarism and Securitisation

Russia has around 5,580 nuclear weapons and the United States 5,428. Each has some 1,600 active deployed strategic nuclear warheads that can be launched within 15 minutes or less. The United States also deploys around 100 air-delivered B-61 variable yield weapons at six locations in five European NATO countries: Belgium, Germany, Italy, the Netherlands and Turkey. These so-called tactical nuclear weapons can be dialled down to as low as 0.3 kilotons, equivalent to 300 tons of TNT (the bomb dropped on Hiroshima on 6 August 1945 was the equivalent of 15,000 tons, 15 kilotons of TNT). Such 'battlefield' weapons are considered 'usable', since the smallest are only 27 times greater than the largest conventional weapon. Russia has an estimated 1,558 five to fifty kiloton tactical nuclear weapon systems, which can be mounted on ballistic or cruise missiles, including the Kh-47M2 Kinzhal ballistic missile.[2] During the Ukraine war, Moscow repeatedly warned of their presence. The confrontation in Europe highlighted again the acute risk of nuclear esclataion. It has assumed the character of a slow-motion Cuban missile crisis, with the world once again facing Armageddon.

In Cold War I, strategic issues were managed and restrained by an increasingly elaborate system of arms control and diplomatic infrastructure, including telephone 'hot lines' between major capitals. In Europe, the Helsinki process gave rise to the OSCE and constraints on conventional arms (the Conventional Forces in Europe, CFE, treaty was signed in November 1990). This architecture has now been dismantled. The Arms Control and Disarmament Agency was disbanded by Bill Clinton in 1997, the 1972 Anti-Ballistic Missile treaty was abrogated by George W. Bush in June 2002, the CFE treaty was gradually voided by Putin and the Intermediate Nuclear Forces treaty signed by Reagan and Gorbachev in 1987 was negated by Donald J. Trump in 2019. The Biden administration extended the New START agreement of 2011 by five years, but it cannot be automatically

---

1 Sergei Lavrov, 'Speech by the Minister of Foreign Affairs of the Russian Federation S. V. Lavrov at the XXXII Assembly of the Council on Foreign and Defence Policy', *Russian Foreign Ministry*, 18 May 2024, https://mid.ru/ru/foreign_policy/news/1951435.
2 For more details, see Lawrence J. Korb and Stephen Cimbala, 'Putin's Tactical Nuclear Exercises: Old Wine in New Bottles?', *The National Interest*, 29 May 2024, https://nationalinterest.org/feature/putin%E2%80%99s-tactical-nuclear-exercises-old-wine-new-bottles-211211.

extended after 2026. Both sides have now withdrawn, although the limits are observed but without mutual inspections. The whole arms control process has run into the sands. Melvin Goodman argues that 'The policy of dual containment of Russia and China carries far greater risk than US policy in the first Cold War'.[3] A new arms race is well underway, with bloated defence budgets and a proliferation of global conflicts. This renders the Cold War II confrontation raw and unmediated.

The issue is not so much NATO enlargement *per se*, since within Europe it acts as the pacifier of traditional rivalries, but the way that it was done. Repeated promises at the time of German unification in 1990 about not enlarging NATO beyond the united Germany were repudiated.[4] NATO's anomalous position – as a US-centred defence system in Europe designed to contain Moscow – was reinforced. The failure to create some sort of overarching security order from Lisbon (or Vancouver) to Vladivostok stoked fears in Moscow and thus precipitated the eventuality that NATO was designed to avert – a revanchist Russia on the war path. Unlike Cold War I, however, Moscow is not the centre of an international communist movement but has become a military challenge to the imperial arm of the Political West. It also represents an ideological challenge to the universal pretensions of the liberal commonwealth. Not only does Russia offer a model of conservative nationalism, defending traditional family values and patriotic moral codes, but it has also assumed the anti-colonial positions of its Soviet predecessor. Espousing defence of the sovereign internationalism at the heart of the Charter International System, Russia aligns with China and states in the Global South to challenge both Western imperial dominance and liberal hegemony.

National security is now defined as preparing for war rather than by fostering peace. NATO engaged in the bombing campaign in Serbia in 1999 without the authorisation of the UN. It was then involved in years-long campaigns in Afghanistan, Iraq and Libya, all conducted in the guise of a struggle against marauding terrorists or dangerous autocrats to install more progressive democratic regimes. Amidst much destruction, none of these campaigns delivered the desired outcomes and in most cases achieved the exact opposite. Having gone 'out of area' to ensure its survival, after 2014 NATO returned to focus on Europe. Defence spending had fallen after Cold War I as European states cashed in the 'peace dividend', but the trend now

---

3 Melvin Goodman, 'The New Cold War Could be Worse', *CounterPunch*, 6 January 2023, https://www.counterpunch.org/2023/01/06/the-new-cold-war-could-be-worse/.
4 Savranskaya and Blanton, 'NATO Expansion'.

reversed. NATO's Newport, South Wales, summit in September 2014 reaffirmed the earlier commitment to spend no less than 2 per cent of GDP on defence. In the United States, defence spending has long been rising, including Barack Obama's plans to modernise the country's nuclear forces. As long as the United States was willing to contribute the bulk of defence expenditure, the European states focused on domestic needs. The price to pay was the relative marginalisation of the European legacy powers, above all France, Germany, Italy and Spain.[5] The EU as a whole, despite much talk of 'strategic autonomy', is relegated to a subaltern role in international politics.[6]

As Cold War II intensified, the long-standing US demand for greater 'burden-sharing' gained added urgency. In the days following Russia's invasion of Ukraine in February 2022, Olaf Scholz's *Zeitenwende* (change of era) speech promised an extra €100 billion to re-arm Germany. The EU turned from a peace project into a 'geopolitical' agent for the militarisation of the continent. Militarism is a broader concept than simply the proportion of budgets spent on defence. The Trumanite 'deep state' endures despite changes of political leadership. Madisonian conventions such as elections, free media and an independent judiciary are subordinated to the 'bipartisan' needs of the security state. Obama White House staffer Ben Rhodes explained policy continuity in terms of 'the Blob', the Washington foreign and defence policy establishment, reproducing itself over generations.[7] The Blob is committed to the maintenance of US global hegemony, whether in the guise of 'leadership' for the more Democratic-oriented part of the establishment, or 'primacy' for the neoconservatives. Both were alarmed when President Trump in his first presidency cast such delicacies aside and declared that the priority was American 'greatness', achieved through trade wars and mercantilist pre-eminence rather than the Cold War system of alliances and bilateral defence commitments. With Biden entering office in January 2021, business as usual was restored. Military Keynesianism was now complemented by a revived industrial policy focused on the energy transition, electric vehicles and the reshoring of industrial manufacturing. In the event, the resources devoted to weakening the Russian military in Ukraine, $75 billion in the first

---

5 The UK is a distinctive case, believing that close alignment with the United States allows it to exercise a degree of 'special' influence with the hegemonic power. The Trumpian disruption came as a shock to this paradigm.
6 For a profound analysis of the dilemmas, although characteristically short on remedies, see Emmanuel Macron, 'Europe Speech', Sorbonne, 25 April 2024, https://www.elysee.fr/en/emmanuel-macron/2024/04/24/europe-speech.
7 Analysed by Stephen M. Walt, *The Hell of Good Intentions: America's Foreign Policy Elite and the Decline of US Primacy* (New York, Farrar, Straus, and Giroux, 2019), pp. 91–136.

20 months, were double the annual investment of Biden's Inflation Reduction Act in energy security and climate change.[8] Money can always be found for war, but not for peace and development.

Defence budgets were ratcheted up amidst talk of a 'pre-war' situation comparable to that of the late 1930s, as Adolf Hitler geared Germany up for war. This justified significant increases in defence expenditure. The US defence appropriation for 2024 was a massive $886bn, including funds for the Pentagon proper and work on nuclear weapons under the aegis of the Department of Energy. If emergency aid for Ukraine and Israel are added, the sum exceeded $900bn for the first time. What President Dwight D. Eisenhower condemned as the 'unwarranted influence' of the military–industrial complex has only grown since his farewell address in January 1961. And this at a time when the US national debt exceeds $35 trillion, some $242,000 per household. China is also engaged in a massive rearmament programme, with its defence budget in 2024 reaching $231bn and total security spending nearing $300bn. The Russian defence and security budget also grew, rising from $75bn in 2022 to reach $140bn in 2024, 6.7 per cent of GDP. This is still far short of the mid-1980s level, when Soviet spending was 13 per cent, helping drive the Soviet system to extinction. By 2024, the Russian military–industrial complex devoured at least a third of governmental expenditure, and total spending on security came to 8 per cent of GDP. Putin repeatedly insisted that this was sustainable, implying that Russia would avoid the Soviet fate.[9] According to the Stockholm International Peace Research Institute, global military spending rose by 6.8 per cent in 2023 to a record $2.4 trillion. Russia's military spending that year rose by 24 per cent to reach $109bn, while the total military spending of NATO countries was an astonishing $1.3 trillion, 55 per cent of the world total. By then, 23 out of NATO's 32 members met the 2 per cent alliance target.[10] The Cold War I average for NATO was 3.5 per cent and in some countries this now became the target.

Militarisation is accompanied by the erosion of the concept of neutrality. Finland joined NATO in 2023, ending its long-standing role as a trusted interlocutor between East and West, followed in 2024 by Sweden. Even Switzerland, pursuing a policy of armed neutrality since 1815, joined

---

8 Robert L. Borosage, 'The Empire Strikes Back', *The Nation*, 4 January 2024, https://www.thenation.com/article/world/the-empire-strikes-back/.
9 For example, 'Vladimir Putin Answers to Media Questions Following the Visit to China', *Kremlin.ru*, 17 May 2024, http://en.kremlin.ru/events/president/news/74065.
10 Alexandra Prokopenko and Alexander Kolyandr, 'Russian Military Spending to Rise & Rise', *The Bell*, 21 June 2024, https://en.thebell.io/russian-military-spending-to-rise-rise/.

sanctions against Russia and thus lost some of its allure as a neutral venue for international organisations. Washington continued to push against Austria's 70-year policy of neutrality, enshrined in the Austrian State Treaty of 1955. As secretary of state Antony Blinken put it, while Austria was 'militarily neutral', it was 'very much not politically neutral'.[11] Militarism also has profound social dimensions. Following the Soviet invasion of Afghanistan in December 1979, the United States boycotted the 1980 Moscow Olympics, and in return the USSR boycotted the 1984 Los Angeles Olympics. In Cold War II, this has become more systematic. Russian field and track athletes were banned entirely from the Paris Olympics in summer 2024, and the rest (only 15 in all) competed as neutrals. They were prohibited from displaying the Russian flag, anthem or national colours. This is accompanied by widespread accusations of doping, some of which levelled against Russia at the time of the Sochi Winter Olympics in 2014 were justified. Other cases simply reflected the increased politicisation of sport, as in the unfair charges against the Russian figure skater Kamila Valieva at the Tokyo Olympics in 2022 and the Chinese swimming team in early 2024.[12]

In the latter stages of Cold War I borders became increasingly porous. Business, tourism and educational exchanges between the blocs were on the rise. Cold War II in this respect is far harsher than the earlier conflict. Not only have most direct flights to Russia and Belarus from Western countries been banned, but enormous pressure is placed on the few remaining routes to Russia, notably via Turkey and Serbia. In December 2023, Finland completely closed its border with Russia, following a number of asylum seekers from the rest of the world entering the country through Russia. A similar crisis in August 2015 was resolved through diplomacy, but this time Helsinki decided on the nuclear option and sealed the border. In 2013 there were 12 million crossings, and even in a time of war there had been over a million crossings in the first seven months of 2023. The border closure was a sign of 'the rapid collapse of the entire structure of bilateral cooperation that had been built over decades'.[13] It is not clear why Russia allowed migrants to approach the border in 2015, but it has been described as a 'classic Kremlin

---

[11] James Carden, 'Biden and Co. Take Aim at Central Europe', *Antiwar.com*, 19 March 2024, https://original.antiwar.com/james-carden/2024/03/18/biden-and-co-take-aim-at-central-europe/.

[12] Rick Sterling, 'NY Times Ignites China Doping Controversy Leading into the Olympics', *Antiwar.com*, 10 May 2024, https://original.antiwar.com/Rick_Sterling/2024/05/09/nytimes-ignites-china-doping-dontroversy-leading-into-the-olympics/.

[13] Arkady Moshes, 'Closure of Russia-Finland Border Heralds End of Pragmatic Cooperation', *Carnegie Endowment for International Peace*, 12 December 2024, https://

mistake', not only destroying functioning cooperation but also heightening Finland's threat perception, setting the country further on the road to NATO membership.[14] Borders everywhere are hardening as part of the backlash against hyper-globalisation and intensifying geopolitical contestation.

Cultural contacts have been ruptured, long-established educational partnerships terminated, and public diplomacy suffocated. The elevation of normal risks into a problem of state security is known as securitisation. It refers to the way that states transform regular political and economic processes into 'security' issues, thus allowing emergency or extraordinary procedures to apply.[15] Cold War II is defined as the wholesale securitisation of states and societies, a process resisted by much of the Global South, who face problems of their own. In a securitised order, budgets are diverted from civilian purposes to face the perceived threat, and ultimately societies are transformed. In Cold War II this means additional resources for the Trumanite state and its equivalents, while the democratic procedures represented by the Madisonian state are curbed and reshaped to face the perceived threat. A profound cold war transformation of states and societies is underway.

Suppression of Dissent

In a cold war, states pay particular attention to internal deviancy and take commensurate measures to suppress dissent. This is a strategy applied across ideological divides, blurring the much-vaunted distinction between democracies and 'autocracies'. The defects of the other are exaggerated, and platforms are established for the propagation of anti-establishment views against the adversary.

In Russia, securitisation since the late 2000s has gradually but inexorably ramped up. The relative liberalism of the Dmitry Medvedev presidency (2008–12) gave way to repression following Putin's return to the Kremlin in May 2012. Unnerved by the scale of the protests against electoral fraud in the December 2011 State Duma election, Putin's third term was marked by illiberalism and the extirpation of independent political opposition. The announcement in September 2011 that he planned to return to the Kremlin

---

carnegieendowment.org/russia-eurasia/politika/2023/12/closure-of-russia-finland-border-heralds-end-of-pragmatic-cooperation?lang=en.

14 René Nyberg, 'Securing Borders after a Breach of Confidence: Russian-Finnish Reflections', *Carnegie Politika*, 5 September 2024, https://carnegieendowment.org/russia-eurasia/politika/2024/09/russia-finland-border-security?lang=en.

15 Barry Buzan, Ole Waever and Jaap de Wilde, *Security: A New Framework for Analysis* (Boulder, Lynne Rienner, 1998).

by swapping positions with Medvedev provoked the White Ribbon and other movements calling for a return to democracy and a 'Russia without Putin'. Putin felt personally affronted by his rejection by a middle class that he had nurtured.[16] Putin's third term represented a 'conservative' counter-revolution, although the idea of conservatism in a country that has been engaged in mimetic modernisation since the time of Peter the Great in the early eighteenth century is inevitably ambiguous.[17] The reaction was accompanied by the intensification of the ideology of Russia as a civilisation-state, set on its own path to modernity.

Relations with the West deteriorated, culminating in the crisis over Ukraine. The Maidan protests beginning in November 2013 ultimately overthrew President Yanukovych and led to the installation in February 2014 of a virulently nationalist, pro-Western and anti-Russian administration. This was followed in short order by Russia annexing Crimea and the beginning of an insurgency in Donbass. Putin returned to the Kremlin for a fourth presidential term in May 2018, with military modernisation and preparations for a long-drawn-out conflict with the West very much on his mind. In 2020, against the background of the Covid-19 pandemic, a constitutional reform consolidated the power of the administrative regime, allowing Putin, as noted, to run for a fifth term in 2024 and possibly even a sixth in 2030. With the launching of the 'special military operation' (SMO) in February 2022, Cold War II turned into a semi-proxy war between Russia and the West. Interstate war returned to Europe, and cold war practices intensified.

Alexei Navalny, who by now had become the figurehead of the political opposition at the head of the Anti-Corruption Foundation (FPK), was purportedly poisoned with a nerve agent in August 2020. On his return from treatment in Berlin in January 2021, he was arrested and sentenced to nine years in a labour camp. In a separate case, he was given an additional 2½ years. His untimely death in February 2024 deprived the opposition of its most charismatic and influential leader. In December 2021, Memorial International and its sister organisation, the Memorial Human Rights Centre, were closed. The court order claimed that they had justified 'extremist and terrorist activities'. The 13-year sentence on Memorial historian Yury Dmitriev was increased by two years. He had discovered a Stalinist killing field in Karelia and was then convicted on trumped up charges of child molestation. Both organisations

---

16 Richard Sakwa, *Putin* Redux: *Power and Contradiction in Contemporary Russia* (London and New York, Routledge, 2014).

17 A point made by Suslov, *Putinism*. See also Paul Robinson, *Russian Conservatism* (DeKalb, Northern Illinois University Press, 2019).

were accused of failing to observe the 'foreign agent' law of 2012. The democratic aspirations of the late 1980s and 1990s were now a distant memory. The Moscow City Court ordered the closure of the Moscow Helsinki Group, Russia's oldest human rights organisation, in January 2023. A month earlier Ilya Yashin, the leader of the PARNAS party from 2012 to 2016 and a member of the municipal council in one of Moscow's districts, was sentenced to 8½ years in prison on the charge of spreading 'fake information', intended to discredit the Russian Army. Opposition activist Vladimir Kara-Murza was arrested in April 2022, and a year later received a draconian 25-year sentence for spreading 'false information' about the army, collaborating with an undesirable organisation and treason.

As in the Soviet period, the number of 'political prisoners' increased. In mid-2022 there were some 500, but intensified wartime repression saw the number rise steeply to some 1,500 by late 2024.[18] The far-right and Russian nationalists, including neo-Nazis, earlier comprised the majority, but now the ranks of political prisoners were swelled by the arrest of trade union, environmental and anti-war activists, with the single largest category, surprisingly, being anarchists of various stripes.[19] Following the mutiny of Evgeny Prigozhin's Wagner private military company in June 2023, 'angry patriots' called for an intensification of the war but were now reined in. One of the leaders of the patriotic movement, Igor Girkin (Strelkov), who led the insurgency in Donbass from April 2014, was jailed on extremism charges (and convicted in absentia by the MH17 tribunal in the Netherlands for the downing of the Malaysian Airlines flight in July 2014). The pressure against the left continued. In January 2024, Sergei Udaltsov, the head of Left Front, was arrested and held in pre-trial detention (SIZO). He had already served a 4½-year jail sentence for participation in the 2011–12 protests, but on his release he supported the annexation of Crimea and then the war against Ukraine. Throughout, he considered himself a 'harsh critic' of Putin.[20] The veteran anti-war socialist and Marxist theorist Boris Kagarlitsky was detained in summer 2023 for an online post he issued in October 2022 about the Kerch bridge explosion, and following a brief period of freedom, in February 2024 the court of appeal imposed a five-year jail sentence.

---

18 The earlier figure is from 'Legal Affairs Committee Calls on Russia to Release 447 Political Prisoners', *PACE*, 24 May 2022, https://pace.coe.int/en/news/8723/legal-affairs-committee-calls-on-russia-to-release-447-political-prisoners.
19 Details of the various groups in Boris Kagarlitsky, 'Broken Windows and Broken Lives', *Canadian Dimension*, 16 April 2023, https://canadiandimension.com/articles/view/broken-windows-and-broken-lives.
20 Denis Kasyanchuk, 'Pro-War Opposition Activist Arrested on Terrorism Charges', *The Bell*, 15 January 2024.

In the same month, the Russian human rights campaigner and chair of the Memorial board, Oleg Orlov, was given a 2½ years sentence for denouncing the Ukraine war and 'discrediting the military'. He condemned the political regime in Russia as 'totalitarian and fascist' and told the court that his view had been vindicated: 'The state in our country again controls not only social, political and economic life, but also claims complete control over culture, scientific thought, and invades private life.'[21] Controls over the media and public discourse had indeed intensified since the start of the war. On 1 March 2022, Roskomnadzor, the media regulator, imposed restrictions on TV Rain (*Dozhd*). Established in 2008, Dozhd was the last independent TV station in Russia, complementing the Echo of Moscow (*Ekho Moskvy*) radio station. The two were accused of failing to follow the new regulations imposed after the invasion by broadcasting 'false information about the nature of the special military operation'.[22] Dozhd relocated to Latvia, but lost its licence to broadcast in December 2002 over its coverage of the war in Ukraine, and ended up in Amsterdam in partnership with *The Moscow Times* (which had also left Russia). In retaliation for the EU banning Russian media, including RIA Novosti, *Izvestiya*, *Rossiiskaya Gazeta* and others, which joined the long list of earlier prohibited outlets such as Pervyi Kanal, REN TV, Rossiya 1, Rossiya 24, Spas, Katehon and many others, the Russian foreign ministry in June 2024 banned dozens of EU media, including national broadcasters, news agencies and newspapers such as *Le Monde*.[23] There appeared to be no limit to the spiral of mutual prohibitions.

In the West, the spiral of repression also intensified. Opposition to the Political West's existence as a military–ideological formation was harassed and even suppressed. Even the illogical claim that NATO enlargement had nothing to do with the war in Ukraine was normalised, even though a raft of Western commentators (including Kennan) had presciently forecast the consequences of the provocative policy. In the EU, the Baltic states have been in the vanguard of repressive measures. In Lithuania, the political activist Algirdas Palatskis speaks movingly of attempts to close down his critique of developments in his country.[24]

---

21 Anastasia Tenisheva, 'I Believe in a Better Future', *Moscow Times*, 27 February 2024, https://www.themoscowtimes.com/2024/02/27/i-believe-in-a-better-future-rights-veteran-oleg-orlov-on-his-25-year-sentence-for-opposing-ukraine-war-a84097.

22 Thom Dinsdale, 'Inside, Out of the Rain', *East-West Review*, Vol. 22, No. 3 (64), 2024, p. 5.

23 For details, see Andrew Rettman, 'Russia Bans EUobserver and Dozens of EU Media', *EUobserver*, 25 June 2024, https://euobserver.com/eu-and-the-world/ar5b99bec6.

24 Al'girdas Palatskis, *Naruchniki na mysl'* (Moscow, Komsomolskaya Pravda, 2022).

In Estonia, in January 2024 the academic Vyacheslav Morozov was arrested on suspicion of activity against the state. Tartu University immediately sacked him, even before the investigation was complete. Morozov worked at St Petersburg State University until 2010, and he retained an apartment and family in the city. In that year, he was appointed professor of European studies (I was on the appointment panel, and in a strong field he was the outstanding candidate), serving as professor of EU–Russia studies from 2016 to 2023, when his title changed to professor of international political theory. He condemned Russia's invasion of Ukraine, but his regular journeys back to St Petersburg evidently raised suspicion. The University of Tartu Rector, Toomas Asser, censured activity that could jeopardise Estonian security. 'It is furthermore worrying that a person now suspected of undermining national security has worked for years at a university – an academic community the moral responsibility of which is to represent peace, academic and democratic values.' Instead of defending academic freedom, the Rector continued: 'I expect us not to underestimate the ability and intent of hostile nations to orchestrate anti-democratic action. We need to retain situational awareness and critical thought as well as pursue full cooperation with our security institutions'.[25] The imperatives of cold war securitisation trumped the hallowed principle of innocent until proven guilty. In June 2024, Morozov was sentenced to six years and three months in jail, accused by the court of having gathered information about Estonian domestic and defence policy, as well as 'people and infrastructure related to it', which he then allegedly shared with Russian intelligence services. Estonian authorities claim that he had been recruited by these agencies while still a student in the 1990s and admitted that the information he had gathered was 'mostly public' and that he did not have access to state secrets.[26] There is sparse evidence in the public domain, and until we know more we can only conclude that the case bears all the signs of a cold war witch-hunt.

Hegemony and Hermeticism

The Atlantic Basin is the heart of the Political West, uniting the EU and the United States in a relationship that is not always harmonious but nevertheless enduring. Transatlanticism prevented the EU from developing the 'strategic

---

25 'ISS Suspects University of Tartu Professor of Action Against Estonia', *ERR News*, 16 January 2024, https://news.err.ee/1609223589/iss-suspects-university-of-tartu-professor-of-action-against-estonia.
26 'Estonia Jails Russian Professor 6 Years for Spying', *Moscow Times*, 18 June 2024, https://www.themoscowtimes.com/2024/06/18/estonia-jails-russian-professor-6-years-for-spying-a85450.

autonomy' desired by its more sovereigntist-minded member states. Attempts to develop a separate defence identity have been stymied ever since the French plan to create a European Defence Community was abandoned in 1954. Instead, security was outsourced to NATO and to the United States. Legacy powers such as France, Germany and Italy have been neutered. They all conduct an active diplomacy, but on crucial foreign and security issues their efforts lack traction – unless reinforced by Washington. This was the case in the run-up to the Ukraine war, with both Berlin and Paris, commendably, looking for a diplomatic solution, but their efforts came to naught. The United States, smarting from defeat in Afghanistan and the chaotic withdrawal from Kabul in August 2021, was in no mood to review Europe's post-Cold War security order. This may change as the United States extends the cold war to Asia, and US domestic resistance to continued European commitments forces a change of priorities. The new generation of European leaders seem only too willing to take up the burden and continue the crusade against Russia, even if it means deindustrialisation (except in the defence sector) and domestic discord. The missionary and didactic approach to foreign policy provokes antipathy and antagonism.

Bloc unity remains the overriding imperative. The curators of Atlanticism are eternally vigilant against any breaches in alliance discipline, above all guarding against any attempt to drive a 'wedge' between the two wings of the alliance. The result has been the disempowerment of the European allies. The idea of pan-continental European unity, dubbed the Gaullist 'heresy', is resolutely condemned. The predominance of Atlanticism foreclosed the option of a genuine pan-European security order. Russia's inclusion in the Political West was also thereby foreclosed, since its membership would necessarily have diluted Transatlantic ties and changed the hierarchy of power. A strengthened pan-continental European dimension would inevitably erode the centrality of Washington. Russia refused to join as a subaltern, but continental unification on the basis of sovereign equality was not something that Washington was ready to contemplate. This pattern is now being repeated on a global scale in relations with China.

This is reinforced by democratic peace theory, the view that liberal democracies do not go to war with each other. This is the Kantian perspective on 'perpetual peace' that radicalised after 1989. The higher the number of democracies, the greater the security of the Political West. The sovereign internationalism at the heart of the Charter International System is displaced by democratic internationalism, and its associated practices of democratism.[27] Democratism is an ideology that stands above democracy

---

27 Richard Sakwa, 'The Perils of Democratism', *Polis: Political Studies*, No. 2, 2023, pp. 88–102; Emily B. Finley, *The Ideology of Democratism* (New York, Oxford University Press, 2022).

and trumps decisions taken at the ballot box when populations, for example, reject the economic neoliberalism that is associated with this model and spurn the geopolitical implications of a unipolar world order. Instead of sovereign equality, democratic internationalism inevitably curbs sovereignty for states that have not yet reached the required civilisational level. It is a charter for sovereign inequality and exposes states to outside intervention. In Cold War I, the 54 US interventions tended to be brutal *realpolitik* affairs.[28] In Cold War II, interventions are garbed in a Wilsonian progressive cloth, to make the world 'safe for democracy'. Condemning political realism for provoking wars, liberal ideology seeks to insert morality into international politics. For democratic internationalists, politics is governed by an ineluctable dialectic of development. In this cosmos, there is no room for a balance of power or spheres of interest, and instead international affairs are governed by the Manichean logic of good versus evil.

In his infamous Chicago speech in April 1999, Tony Blair justified the bombing of Yugoslavia by denying the Westphalian principle of sovereign equality. He argued that globalisation had made the world more interdependent, hence 'We are all internationalists now, whether we like it or not. [...] We cannot turn our backs on conflicts and the violation of human rights within other countries if we want still to be secure'.[29] International law was now to be supplemented by an ill-defined yet energetic body of humanitarian law. In certain cases this is entirely appropriate, when sanctioned by the UN, but when applied in a discriminatory and arbitrary manner by the rules-based international order, it only exacerbates conflict. The expansive dynamic of a values-based foreign policy tolerates no resistance, generating conflict and war. This is a doctrine that celebrates peace as the dominance of a particular geopolitical constellation.

There is little scope for political dialogism, in which both parties change as a result of interaction – in other words, diplomacy. A classic case is the refusal of the Political West to recognise the outcome of the 2006 elections in Gaza, won in a fair contest (as monitored by the EU) by Hamas. The election was disregarded by institutional actors. Richard Falk notes that the 'incident once more illustrates the primacy of geopolitics in relation to democratic values whenever there is a serious policy clash'.[30] John Gray argues that

---

28 Analysed by Lindsey A. O'Rourke, *Covert Regime Change: America's Secret Cold War* (Ithaca and London, Cornell University Press, 2018).
29 Tony Blair, 'Doctrine of the International Community', Chicago, 22 April 1999, http://www.britishpoliticalspeech.org/speech-archive.htm?speech=279.
30 Richard Falk, 'Exposing the Binding Chains of Discursive Bondage', *International Politics*, Vol. 60, No. 3, 2023, p. 772.

> The fundamental threat to freedom in the West comes not from Marxism, postmodernism or even the increasing sway of autocratic regimes in boardrooms and universities, but from within liberalism. From being an empirical philosophy, open in principle to learning from experience, it has become a self-referential world-view that screens out forbidden truths.[31]

Liberal hegemony is projected outwards, but in cold war conditions it is no less focused on 'manufacturing consent', accompanied by measures to suppress dissenting voices. When the head of the German navy, Vice Admiral Kay-Achim Schönbach, argued that Crimea was irretrievably lost and that Russian security concerns should be treated with respect, he was forced to resign in January 2022. His was not the only case.[32] The journalist Peter Hitchens puts it well:

> Are we the baddies? What if the Ukraine war is just as stupid and wrong as the Iraq war, but the state propaganda has been more successful and hardly anybody has realised [...] yet? Many people to this day still think the damaging and morally dubious Western attacks on Serbia and Libya were justified. Many still think the gory attempt to destroy Syria was a good thing. It took ages for opinion to swing on the Vietnam war, back in the 1960s.[33]

News and public opinion management leads to the homogenisation of the public sphere. Manufacturing consent 'entails the use of propaganda to manipulate public opinion in ways that benefit the establishment without the need for overt force'. Foreign policy is overwhelmingly elite driven, so the challenge is to justify foreign policy in moral terms. Narrative management is required to overcome the resistance of ordinary citizens to interventions that would otherwise be regarded as pointless and expensive. Therefore,

> to gain traction for interventions not in the people's interests, a tale must be told. To succeed, this tale must fit with pre-existing and common tropes that elicit fear, anger, or compassion, the predominant two

---

31 John Gray, 'These Times: Progressives are Using the Law to Attack Free Speech in a Bid for Unchecked Power', *New Statesman*, 26 April–2 May 2024, p. 27.
32 Diesen, *The Ukraine War*, p. 214.
33 Peter Hitchens, 'If We Don't want Death, Blackouts, and Busybodies in Every Corner of Our Lives, End This Brainless March to War', *The Mail on Sunday*, 27 January 2024, https://www.dailymail.co.uk/debate/article-13013261/PETER-HITCHENS-death-blackouts-brainless-march-war.html.

being: 1) the infectious subversive trying to change the holy status quo and 2) the righteous David fighting a repressive Goliath.

This opens up traps of its own. The Mujahideen in Afghanistan were heroized when fighting Soviet forces in the 1980s, then demonised when the Taliban took power in 1996, but they once again became brave freedom fighters when Islamic militants fought against Muammar Gaddafi in Libya or Bashar al-Assad in Syria. Today, 'plucky underdogs like Ukraine and Taiwan [have] to be backed against evil empires'. This narrative did not work so well when Israel 'killed more Palestinians in one month than Russia killed Ukrainians in 592 days of war'. Not surprisingly, Western diplomats complained that 'We have definitely lost the battle in the Global South'.[34]

Opposition to cold war militarisation and securitisation is smeared in a manner reminiscent of J. Edgar Hoover's dismissal of the civil rights movement as a communist operation. As former House speaker Nancy Pelosi put it, 'Make no mistake, this [demonstrations against the slaughter in Gaza] is directly connected to what he [Putin] would like to see. Same thing with Ukraine. It's about Putin's message'.[35] Pelosi admonished Code Pink, an anti-war movement protesting against Israel's military operation in Gaza, telling them 'Go back to China where your headquarters is', a reference to an earlier *New York Times* article insinuating, without proof, a link between the group (and others) and the Chinese government.[36] A dense network of Western think tanks and allied mainstream media reinforce the narrative. Often working in collusion with security agencies and funded by defence industries, this ensures a remarkable uniformity in thinking on national security issues. The struggle for domestic hegemony marginalises formerly critical groups, including peace movements, faith-led pacifism and anti-militarism.

In Britain, the trade union movement since the Thatcher years has been relatively depoliticised. Although a focus on the welfare of union members rightly should be the priority, unions are nevertheless a core civil society association and it would not be inappropriate for them to have a view on fundamental issues of war and peace. Instead, the communicative monopoly shapes domestic

---

34 Kadira Pethiyagoda, 'Interventionism's Moral Narrative Has Crumbled', *The National Interest*, 9 January 2024, https://nationalinterest.org/feature/interventionism%E2%80%99s-moral-narrative-has-crumbled-208482.
35 Dana Bash interview with Nancy Pelosi, *CNN*, 28 January 2024, https://transcripts.cnn.com/show/sotu/date/2024-01-28/segment/01.
36 'A Global Web of Chinese Propaganda Leads to US Tech Mogul', *New York Times*, 5 August 2023, https://www.nytimes.com/2023/08/05/world/europe/neville-roy-singham-china-propaganda.html.

political life. The *Guardian* newspaper, once known for critical analysis and support for peace, shifted into the militant liberal interventionist camp, accompanied allegedly by a purge of 'dissident' voices at the beginning of Cold War II in 2014.[37] The Labour Party leader Keir Starmer even went so far as to assert that opposition to NATO was incompatible with party membership, despite the fact that anti-war and peace movements have long been part of the hallowed tradition of the British labour movement. Starmer imposed Leninist-style discipline, transforming what had traditionally been a broad and diverse movement into a more monolithic and disciplined organisation. The result was a decisive victory in the July 2024 election, overturning an enormous Conservative majority, but the party then lost its intellectual vitality. The traditional Atlanticism of the Labour Party now turned to fighting the renewed cold war rather than ending it, exposing divisions in the party that could threaten its existence.

This internal development reflected the broader change in the post-Cold War conduct of international affairs. Realists apply principles such as the balance of power and spheres of interest, but after 1989–91 Russia was considered too weak and irrelevant for its strategic concerns to be taken into account. Instead, ideological categories predominated. Values rather than interests shaped the narrative. Values had certainly not been absent in Cold War I, but defence of 'free world' was tempered by realist concerns, above all respect for postwar spheres of interest. Conflict was limited to what was then called the Third World. After 1989–91, geopolitical compromise was considered not only anachronistic and unnecessary but as somehow fundamentally illegitimate. The Political West's military–political institutions were not only free to expand but had a duty to bring freedom to the world. Resistance was recidivist and only demonstrated the indispensability of the democratic mission. Russian defiance only proved the necessity of the policies that provoked the resistance, a circularity that is dangerous and hubristic. Hermeticism, the inability to process information, views and perspectives coming from outside the system, reached dangerous levels.

In Greek myth, Hermes acts as the herald of the gods. The winged messenger moves easily between the human and the divine worlds. Over time, hermeticism came to mean the gulf between the materially based human world and the life of the soul. The doctrine of the *prisca theologia* asserts the existence of a single, true theology, manifested in all religions since antiquity. The associated concept of alchemy, or the operation of the sun, is concerned

---

[37] The allegation is made by John Pilger, reported by Caitlin Johnstone, 'What MSM Can No Longer Say', *Consortium News*, 30 January 2023, https://consortiumnews.com/2023/01/30/caitlin-johnstone-what-msm-can-no-longer-say/.

not only with turning base metal into gold but above all represents an enquiry into the spiritual constitution of life, of matter and material existence through the study of the mysteries of birth, death and resurrection. In contemporary terms, hermeticism suggests that the mysteries of international politics have been resolved for all time, hence all that remains is the application of this deep knowledge (gnosis). The hyper-normalization of this reality renders everything else false and unreal. This is the thinking at the heart of the Straussian neoconservative project, practiced by its epigones such as William Kristol and Victoria Nuland. Formerly Republicans, the migration of such neocons to the Democrats demonstrates the way that in foreign policy the two parties effectively fused. The base lead of earlier pragmatism and realism has been transformed into the gold of democratic internationalism. The stubborn resistance of recalcitrant powers is to be overcome not by engagement, dialogue or diplomacy but by confrontation and the reinforcement of hegemony. Coercion is the midwife of the new world order, with recalcitrant powers to be disciplined. Heterodox ideas threaten the purity of the vision and must be resisted at all costs. Strauss-inspired foreign policy on principle refuses dialogue and engagement with adversaries, other than minimally necessary interactions. The Straussian neoconservative transformation of US foreign policy became an era of NATO enlargement and perpetual war.

All this adds up to the Political West becoming increasingly hermetic, closed to the concerns of others and condemning intrusions from outside the 'golden circle'. Democratic internationalism generates a tutelary and hierarchical, exclusive and pedagogical approach. Just as democratism subverts democracy, so hermeticism undermines diplomacy.

Anti-Diplomacy and Demise of Dialogue

Dialogue and diplomacy can only be conducted on the basis of respect for the sovereignty of others, however deep the disagreement. In his marvellous study of diplomatic professionalism, former ambassador Chas Freeman notes that 'Tact is the knack of making a point without making an enemy'.[38] Hegemonic ideology subverts diplomacy, and moralistic thinking undercuts the foundations for agonistic engagement. Cold war ideologisation of international relations shifts international politics from the rational pursuit of national interests, however constructed, to idealistic crusades – tempered by the double standards characteristic of all such projects. Cold War II is characterised

---

38 Chas W. Freeman, 'On Diplomatic Professionalism', July 2024, https://chasfreeman.net/on-diplomatic-professionalism/.

by acute diaphobia, the fear of dialogue. Dialogue with an adversary grants them an undeserved legitimacy and rewards bad behaviour with recognition. Diplomacy is a gift that can be withdrawn. Diplomacy becomes just another weapon in the arsenal of democracy. Substantive engagement is equated with appeasement, and any concession tantamount to a defeat.

By this logic, diplomacy becomes meaningless and redundant. If all substantive issues at the end of history have been resolved, what is there left to talk about? Equally, if dialogue is equated with appeasement, then in this Manichean world the only option is defeat of the opponent. Mortal combat is conducted in the communicative sphere, but when all else fails then the Hobbesian struggle is transferred to the battlefield. If political evolution has reached its logical end point, with Western modernity the only viable and legitimate form of political community, then anything outside by definition is not on 'the right side of history' and part of the jungle. If there is no legitimate alternative form of modernity or development other than the one advanced by the Political West, then it is incumbent on the West to universalise its experience and share its bounty with the rest of the world, a revival of the 'civilising mission' of nineteenth century liberal imperialism. A global Monroe Doctrine is then imposed, a universalism that brooks no islands of particularism. The logic is impeccable, which in the nuclear age inevitably generates cold war forms of politics.

Michael Doyle notes the way that cosmopolitan liberals in Cold War I opposed non-liberal states not so much because of what they did, but what they were (the essence of cold war politics): 'Liberalism creates both the hostility to communism, not just to Soviet power, and the crusading ideological bent of policy. Liberals do not merely distrust what [the communists] do; we dislike what they are – public violators of human rights'.[39] Today, this animus is directed against illiberal states, part of the putative Fifth International of autocracies. For example, the European Parliament ruled that Russia's presidential election of 15–17 March 2024, in which Putin was returned for a fifth term, was illegitimate, a motion supported by 493 out of 522 members, with only 11 voting against and 18 abstaining. The resolution also held Putin personally responsible for Navalny's death.[40] Diplomacy is subordinated to ideological imperatives. This reinforces the hermeticism of the Political West. The practices include the following:

---

39 Michael Doyle, 'Kant, Liberal Legacies, and Foreign Affairs, Part 2', *Philosophy & Public Affairs*, Vol. 12, No. 4, 1983, p. 330.
40 'European Parliament Rules Russia's Presidential Election Illegitimate, Calls Putin a "Murderer"', *Intellinews*, 26 April 2024, https://www.intellinews.com/european-parliament-rules-russia-s-presidential-election-illegitimate-calls-putin-a-murderer-322967/.

First, the Cold War II attack on the diplomatic infrastructure is unprecedented. This is very different from Cold War I, where in the post-Stalin era backchannel (Track 2) diplomacy kept lines of communication open. At the height of the Cuban missile crisis in October 1962, attorney-general Robert Kennedy was in constant contact with the Soviet ambassador in Washington, Anatoly Dobrynin. The president, John F. Kennedy, exchanged letters with the Soviet leader, Nikita Khrushchev, before, during and after the crisis.[41] By contrast, in Cold War II even contact with ambassadors is considered 'collusion', as was the case at the height of the 'Russiagate' mania directed against Trump in 2016. Communications with the Russian ambassador, Sergei Kislyak, was condemned.[42] This damaging proscription is reinforced by repeated expulsions and closure of diplomatic and cultural facilities. Diplomatic infrastructure is a particular target. In December 2016, in one of his last acts as president, Barack Obama expelled 35 Russian diplomats and closed Russian vacation estates in Maryland and New York, which the US side claimed were being used for intelligence purposes. In a delayed response, half a year later Moscow demanded parity and ordered the United States to reduce its presence in Russia to 455 employees.

In response, the United States also demanded 'parity' in the number of institutions and on 1 September 2017 the Russian consulate in San Francisco and trade missions in New York and Washington were closed. The staff in San Francisco were given only two days' notice to move out. Obama's assault was continued by Trump, who naturally has little time for the niceties of traditional diplomacy. A year after first entering office, 46 ambassadorships were still vacant. The expulsions continued following the poisoning of the former Russian double-agent Sergei Skripal and his daughter Yulia in Salisbury, England, in March 2018. Following a series of tit-for-tat expulsions, Moscow forced the closure of the British Council in Russia, although some of its function were brought in-house under the aegis of the embassy. In 2024, London expelled the Russian defence attaché and removed diplomatic status from several premises owned by Russia, including Seacox Heath, a castle on the Kent–Sussex border. The *danse macabre* continues, accompanied by threats to downgrade diplomatic representation more broadly. The next step would be to break off diplomatic relations in their entirety, an unthinkable action except in wartime, but now an entirely plausible eventuality

---

41 Jeffrey D. Sachs, *To Move the World: JFK's Quest for Peace* (London, The Bodley Head, 2013), pp. 34 and *passim*.

42 Richard Sakwa, *Deception: Russiagate and the New Cold War* (Lanham, Lexington Books, 2022), pp. 7, 199–224 and *passim*.

Second, the practice of boycotts. A signal example is the 57-member OSCE ministerial meeting in Skopje, North Macedonia, on 30 November 2023. The Helsinki meeting of the OSCE's predecessor, the Conference on Security and Cooperation in Europe (CSCE), in August 1975 adopted the Final Act and signalled serious engagement by all the European states and the United States and Canada to manage and ultimately overcome the logic of cold war. The CSCE's normative framework provided the framework to end Cold War I in 1989. It was also anticipated to become the institutional framework for an inclusive and indivisible post-Cold War peace order. It was not to be. Instead, NATO amplified its ambitions to become the premier collective *defence* body, marginalising what had become the OSCE in December 1994. This left an enormous gap where a pan-European *collective security* order should have been. The great English School scholar and diplomat, Adam Watson, lamented the fragmentation of the pan-European security architecture, which in his opinion should have included Russia.[43] Cold War II passions were fostered in this void. By the time of the Skopje meeting, there could be no agreement on even a relatively straightforward issue as who would occupy the rotating chairmanship. With the existence of the OSCE in the balance, Russian foreign minister Lavrov attended. This prompted a boycott by Ukraine, Poland, Latvia, Lithuania and Estonia. With the European security order in tatters, the faint hope that the OSCE could provide a pathway to peace, as it had done at the end of Cold War I, was frustrated.

Third, the politicisation of international institutions. Moscow, and increasingly Beijing, complain about the way that the Political West seeks to 'privatise' what were meant to be universal platforms dealing with the common problems of humanity. Instead, Russian and Chinese representatives are prevented from gaining leadership posts or even of joining executive boards. By 2021, China led four of the UN's 15 specialised agencies: the Food and Agriculture Organization, the International Telecommunications Union, the UN Industrial Development Organization and the International Civil Aviation Organization. This prompted a coordinated response by the Political West, fearing that the so-called 'revisionist' powers were subverting liberal order from within. China was blocked from assuming more leadership roles. In November 2023, Russia for the first time failed to be elected to the board of the Organisation for the Prevention of Chemical Weapons. It was denied representation on the ICJ and the UN Human Rights Commission.

---

43 Filippo Costa Buranelli, 'Beyond the Pendulum: Situating Adam Watson in International Relations and the English School', *International Politics*, October 2023, online version.

The rules-based order increasingly inserts its 'rules' where international law and conventions should apply. The result is arbitrariness and the further erosion of the credibility of the Charter International System. Lingering elements of the spirit of 1945 dissipated.

Fourth, NATO enlargement is one of the greatest acts of anti-diplomacy in history. In the words of one reflective analysis,

> Washington's message to Moscow could not have been clearer or more disquieting: Normal diplomacy among great powers, distinguished by the recognition and accommodation of clashing interests – the approach that had defined the US-Soviet rivalry during even the most intense stretches of the Cold War – was obsolete. Russia was expected to acquiesce to a new world order created and dominated by the United States.[44]

This came to a head in the Russo-Ukrainian war, when Washington's stated goal was to inflict maximum pain on Russia. Biden's demand that his counterpart, in command of the world's largest nuclear arsenal, be removed from power 'seriously crimps opportunities for diplomacy and dialogue while ushering in death and destruction'. After 1,000 years, Russia was not going anywhere and neither was the United States.[45] This explains why Todd argues that World War III has already begun:

> It's obvious that the conflict, which started as a limited territorial war and escalated to a global economic confrontation between the whole of the West on the one hand and Russia and China on the other hand, has become a world war.

Neither side could let go, hence 'we are now in an endless war, in a confrontation whose outcome must be the collapse of one or the other'.[46] Both sides call for 'total victory' and condemn those calling for a negotiated resolution.

Fifth, if values are placed at the heart of interstate relations, then diplomacy tends towards the crusader spirit. Nineteenth-century liberal imperialism

---

44 Benjamin Schwarz and Christopher Layne, 'Why Are We in Ukraine?', *Harper's Magazine*, June 2023, https://harpers.org/archive/2023/06/why-are-we-in-ukraine/.

45 Thomas Emanuel Dans, 'Why Was Tucker Carlson's Putin Interview the First Time Americans Heard the Russian Viewpoint?', *The American Conservative*, 13 February 2024, https://www.theamericanconservative.com/americans-most-dangerous-blind-spot/.

46 Rob Lownie, 'Emmanuel Todd: World War Three Has Already Begun', *UnHerd*, 16 January 2023, https://unherd.com/newsroom/emmanuel-todd-world-war-iii-has-already-begun/.

appealed to a 'standard of civilisation', with disastrous consequences.[47] Democratic internationalism reinserts a Western narrative of superiority and establishes a teacher–pupil relationship with the world outside of the Political West. It reasserts the civilisational discourse that accompanied the rise of the West in the first place some 500 years ago, with all the achievements of the Renaissance and Enlightenment but also the gruesome cruelties of imperialism and colonialism. The Political West reproduces this style of imperial thinking. Europe's high representative for foreign policy, Borrell, put it rather brutally: Europe is a garden surrounded by a jungle.[48] The echo of Joseph Conrad's *Heart of Darkness* is unmistakeable. In this model, the Political West claims to be the recipe to cure the alleged ills of the lesser developed countries. Critique of this liberal imperialism does not mean that values are not important in international politics, but asserts that they are more credible when practised by those who profess them. As Freeman argues, 'Hypocrisy begets both distrust and contempt'.[49]

Sixth, the outcome is 'democratism', the instrumental deployment of values in the pursuit of geopolitical goals. This generates an entire 'democracy promotion' industry, which typically seeks to mobilise 'civil society' against regimes deemed unacceptable. Worse, support for civil society undermines the work of governmental agencies, thus eroding the coherence of state development in its entirety. This was famously the case earlier in Kyrgyzstan, when NGOs were explicitly directed not to work with local government authorities, on the grounds that they were corrupt. However, corruption too often is term used to describe informal practices that in the context may deliver public goods in the absence of legal-rationalist bureaucracies. Democracy promotion blends into regime change operations, as in Ukraine. Again, this does not mean that democracy is not important, but democratism is something very different. As we have seen, the pursuit of geopolitical goals in the guise of advancing values generates double standards. The classic principles of self-determination and pluralism based on sovereign internationalism are subverted by the instrumental promotion of democratic norms. Double standards become a mode of engagement in international affairs.

---

47 Gerrit W. Gong, *The Standard of 'Civilization' in International Society* (Oxford, Clarendon Press, 1984).
48 Josep Borrell, European Diplomatic Academy, 'Opening Remarks by High Representative Josep Borrell at the Inauguration of the Pilot Programme', 13 October 2022, https://www.eeas.europa.eu/eeas/european-diplomatic-academy-opening-remarks-high-representative-josep-borrell-inauguration-pilot_en.
49 Freeman, 'On Diplomatic Professionalism'.

All this adds up to something very different from the classical tradition of diplomacy. The former British diplomat posted to Moscow, Ian Proud, put it well when he argues 'It's not the job of diplomacy to fix Russia, but to live at peace with it and to ensure it is at peace with its former Soviet neighbours. On that, we have singularly failed.'[50] He notes how the British foreign secretary, Philip Hammond, considered Russia 'an enemy to be countered, not a nuclear-armed regional power to be negotiated with'. The sanctions imposed from 2014 'were valued primarily for the political signal they sent', irrespective of whether they materially changed Russian behaviour or promoted a resolution of the Ukraine conflict.[51] He argues that 'The dumbing down of diplomacy started under New Labour, seduced by the notion that modern diplomats needed little more than a laptop', rather than detailed country knowledge and language skills.[52] The fear was that 'diplomatic engagement with Russia would show weakness rather than resolve'.[53] This misses the point: 'Real diplomacy seeks to balance competing interests to prevent conflict.'[54] Instead, the very idea that interests could conflict and should therefore be managed was lost in the hubristic illusions and false universalism fostered by 'victory' in Cold War I.

Instead of focusing on core strategic concerns, Washington simultaneously alienated Moscow and Beijing. Any conceivable Sino-US war would be catastrophic for all concerned. An alternative was to hand:

> The best route to preventing a future Chinese invasion of Taiwan would be to revive Washington's 'one China' policy that calls for China to commit itself to a peaceful resolution of Taiwan's status and for the US to forswear support for that island's formal independence. In other words, diplomacy, rather than increasing the Pentagon's budget to 'win' such a war, would be the way to go.[55]

The war fever of the early 2020s intensified anti-diplomacy. Anti-diplomacy subverts the conflict-managing rationale of genuine diplomacy. Multilateral engagement becomes an instrument in a predetermined dialectical frame, rather than a mode of dialogical engagement in which all sides change.

---

50 Personal correspondence, 14 December 2023.
51 Ian Proud, *A Misfit in Moscow: How British Diplomacy in Russia Failed 2014–2019* (Copyright Ian Proud, 2023), p. 68.
52 Proud, *A Misfit in Moscow*, pp. 71–72.
53 Proud, *A Misfit in Moscow*, p. 88.
54 Proud, *A Misfit in Moscow*, p. 95.
55 William Hartung, 'The World Weeps While the Military Industrial Complex Keeps Winning', *Responsible Statecraft*, 19 January 2024, https://responsiblestatecraft.org/defense-industry-war-pentagon/.

Chapter 5
SANCTIONS AND MORAL ECONOMY

Sanctions undermine the liberal order that they are intended to protect. By challenging the principle of innocent until proven guilty, the Political West erodes its moral standing not only in target countries but across the Global South. Undermining the property and legal rights of individuals and states damages not only economic interdependence but also the very idea of deeply interconnected economies. The trend towards deglobalisation accelerates as states seek to insulate their economies and make them more resilient by shortening supply chains, increasing localisation and import substitution.[1] The geopolitical effects are also severe. Sanctions on Japan precipitated the attack on Pearl Harbour in December 1941. Unilateral coercive measures, as sanctions are better called, act as a form of ersatz war, entrenching the growing hostility between Russia and the West, a process that was later repeated vis-à-vis China. In his study of peasant rebellions in Southeast Asia, James C. Scott examined the moral economy of economic activity and relationships.[2] The term is applied here to highlight the morally contentious ground on which sanctions are applied today. Without procedural justice and impartiality, not only the legitimacy of the sanctions but that of the sanctioning states themselves is questioned. No less important, sanctions contribute to the overall deterioration in the geopolitical environment, indefinitely locking states into patterns of hostility.

Sanctions from Hell

The modern era of sanctions was launched by Congress's adoption of the Magnitsky sanctions in December 2012, followed by Obama's expulsion of diplomats in 2016. Putin's 'cronies' became an easy although dangerously

---

1 Richard Connolly, *Russia's Responses to Sanctions: How Western Sanctions Reshaped Political Economy in Russia*, Valdai Paper No. 94, November 2018, http://valdaiclub.com/a/valdai-papers/russia-s-response-to-sanctions-how-western-sanctio/.
2 James C. Scott, *The Moral Economy of the Peasant* (New Haven, Yale University Press, 1976).

unspecific target, along with assorted oligarchs and genuine criminals. In July 2017, Congress adopted the landmark legislation, 'Countering America's Adversaries through Sanctions Act' (CAATSA). The CAATSA sanctions limited the president's ability to ease or lift earlier ones. Obama's sanctions had been introduced by executive order, but they were now codified in statute and therefore cannot be rescinded by presidential decree.[3] The target was no longer alleged Russian crimes but the Russian corporate economy as a whole. This came on top of the cessation of most military-to-military contacts in the wake of the 2014 Ukraine crisis with the exception of 'deconfliction' procedures in Syria. A reluctant Trump had no choice but to sign the measure. CAATSA is a sprawling catch-all law, effectively 'expropriating' the management of foreign policy from the White House. It created a punitive dynamic liable to poison relations between Russia and the United States for generations to come. The law extended sanctions to countries outside Russia (extraterritoriality) where US corporations or persons provided goods, services and technology for certain projects 'in which a Russian firm is involved', raising the concerns of European leaders and companies, notably those involved in building the Nord Stream 2 gas pipeline under the Baltic Sea from Russia to Germany.[4] Congress feared that Trump would weaken or even reverse the Obama-era legislation and hence closed ranks in a bipartisan manner against the president.[5] CAATSA marked a watershed in Russo-US relations and in the management of global affairs in general.[6] The anti-democratic attempt to make policy 'Trump-proof' continued into the Biden era.

On 6 April 2018, Trump imposed the most devastating sanctions yet seen, in part in response to the Skripal affair and the alleged use of chemical weapons in Douma in Eastern Ghouta on the outskirts of Damascus. They targeted what the United States claimed were individuals and companies that aided or benefitted from what were considered the Kremlin's 'malign activities' around the world, including the alleged interference in the 2016 US

---

3 Obama imposed executive sanctions on 6 March and 18 December 2014, 1 April 2015, and 26 July and 29 December 2016.
4 Wolfgang Ischinger, 'Why Europeans Oppose the Russia Sanctions Bill', *Wall Street Journal*, 17 July 2017, https://www.wsj.com/articles/why-europeans-oppose-the-russia-sanctions-bill-1500232733.
5 Mikhail Alexeev, 'Why Trump's Bid to Improve US-Russian Relations Backfired', *Ponars Eurasia*, February 2018, http://www.ponarseurasia.org/memo/why-trumps-bid-improve-us-russian-relations-backfired-congress.
6 For an excellent analysis, see Konstantin Khudoley, 'Russia and the US: The Way Forward', *Russia in Global Affairs*, No. 4, 2017, http://eng.globalaffairs.ru/number/Russia-and-the-US-The-Way-Forward-19263.

presidential election, supplying weapons to Syrian president Bashar al-Assad and subverting Western democracies. The US Treasury Department imposed sanctions on seven Russian oligarchs, 12 companies they either owned or controlled and 17 senior Kremlin officials. Those sanctioned could not do business in the United States or gain access to financial markets. Oleg Deripaska, the head of one of the world's largest aluminium companies, Rusal, was targeted 'for having acted or purported to act for or on behalf of, directly or indirectly, a senior official of the Government of the Russian Federation'.[7] The disruption caused havoc in the aluminium market, forcing a partial reversal to allow Deripaska to divest himself of his majority interest in Rusal. The company, like some others, proved 'too big to sanction'.[8] In December 2019, the US Senate foreign relations committee adopted a resolution calling for 'sanctions from hell' to be imposed on Russia for its alleged electoral interference, 'malign' actions in Syria and aggression against Ukraine.[9] These sanctions were imposed following Russia's invasion of Ukraine in February 2022.

The prime minister, Dmitry Medvedev, condemned the April 2018 sanctions as 'outrageous and obnoxious' but stressed that they forced Russia to rethink its place in the world. He considered the containment of Russia an enduring strategy of the West, which it would continue to pursue regardless of how the country may be called: 'They did this with regard to the Russian Empire, and they did this many times with regard to the Soviet Union and Russia'. Medvedev's argument highlights how Cold War II is embedded in a much longer pattern of hostility between Russia and the West, which for many goes back to Russia's insertion into the European state system in the eighteenth century, while Russophobia has an even longer history. Medvedev insisted that Russia would adapt and respond through import substitution and improvements to its own social institutions. He took it for granted that 'sanctions will remain in place for a long time'.[10] This view was shared by the Russian public, with 43 per cent at that time believing that they would not be

---

7 Sabra Ayres, 'Russia Feeling the Financial Bite of US Sanctions', *Los Angeles Times*, 10 April 2018, p. A3.
8 Jeanne Whalen and John Hudson, 'Too Big to Sanction? US Struggles with Punishing Large Russian Businesses', *Washington Post*, 27 August 2018.
9 'US Lawmakers Pass Russia "Sanctions Bill from Hell"', RFE/RL, *Russia Digest*, 18 December 2019, https://www.rferl.org/a/u-s-lawmakers-to-discuss-russia-sanctions-bill-from-hell-/30331992.html.
10 'Excerpts from Dmitry Medvedev's Interview with Vesti and Subbotu Programme', 28 April 2018, http://www.publicnow.com/view/.

lifted in the next few years.¹¹ Putin noted that 'We are not surprised by any restrictions or sanctions: this does not frighten us and will never force us to abandon our independent, sovereign path of development'. And he went on to declare: 'I believe that either Russia will be sovereign, or it will not exist at all.'¹²

A post-Western Russia is taking shape, increasingly estranged from the Political West but seeking to retain its European identity, although as always insisting that Russia represents a more authentic and better Europe.¹³ The rupture with the Political West is complete. As Dmitry Trenin, the former director of the Moscow Carnegie Centre, later put it:

> having re-established the supremacy of national legislation over international treaties, Moscow now cares little about what its adversaries can say or do about its policies or actions. From Russia's standpoint, not only can't the West be trusted any longer; the international bodies that it controls have lost all legitimacy.¹⁴

Moscow remains committed to the Charter system and the UN, as Putin stressed at the Valdai Club meeting in October 2023, but if that were to change then Russia really would become a fully revisionist power.¹⁵

Washington had long been concerned by Europe's energy dependency on Russia. The 'Protecting Europe's Energy Security Act' adopted by Congress in 2019 as part of the 2020 National Defence Authorisation Act was reinforced the following year.¹⁶ The goal was to prevent the completion of Nord Stream 2 and thus was directed as much against Germany as Russia. Energy-related sanctions hark back to the Cold War days of the early Reagan period,

---

11 'Over 40% of Russians Believe Western Sanctions Likely to Remain for Years', *Sputnik*, 29 April 2018, https://sputniknews.com/russia/201804291064013398-sanctions-lift-poll/.

12 Vladimir Putin, 'Interview with China Media Group', *Kremlin.ru*, 5 June 2018, http://en.kremlin.ru/events/president/news/57684.

13 Cf. Iver B. Neumann, *Russia and the Idea of Europe: A Study in Identity and International Relations* (London, Routledge, 2016).

14 Dmitry Trenin, 'Russia Is Undergoing a New, Invisible Revolution', *RT.com*, 2 April 2024, https://www.rt.com/russia/595266-ukraine-west-pushed-russia/.

15 Vladimir Putin, 'Valdai International Discussion Club Meeting', 5 October 2023, http://en.kremlin.ru/events/president/news/72444. In asking the question, it was important for me to receive confirmation that Putin remained committed to the UN system, despite its manifest failings.

16 Ivan Timofeev, *Sanctions against Russia: A Look into 2021* (Moscow, RIAC Report No. 65. 2021), p. 13, https://russiancouncil.ru/en/activity/publications/sanctions-against-russia-a-look-into-2021/.

when Europe resisted American pressure and provided the Soviet Union with the technology to complete large-bore energy pipelines. The European energy crisis from late 2021 was exacerbated by Russia's refusal to ramp up gas supplies, although contracted quantities were supplied. Russia sought new long-term contracts and regulatory approval of Nord Stream 2. Russia's philosophy since the early 1970s had been 'meet the contract at all costs'. However, when it stopped supplies to Ukraine in early 2006 and again in early 2009, Ukraine simply diverted supplies destined for Europe for its own needs, leaving Europe in the cold. Russia's reputation for reliability was irreparably damaged, and the myth of the Russian 'energy weapon' was born. Moscow intensified its long-term strategy of avoiding unreliable transit states.

The two lines of Nord Stream 1 were completed in 2012 and of Nord Stream 2 in August 2021 but delays in regulatory approval meant that the latter never came on stream. Three of the four lines were blown up on 26 September 2022, for which the CIA working with Norwegian special services has been held responsible.[17] A number of fanciful versions were later advanced to explain 'one of the most significant acts of industrial sabotage in history', depriving Germany of the gas that had powered its heavy industries for a generation. Worse, the perpetrators not only enjoyed a surprising degree of immunity but above all knew that 'they would get away with it. [...] The latter points to deeper forces operating within a society or even a civilisation'.[18] In the first instance, it confirms the operative double standards identified earlier, but also exposes the 'deeper forces' identified in this book. One of those is the long-term Washington imperative to prevent a new Rapallo, a German-Russian alliance that would upend global geopolitics in their entirety by moving away from the Atlanticism at the heart of the Political West since 1945 towards a more dynamic post-American European continentalism.

Russia imposed a range of counter-sanctions, including those of August 2014 (and later extended) on food imports from sanctioning countries. In June 2018, Putin signed legislation allowing 'counter-measures against unfriendly actions' by the United States and other foreign countries, effectively an upgrade of a December 2006 law providing for 'special economic measures'. The new law weakened earlier responses mooted by impassioned deputies in parliament, which would have damaged Russia more than the sanctions

---

17 Seymour Hersh, 'How America Took Out the Nord Stream Pipeline', *Substack*, 8 February 2023, https://seymourhersh.substack.com/p/how-america-took-out-the-nord-stream.

18 Henry Johnston, 'Blast from the Past: Why the Nord Stream Sabotage May Yet Have its Day of Reckoning', *RT.com*, 28 August 2024, https://www.rt.com/business/603110-nord-stream-blast-from-past/.

themselves.[19] The country's economy was reoriented to ensure greater resilience and autonomy. The role of the state in the economy was further increased, and import substitution was intensified as self-reliance became the guiding principle.[20] The EU's sanctions between 2014 and 2021 were renewed every six months, on the grounds that Russia was not fulfilling the Minsk Accords on regularising the status of the two Donbass republics.

Following Russia's invasion of February 2022, the US Treasury Department and equivalent bodies in the European Commission (EC) imposed a set of measures against Russia that were unprecedented in their scope and intensity. The sanctions came in five main forms: hits against financial institutions and services; cutting Russian energy exports; bans on the importation of manufactured items (especially dual-use technologies) that could support Russia's war effort; the withdrawal of Western companies from the Russian market; and the imposition of sanctions on individuals. Russia was in danger of turning into a larger version of North Korea. Three decades of economic integration with the West were reversed in a matter of months. On 8 March 2022, Biden announced a ban on all Russia oil and natural gas imports to the United States, and the EU gradually followed suit. Severe financial sanctions were imposed by the United States, EU and UK, including unexpectedly against the Central Bank of Russia (CBR), thus freezing half of Russia's 'war chest' reserves of $630bn, some $300bn held in dollars and other currencies abroad. Seven major banks were barred from accessing SWIFT, the interbank messaging service that acts as the nerve centre of the international financial system, and transactions with many major Russian SOEs were blocked. An extensive list of 'oligarchs' were also sanctioned, a category as broad as it was vague, and extraterritorial sanctions were imposed on third parties who allegedly supported Russia's war economy. By January 2024, Russia was subject to over 28,000 sanctions, over 16,000 of which were imposed on individuals, nearly 10,000 were imposed on companies and 3,200 were against institutions.[21] Russia responded by diverting exports formerly entering European markets to China, India and elsewhere in the Global South,

---

19 Ivan Timofeev, 'Fighting Sanctions: From Legislation to Strategy', *Valdai Club*, 18 June 2018, http://valdaiclub.com/a/highlights/fighting-sanctions-strategy/.

20 This is analysed by Richard Connolly, *Russia's Response to Sanctions: How Western Statecraft Is Reshaping Political Economy in Russia* (Cambridge, Cambridge University Press, 2018).

21 Michael Corbin, 'Did the West "Crush" Russia's Economy for Invading Ukraine?', *Responsible Statecraft*, 14 February 2024, https://responsiblestatecraft.org/russia-sanctions-ukraine/.

allowing parallel imports through third countries and reshaping the domestic economy towards 'military Keynesianism'.

Contesting Sanctions

All major states deploy sanctions as an instrument of statecraft, but the United States is by far the global leader. America became 'addicted' to sanctions, with one wave following another. For example, between 5 January 2020 and 10 January 2021, it was responsible for 52 per cent (449 out of 850) sanction events. China and Russia were minnows in the field, with China accounting for 12 events and Russia for 16. Remarkably, the UN accounted for only 58, even though the Security Council is the only legitimate source of multilateral restrictive measures.[22] Most of the sanctions against Russia are associated with Ukraine, often imposed on individuals who have nothing to do with the conflict but who are targeted for political reasons, such as the ubiquitous 'ties' to the Russia leadership – it seems that anyone who is anyone in Russia is 'close to Putin'. Never before has a major country been hit with such an all-encompassing economic attack outside of the formal declaration of war. However, as it became clear that the international financial system could be weaponised in the pursuit of particular goals, non-Western powers hastened to build an alternative financial architecture to protect themselves. The anti-Russian sanctions demonstrate that the international economic architecture can be deployed against adversaries through primary or secondary sanctions, rendering everyone vulnerable. Hence, the global scramble to insulate against the Political West's economic warfare.

Sanctions serve as the alternative not only to war but also to diplomacy. Sanctions against Iraq, Iran, Syria and Afghanistan provoked countless deaths, but when applied against Russia they threaten not only physical suffering but also the dismantling of the entire Charter International System as constituted after 1945. They also threaten globalisation and the dominance of the Political West. Non-Western states are withdrawing sovereign reserves in case they, too, are hit with sanctions and their funds impounded. The dollar is losing its accustomed primacy. Russia, China, India and other states increasingly trade in their own currencies, amidst much talk of devising an alternative currency and digital variations. Sanctions are increasingly perceived as punitive, even vindictive, and pursued even when they are unlikely to achieve

---

22 Timofeev, *Sanctions against Russia*, p. 7.

any tangible benefit.[23] Worse, the possible harms are evident. When sanctions are imposed without due cause and without a substantive evidentiary basis, with appropriate rights of appeal on the basis of the classic common law principle of innocent until proven guilty, then the whole sanction system is liable to stand accused of bias and injustice. The foundations of the rule of law are undermined.

The UN is the only legitimate source of universal sanctions and other interventions. The imposition of unilateral coercive measures by the United States and its allies, including secondary sanctions, is an example of the usurpation of the prerogatives of multilateral institutions, a development contested by the rising powers of the Political East. The weaponisation of the economic instruments of coercion, in the form of sanctions and other punitive measures falling short of kinetic conflict, has intensified in recent years. Sanctions are typically considered a relatively cost-free alternative to military action or other forms of pressure. Sanctions obviously work best when they offer an incentive to behave in a manner desired by the sanctioning power, including a clear set of criteria for their revocation. Cold War II is distinctive because means have typically been decoupled from ends. The means has been more sanctions, but the defined end has usually been unclear. What Washington calls 'malign activities' are perceived elsewhere as the legitimate defence of national interests. They became part of broader containment strategies applied against countries such as Cuba, Iran, North Korea, Venezuela, Russia and increasingly China. They are no longer connected to a designated cause with a specific outcome but have become part of an enduring war of attrition.

The principle that the UN is the main source of legitimate sanctions is breaking down, and their widespread application by Western powers is yet another indication of the great substitution. In the United States, Congress and the White House compete to see who can be tougher, while the EU has been implacable in seeking to impose costs on Russia for its war in Ukraine. Sanctions represent a type of 'foreign policy on the cheap', imposed – until recently – with minimal domestic blowback effects. It allows the functional equivalent of war to replace diplomacy, targeting civilian populations without the restrictive protocols regulating conventional warfare. They are overwhelmingly targeted against countries that challenge the United States in one way or another, although their use is not restricted to one country. They assert the primacy of the Political West to force adversaries to accept US

---

23 Owen Matthews, 'Sanctions against Russia Have Backfired', *The Spectator*, 25 November 2023, https://www.spectator.co.uk/article/sanctions-against-russia-have-backfired/.

hegemony. Sanctions are easy to impose but hard to lift and thus become part of the repertoire of 'forever wars'.[24] Imposed often in defence of human rights, there is little evidence that they improve conditions, and in some cases only provoke further repression and exacerbate the problem they are intended to resolve. As Paul Robinson notes, the emphasis on deontological ethics – the Kantian appeal to absolute ethics and right intentions – overshadows the utilitarian tradition associated with Jeremy Bentham, where the focus is less on what sanctions are intended to do but on the actual results.[25] On this metric, the sanctions of our age have been overwhelmingly counterproductive: not only not achieving their intended goals, but prompting outcomes antithetical to their stated purpose.

The Ukraine War and Collective Guilt

When illegitimate legal devices and national security considerations are deployed to harm adversaries, the means contradict the ends. This drifts into the territory where law is instrumentalised to pursue political goals. Jeremy Peterson's classic analysis describes a show trial as including the following elements: denying the accused the opportunity to tell their side of the story; denying the accused the opportunity the right to counsel; denying the accused the opportunity to obtain exculpatory evidence; denying the accused the opportunity to challenge the prosecution's evidence; failing to limit the record to relevant evidence or failing to admit relevant evidence; not providing a clear definition of the crime attributed to the accused; lacking sufficient proof requirements and diminished independence or competence of decision-makers. In sum, if a trial lacks 'risk' (meaning there is no chance of the accused being found 'not guilty') and the demonstration effect preoccupies the participants' minds, then Peterson argues that the process lacks legitimacy.[26]

The fundamental common law principle of innocent until proven guilty was fundamentally repudiated by Magnitsky Rule of Law Acts, beginning with the one imposed by the US Congress in December 2012. Individuals

---

24 Krishan Mehta, 'Sanctions and Forever Wars', *American Committee on US-Russia Accord (ACURA)*, 4 May 2021, https://usrussiaaccord.com/acura-viewpoint-sanctions-and-forever-wars-by-krishen-mehta/.
25 Paul Robinson, 'How Western Sanctions Drove Belarus Closer to Moscow', *Canadian Dimension*, 1 April 2023, https://canadiandimension.com/articles/view/how-western-sanctions-drove-belarus-closer-to-moscow.
26 Jeremy Peterson, 'Unpacking Show Trials: Situating the Trial of Saddam Hussein', *Harvard International Law Review*, Vol. 48, No. 1, Winter 2007, pp. 257–92.

are placed on blacklists without the sanction of the courts. In the absence of a judicial process, the evidence of alleged malfeasance cannot be challenged and there is no right of appeal. Obama understood the implications, and that is why he sought to prevent the adoption of the Congressional legislation in 2012.[27] The pursuit of justice through blacklists and sanctions is exposed as political chicanery and thus discredits the sanctioning authorities. The Russiagate allegations in the United States, asserting that Trump in some way colluded with Putin to win the 2016 presidential election, have been exposed as a cynical act of deception, masterminded by the Hillary Clinton camp.[28] The whole renewed cold war cycle of sanctions and countersanctions began with an act since exposed as fraudulent. Cold War II intensified, and with growing mistrust on all sides, the slide to war in Ukraine accelerated. Thereafter, the imposition of draconian sanctions on Russia asserted the principle of collective guilt – effectively repudiating the Geneva conventions. In his famous work *The Question of German Guilt*, Karl Jaspers identified four types of guilt: criminal, the commitment of overt acts, requiring conviction in a court of law; political, acquiescence in the acts of a regime, imposed on a defeated party (as in the case of Germany) by the victors; moral, a private judgement among friends; and a fourth category which he labelled metaphysical – universally shared by a people who do not do all that is possible to withstand evil.[29] Jaspers' examination of Germany's war guilt has profound resonance in a Russia at war in Ukraine.[30]

Regional geopolitics play an important part in stimulating cold war practices. The anti-Russian positions adopted by the EU and the UK were in part driven by the intense Russophobia of the Baltic republics, Poland, Romania and some other former Soviet bloc states. Historical grievances in the former Soviet and Soviet bloc states are real and painful, but the EU had once been considered a peace project – a way of reconciling former foes to create conditions where war between them is impossible. Instead, the EC in Cold War II became an active agent in fomenting anti-Russian hostility. Instead of looking for ways of negotiating a new peace order, the EC intensified the logic of conflict. This was particularly stark in the 'geopolitical' Commission headed

---

27 As admitted by Bill Browder, the indefatigable advocate of punitive sanctions against Russia. Bill Browder, *Red Notice: How I became Putin's No. 1 Enemy* (London, Bantam Press, 2015).
28 Sakwa, *Deception*.
29 Karl Jaspers, *The Question of German Guilt*, 2nd rev. edn (New York, Fordham University Press, 2000).
30 See, for example, articles by Oleg Aronson, Andrei Arkhangel'skii and Mikhail Mayatskii in Nikolai Plotnikov (ed.), *Pered Litsom Katastrofy* (Berlin, Hopf, 2023).

by Ursula von der Leyen from 2019 Much of this verges on outright racism, designed to counter any diplomatic rapprochement with Russia or negotiated settlement to the Ukraine war. This drew on decades if not centuries of anti-Russian propaganda. As always, this advances two contradictory positions, known as 'Russophrenia'. Russia is simultaneously presented as an ominous threat looming over Europe, while at the same time it is a basket case on the verge of disintegration. US senator John McCain famously described Russia as a 'gas station masquerading as a country'.[31] For Russia's critics, it is always 1938. From this perspective,

> Efforts to appease Putin are fundamentally flawed. Russia's foreign policy is not a response to a series of legitimate and isolated grievances that can be addressed in a rational manner; it is a product of the country's deeply imperialistic political culture and authoritarian state institutions. Any attempt to make sense of Putin's Russia that fails to recognize this reality is tantamount to ignoring the fact that Hitler's Germany was a Nazi state.[32]

This essentialisation of Russia is historically incoherent, since the country (in its various manifestations) on numerous occasions was a responsible diplomatic and even military partner, and academically flawed, since any serious study of post-Cold War Russia demonstrates an openness to partnership. From the beginning, as Jeffrey Sachs among many others demonstrates, this was thwarted by Washington's hegemonic ambitions. In refusing to support Russia after the Soviet collapse, 'the US was far more interested in Russia's subservience to NATO than it was in stable relations with Russia'.[33]

The monological *reductio ad hitlerum* typically puts an end to discussion, but what if the security concerns were genuine? After all, leaders since Gorbachev and Yeltsin had warned against unmediated NATO enlargement, joined by

---

31 John McCain, 'Russia Is a "Gas Station Masquerading as a Country"', *The Week*, 8 January 2015, https://theweek.com/speedreads/456437/john-mccain-russia-gas-station-masquerading-country.

32 Dennis Soltys and Alexander Motyl, 'The West Must Not Let Millions of Ukrainians Freeze to Death', *Atlantic Council*, 30 October 2022, https://www.atlanticcouncil.org/blogs/ukrainealert/the-west-must-not-let-putin-freeze-millions-of-ukrainians-to-death/.

33 Jeffrey D. Sachs, 'How the Neocons Chose Hegemony over Peace Beginning in the Early 1990s', *IDN*, 4 September 2024, https://indepthnews.net/how-the-neocons-chose-hegemony-over-peace-beginning-in-the-early-1990s/.

a range of American diplomats and commentators.[34] Moscow feared that the ultimate effect would be to keep Russia permanently weak. James Carden argues that 'Specific American policy choices (made with the acquiescence of America's NATO allies in Europe) pursued over the course of that decade [the 1990s] have led to where we are today', hence 'things didn't have to be this way'.[35] If that is indeed the case, then the standard formula in refusing to engage with Russian concerns – that to do so would represent 'appeasement' and that capitulation to the demands of an aggressor only whets their appetite – is not only mistaken but fundamentally dangerous, adding fuel to the fire of resentment and sense of exclusion. Such an approach a priori closes down the scope for diplomacy and feeds the distrust that intensifies a security dilemma. Facing down an aggressor is appropriate in certain circumstances, but is the breakdown of the European security order such a case? Most leaders of the Political West are resolute in their view that the invasion of Ukraine in 2022 is indeed an instance when aggression has to be countered militarily.

Moscow's security and other concerns are categorised as attempts to compensate for economic stagnation and declining living standards. This is the standard 'diversionary' formula, where an embattled regime seeks to buy peace at home by fighting abroad. As Shakespeare put it in *Henry V*, 'To busy giddy minds with foreign quarrels'. The Russian economy had indeed failed to generate sustained growth since at least 2013, exacerbated later by sanctions, yet healthy growth of 3.5 per cent was registered in the first quarter of 2022, demonstrating that the country was pulling out of the economic doldrums. Structural realist accounts are the most convincing: foreign and security policies were generated by developments in international politics rather than emanating in a deterministic manner from domestic political or historical-cultural concerns. An aversion to liberalism or democracy had nothing to do with the rise of an anti-Western policy. Instead, it was rooted in a growing Russian perception of threat from NATO and the West, a perspective that has been systemically suppressed in Western public consciousness. Pragmatic realism would have provided a surer guide on how to respond than the 'idealist' condemnation of Russia and dismissal of its concerns. This does not justify the 'special military operation', but recognises it as a strategy of coercive diplomacy intended to bring Ukraine and its Western backers to

---

34 Reviewed in Richard Sakwa, *Russia against the Rest: The Post-Cold War Crisis of World Order* (Cambridge, Cambridge University Press, 2017), pp. 77–90.
35 James W. Carden, 'November 1992: The Hinge of History', *ACURA Viewpoint*, 8 November 2022, https://usrussiaaccord.org/acura-viewpoint-james-w-carden-november-1992-the-hinge-of-history/.

the negotiating table. Views within Russia and those held by Russians abroad are complex and divided. Ascribed guilt, by mere dint of being Russian, is a dangerous slope and in certain cases smacks of racism.

Even individuals and institutions opposed to the war and to the Putin-led regime have fallen into the crosshairs of the sanctions 'cancellation' mania. The negation of all things Russian has become the default setting. For example, all Russians, even those opposed to the regime, were banned from the Polish Economic Forum in September 2022. Held annually, latterly in Karpacz in Lower Silesia, this is a broad gathering of politicians and business leaders. It provided a venue for Russian oppositionists to meet each other and Western experts and scholars (including me), but from 2022 the ill-advised ban, justified by concern for the feelings of Ukrainian participants, deprived them of this opportunity. Another example of the pernicious consequences of the imposition of collective guilt on a whole nation is the *'Dozhd* conundrum' – the independent media channel relocated to Latvia at the beginning of the war after stopping its operations in Russia because of the threat to its journalists from the draconian wartime censorship laws. Promoting an email address which encouraged *Dozhd* viewers to share information about illegal conscription and inadequate provision for soldiers at the front, one of its journalists, Alexei Korostelev, stated: 'we hope that we were able to help many soldiers, for example with equipment and basic amenities'. Following an uproar, he was sacked – but that did not help.[36] Earlier, the station described the Russian army as 'ours' and published a map showing Crimea as part of Russia. In December 2022, Latvia stripped *Dozhd* of its local broadcasting license on the far-fetched grounds that the channel jeopardised national security.

The incident has worrying connotations. It suggests that there can be no 'good Russians' and even if there are a few, they are so statistically insignificant as to be hardly worth bothering about. Even they, it was implied, have a hidden 'imperialist' agenda, even if they support liberal causes. Those who had gone abroad to avoid becoming implicated in Putin's stratagems should have stayed at home to overthrow him there. There is no avoiding the conclusion: to be Russian today means bearing the mark of Cain and enduring the appropriate sanctions. Paradoxically, as the liberal commentator Kirill Rogov points out, 'this position actually echoes the key Kremlin-promoted narrative that Putin and Russia are one and the same. Neither narrative

---

36 'The Dozhd Conundrum', *The Bell*, 12 December 2022, https://thebell.io/the-dozhd-conundrum.

leaves any space on the map for a different kind of Russia'.[37] The campaign to 'cancel Russia' invalidates the views of those who believe in a very different country, one in which the promise of Russia's democratic revolution in the late Soviet years finally comes to fruition.

The Ukraine war poses ethical dilemmas of the highest order. This was the case with German Gref, the former economics minister who was appointed chief executive of the state-owned Sberbank in 2007. Gref was one of the liberal contingent that Putin brought with him from St Petersburg. On taking charge, Gref reshaped Sberbank from a lumbering Soviet-style institution into one of the most dynamic and innovative banks in the world. Gref is fascinated by advanced technologies, and his enthusiasm transformed the bank. A month before the invasion, Gref presented a 39-page document at a meeting of top economic advisers with Putin at his residence in Novo-Ogaryovo, on the outskirts of Moscow. He briefed the president on the likely effect of Western sanctions and strongly advised against military action. This was in keeping with the sentiments of Russian technocrats, who understood that military action would jeopardise Russia's economy for years to come. The invasion left Gref, like so many of his peers, dumbfounded and in shock.[38] Everything that they had built over the last decades was threatened.

Hit by devastating sanctions, the technocrats at the CBR, Ministry of Finance and elsewhere worked to save the economy, which they did remarkably successfully. Instead of an anticipated 10–15 per cent fall in GDP, the decrease in 2022 was just 2.1 per cent and in 2023 growth of 3.6 per cent was registered, which continued into 2024. The bank's head, Elvira Nabiullina, sought to leave her post but Putin convinced her to stay. Her deputy responsible for macroeconomic policy, Ksenia Yudaeva, felt that she had a moral obligation to remain in office to protect the interests of the Russian people. This drew severe criticism from her former colleague, Konstantin Sonin, an economics professor at Chicago University, who urged her to resign. When she insisted on carrying on, Sonin broke off all relations with her, although she did resign later.[39] The statist technocrats kept the more hard-line protec-

---

37 Kirill Rogov, 'Misadventures in Late-Stage Putinism: Dozhd and the Conundrum of Exile', *The Moscow Times*, 13 December 2022, https://www.themoscowtimes.com/2022/12/13/misadventures-in-late-stage-putinism-dozhd-and-the-conundrum-of-exile-a79658.

38 Max Seddon and Polina Ivanovo, 'How Putin's Technocrats Saved the Economy to Fight a War they Opposed', *Financial Times*, 16 December 2022, https://www.ft.com/content/fe5fe0ed-e5d4-474e-bb5a-10c9657285d2.

39 'The Banker's Dilemma: How Elvira Nabiullina and Her Team ave Tried to Save Russia's Economy Amid War and Sanctions', *Meduza*, 7 July 2022, https://meduza.io/en/feature/2022/07/07/the-banker-s-dilemma.

tionists and militarisers at bay and skilfully negotiated the perils of all-out economic warfare. Their actions saved the Russian economy, at least in the short term, maintaining living standards and macroeconomic and political stability. The alternative was chaos, possibly leading to a hard-line coup – resulting in an escalation of the war in Ukraine and against the West.

Entrepreneurs, activists and others who found themselves abroad were rejected by the regime. They were virulently condemned by Putin in an emotional speech on 16 March 2022: 'Those who earn money here with us but live there' were categorised as part of the 'so-called fifth column' and 'national traitors'. Such people, in his view, 'are mentally located there, and not here, are not with our people, not with Russia'. However, the Russian people 'will always be able to distinguish true patriots from scum and traitors, and simply spit them out like a gnat that accidentally flew into their mouths, spit them out on the pavement'.[40] Sanctions are ill-conceived when they offer no incentive for defections from the regime. There is almost no conceivable route in which they can have the desired effect of stopping the war. The greater the external pressure, the greater the resolve to prosecute the war to some sort of acceptable conclusion. The war was Putin's, but it became the Russian people's as well. A resolute contingent of some 10–15 per cent oppose the war; the majority are not enthusiastic but accept the conflict as a grim necessity, while at the other end of the spectrum some 15 per cent demand victory at any cost.[41]

Anticipation that a change of regime in Moscow will provide a route to victory is ill-conceived. The disintegration of a nuclear-armed state jeopardises the very existence of humanity. State disintegration in Russia is hardly an appropriate solution. Diplomacy does not represent appeasement but the only rational and humane way forward. Within Russia, sanctions are considered arbitrary and unjust, and only consolidates support behind the regime, if not for the war itself. At the start of the war, Putin enjoyed no more than 61 per cent popular support but Levada Centre polls suggest that it later rose to around 80 per cent.[42] Polling in wartime conditions amidst severe repression against not only critics but any open debate about the war (even the term is penalised) is deeply problematic, but independent observers suggest that the results reflect the reality. This is in part the result of the 'rally round the flag'

---

40 Vladimir Putin, 'Meeting on Socioeconomic Support for Regions', *Kremlin.ru*, 16 March 2022, http://en.kremlin.ru/events/president/news/67996.
41 Denis Volkov and Andrei Kolesnikov, 'Alternate Reality: How Russian Society Learned to Stop Worrying about the War', *Carnegie Endowment for International Peace*, 28 November 2023, https://carnegieendowment.org/2023/11/28/alternate-reality-how-russian-society-learned-to-stop-worrying-about-war-pub-91118.
42 'Putin's Approval Rating', *Levada Centre*, https://www.levada.ru/en/ratings/.

effect, but it also reflects a refusal to submit to external pressure. Sanctions do little to end the war but are interpreted by critics as yet another instance of anti-Russian behaviour, devoid of a clear connection between the measures and outcomes. Categorised as gesture politics, they undermine the ability to achieve the declared goals – an end to the war in Ukraine on reasonable and realistic terms.

Sanctions have become an instrument of hegemonic assertion and a symbol of 'resolve', demonstrating fealty and commitment to a cause that overrides other considerations. The intensity of geopolitical confrontation, culminating in the long-anticipated war in Ukraine, means that wartime 'emergency' considerations apply. A state of emergency has not been declared, yet exceptional procedures are deployed. Sanctions, financial oversight regulations, extraterritorial impositions and the law have been 'securitised' – a situation in which normal evidentiary standards and rules are trumped by the exigencies of the emergency. As Carl Schmitt argued long ago, the sovereign is the one who can decide on the 'state of exception'.[43] This is dangerous for the long-term legitimacy and security of the Political West itself. By failing to observe the highest standards of liberal democracy and individual civil rights, ground is relinquished on which the fundamental struggle against authoritarianism should logically be waged. Every act of subversion of democracy and civil rights represents a victory for the enemies of freedom. Only by defending the impartial pursuit of natural law and justice can the gulf between ends and means be overcome.

---

43 Carl Schmitt, *The Concept of the Political* (Chicago, University of Chicago Press, 1996).

Chapter 6

MISCOMMUNICATIONS

There is not yet a spy literature of Cold War II comparable to that of the first. There is not yet a John Le Carré or even an Ian Fleming. This conflict is not couched in the allure of dangerous operations behind enemy lines, the subtle psychology of propaganda campaigns or the agonised dilemmas of those caught in the middle.[1] A silent but significant minority repudiate the logic of cold war, especially when it diverts attention from the multitude of pressing issues that face humanity and is driven by security concerns that require a diplomatic rather than a military response. To adapt Karl Marx's well-known aphorism, if Cold War I was a tragedy, the second is indeed a farce, although a dangerous one. At its heart is the struggle to control narratives, to shape popular perceptions of reality.

This is an age-old endeavour, but in Cold War II the misrepresentation of situations is exacerbated by the decline of high modernist ideals of fact-based journalism and impartial scholarship.[2] Western media act less like 'watchdogs as to their own government's foreign policy. Rather, they act as a handmaiden.'[3] Jacques Baud even goes so far as to argue that Western societies are governed by fake news. He argues that the refusal to conduct impartial investigations of critical events, such as Bashar al-Assad's use of chemical weapons in Syria or Putin's attempts to destabilise Western democracies (notably in the Russiagate case in the United States), shapes the foreign policy of Western countries. Having worked for the UN and NATO, he witnessed at first hand

---

1 There is, however, a burgeoning cinematography of the conflict, although much of it with a retro feel. See Dmitry Kuzmin, 'War and Peace on the Silver Screen', *RT.com*, 28 April 2024, https://www.rt.com/pop-culture/596657-spy-games-in-cinema/.
2 Analysed by Tabe Bergman and Jesse Owen Hearns-Branaman (eds), *Media, Dissidence and the War in Ukraine* (London, Routledge, 2023).
3 Tabe Bergman, 'Confronting Censorship: on Media Bias and the War in Ukraine', *Pearls and Irritations*, 4 September 2024, https://johnmenadue.com/confronting-censorship-on-media-bias-and-the-war-in-ukraine/.

the inability to understand the logic of the adversary, the lack of general culture, the absence of sensitivity to the holistic dimension of conflicts, a total lack of imagination in finding alternatives to the use of force to solve sometimes simple problems.[4]

He notes how 'suppositions become certainties and prejudices become realities', with the sad outcome: 'We do not understand war, so we cannot understand peace.'[5] The prejudices generated by fake news rebound to generate 'the terrorism that is killing us'.[6] It is not only terrorism that is generated but cold war as a form of international politics. Cold wars are driven by the refusal to recognise the legitimacy of the other, and conducted by undermining the adversary's ability to function while discrediting both their policies and their very existence. They reflect fundamental conflicts over the meaning of world order and the desirable good life. They are ultimately avoidable and unnecessary, although no less tragic for that.

Sources of Narrative Management

Sigmund Freud's nephew Edward Bernays demonstrated that the public can be made docile and compliant via mass-scale psychological manipulation.[7] Contemporary information management is shaped by three processes, which intersect and amplify each other. The first is generated within the Political West and is designated by various terms, beginning with the notion of a 'cultural war' introduced by Patrick Buchanan at the 1992 Republican convention, which he described as a battle for 'the soul of America'.[8] This has morphed into 'cancel culture', 'woke wars' and other terms (including the now defunct notion of 'political correctness') that characterise identitarian forms of politics.[9]

The so-called culture wars pit one section of society against another, based on such issues as gender, sexual orientation, gender dysphoria, race and ethnicity, and the affirmation of world views on their basis. The culture war in

---

4 Jacques Baud, *Governing by Fake News: 30 Years of Fake News in the West* (Paris, Max Milo Editions, 2023), p. 13.
5 Baud, *Governing by Fake News*, p. 14.
6 Baud, *Governing by Fake News*, p. 18.
7 See his classic, Edward Bernays, *Crystallizing Public Opinion* (New York, Boni and Liveright, 1923).
8 Lee Siegel, 'Trump Has Mainstreamed the Radical Right', *UnHerd*, 13 July 2024, https://unherd.com/2024/07/trump-has-mainstreamed-the-radical-right/.
9 For a critique, see Mark Lilla, *The Once and Future Liberal: After Identity Politics* (London, Hurst, 2017).

the United States is defined as a struggle between those defending traditional values against advocates of individual freedoms and a progressive culture of change.[10] The right wing has embraced free-speech absolutism, while the legacy left is now identified with the policing of 'right-think' in public life. Factions across the political spectrum practice norm enforcement, exacerbating polarisation and the persecution of individuals who are perceived to have breached an appropriate standard. This is accompanied by 'context collapse' and 'rapid mob activation'. A historical tweet or perceived inappropriate comment or joke under 'the reign of cancel culture [...] can amount to a near total reputational destruction, cascading across all realms of individuals' lives while according them an unwanted public profile'.[11]

The dialogue of the deaf in domestic politics is projected outwards in the form of monological interactions with international interlocutors. Issues become non-negotiable, giving rising to deontological forms of politics – in which principles or ideologies become absolute, eroding the scope for pragmatic problem-solving and diplomacy.[12] In 2024, the ROC declared the Ukraine conflict a 'Holy war' against Western 'globalism' and 'Satanism'. The decree presented Russia as a great power engaged in a civilisational contest with the West. Ukraine was to be purged of its hostile Russophobic political regime controlled from outside.[13] From 2012, Russia began to identify as a 'civilisation state' and thereby prioritised culture, traditions and history over more civic conceptions of national identity.[14] Cold War II contestation between liberal forms of human community and more communitarian representations of national identity is entwined with the struggle between visceral forms of nationalism. Neither are susceptible to mediation through diplomacy.

---

10 James Davison Hunter, *Culture Wars: The Struggle to Define America* (New York, Basic Books, 1991).
11 Geoff Shullenberger, 'How Cancel Culture Lost Its Power: The Right Should be Wary of Norm Enforcement', *UnHerd*, 19 July 2024, https://unherd.com/2024/07/how-cancel-culture-lost-its-power/.
12 The model helps explain the deterioration in EU-Russian relations. See Cristian Nitoiu and Florin Pasatoiu, 'Hybrid Geopolitics in EU-Russia Relations: Understanding the Persistence of Conflict and Cooperation', *East European Politics*, Vol. 36, No. 4, October 2020, pp. 499–514.
13 'Nakaz XXV Vsemirnogo russkogo narodnogo sobora "Nastoyashchee i budushchee Russkogo mira"' ['Order of the XXV World Russian People's Council "The Present and Future of the Russian World"'], 27 March 2024, http://www.patriarchia.ru/db/text/6116189.html.
14 Andrei P. Tsygankov, 'Crafting the State-Civilization', *Problems of Post-Communism*, Vol. 63, No. 3, 2016, pp. 146–58.

The terrain of political contestation has shifted towards the rights-based activation of identity as the basis of politics, marginalising more traditional concerns with class, inequality and various forms of socialist progressivism.[15] Marxists predicted that class conflict would ultimately lead to revolution, but it is the intense polarisation provoked by culture wars that now generate civil discord.[16] As far as cultural conservatives are concerned, the so-called 'liberal-left' dominates through the instruments of the 'administrative state', recreating neo-communist patterns of authoritarianism that are as intolerant of dissent as the old Soviet bloc. The ideological puritanism of culture war politics is then projected onto international affairs. This was a notable feature of the Obama administration. Obama refused to attend the Sochi Winter Olympics in spring 2014 because of Russia's adoption of a law restricting so-called LGBT+ propaganda to minors, while his secretary of state, Hillary Clinton, shaped much of US foreign policy around these issues.[17]

The second ground of communicative conflicts is generated by geopolitical contestation and great power struggles. This has a long pedigree. In June 1917, the US Congress passed the vague and all-encompassing Espionage Act, and in the wake of the Bolshevik seizure of power that October the 'red scare' resulted in the imprisoning or exile of left-wing radicals. The Act was used in 1919 to imprison the Socialist leader Eugene Debs, as well as Victor Berger, a Socialist member of the House of Representatives. The anarchist Emma Goldman was forced into exile, and a criminal case was devised against Nicola Sacco and Bartolomeo Vanzetti, who were later executed. The House Un-American Activities Committee (HUAC) was created in 1938 to investigate disloyalty on the part of citizens and public employees' organisations with alleged Communist ties. The McCarthyite scare lasted a bare five years between 1950 and 1955, and HUAC was finally wound up in 1975, whereas today a whole network of shadowy agencies has been mobilised for the long term.

The enemy is no longer an ideology (communism) bound up in a state (the Soviet Union), but states (Russia, China and some others) opposing the hegemony of the West. Matt Taibbi notes

---

15 A point made by Richard Rorty, and he identified the domestic sources of such a progressive politics, *Achieving Our Country: Leftist Thought in Twentieth Century America* (Cambridge, MA, Harvard University Press, 1998).

16 James Davison Hunter, *Before the Shooting Begins: Searching for Democracy in America's Culture War* (New York, Free Press, 1994).

17 Hillary Rodham Clinton, *Hard Choices: A Memoir* (New York, Simon & Schuster, 2014), describes her work as secretary of state, while her *What Happened* (London, Simon & Schuster, 2017) tries, but fails, to explain her loss to Trump in November 2016.

Civil society institutions, the media, politicians, and government are supposed to maintain distance from one another in a democracy. The Censorship-Industrial Complex shows an opposite instinct, for all these groups to act in concert, essentially as one giant, incestuous intelligence operation – not of the people, but paternalistically "for" the people, or so they believe.

Targets are more diffuse and widespread. The struggle between communism and capitalist democracy was straightforward and easily understood, but the amorphousness of the struggle against alleged disloyalty and alignment with the enemy today renders the struggle more pernicious, pervasive and damaging. Criticism of US or EU foreign policy is dismissed as 'Russian propaganda'. Those questioning whether international politics are inherently conflictual are dismissed as dupes of Chinese 'win-win' diplomacy. Deviation from mainstream narratives is condemned as disinformation or 'conspiracy thinking'. Trump era 'anti-populism' gave birth to

> a new brand of paranoid politics [...] creating a single political cartel to protect against 'contagion' of mass movements [...] this explains why so many 'anti-disinformation' campaigns describe language as a kind of disease, e.g. 'infodemic', 'information pollution', and 'information disorder'.[18]

Dangerous ideas are pathologised and considered a sickness.

The third process is the long-term 'clash of civilisations'. In the 1990s, the American political scientist Samuel Huntington argued that conflict based on ideological contestation would give way to civilisational struggles, based on ideational-religious blocs.[19] The idea was valid, but his view of geopolitics as based on religious affiliation was crude and deterministic. A broader view is required. The 500-year dominance of the Civilisational West, the era of colonialism and imperialism, is coming to an end. The Political West seeks to perpetuate the West's hegemony by imposing its new 'standard of civilisation', but the West's accustomed military and economic supremacy is eroding. The United States remains the pre-eminent military power, but its economic and financial dominance is waning. China and Russia, moreover, pose a military challenge the like of which the West has not faced over the last

---

18 Matt Taibbi, 'Report on the Censorship-Industrial Complex', *Racket News*, 25 April 2023, https://www.racket.news/p/report-on-the-censorship-industrial.

19 Samuel P. Huntington, 'The Clash of Civilizations?', *Foreign Affairs*, Vol. 72, No. 3, Summer 1993, pp. 23–49; Samuel P. Huntington, *The Clash of Civilizations and the Remaking of World Order* (New York, Simon & Schuster, 1996).

Information Management

The confluence of these three streams shapes the informational environment, exacerbates cross-cutting currents of polarisation and degrades the discursive environment. Brave souls who take a stand against the mainstream tide are pilloried and excoriated. Careers and livelihoods are blighted.[20] Certain issues are out of bounds. One of these is critical analysis of the character and future of the Atlantic alliance system. In Cold War I, leaders on both sides of the Atlantic as well as media commentators, academics and others questioned the purpose of the alliance, discussed the negative features of dependence on the United States for security and advocated alternatives. Eisenhower himself warned that if 'in 10 years, all American troops stationed in Europe for national defense purposes have not been returned to the United States, then this whole project will have failed'.[21] Like Trump, he called for more burden-sharing between alliance members. Instead, today there is an 'ahistorical sense of policy inevitability', the hyper-normalization mentioned earlier. If the character of American security commitments was questioned 'in far more perilous times', then they should be now.[22]

The outcome is stark. Military budgets expand, and the security services once again deploy their dark arts. Jeffrey Sachs argues that 'the US played a major covert role in the violent coup that brought down Yanukovych and pushed Ukraine into a decade of bloodshed but to this day, we don't know the details'. He also notes that the CIA covertly trained the special operations forces of the post-coup regime, thus helping fuel the bloodshed. The White House in 2011 ordered the CIA to overthrow Bashar al-Assad in Syria.[23] The

---

20 Olga Baysha (with Kamilla Chukasheva) describes her experience of being shouted down at an academic conference (Ch. 7), and Tim Hayward, a Scottish professor of philosophy, was attacked for a tweet of 11 March 2022: 'As long as we're still able to hear two sides of the story we should continue striving to do so', linking to a Russian source (Ch. 8), in Bergman and Hearns-Branaman (eds), *Media, Dissidence and the War in Ukraine*.

21 Quoted by Eugene J. Carroll, 'NATO Expansion Would be an Epic "Fateful Error"', *Los Angeles Times*, 7 July 1997, https://www.latimes.com/archives/la-xpm-1997-jul-07-me-10464-story.html.

22 Brandan P. Buck, 'Fact Check: NATO Was Never Out of Bounds', *Responsible Statecraft*, 16 February 2024, https://responsiblestatecraft.org/trump-nato/.

23 Jeffrey D. Sachs, 'How the CIA Destabilizes the World', *Common Dreams*, 12 February 2024, https://www.commondreams.org/opinion/cia-destablizes-the-world.

CIA has also been held responsible for the destruction of the Nord Stream gas pipeline in September 2022. Sachs points out that only once since its foundation in 1947 has the CIA been held to account, in the Church Committee hearings of 1975. He argues that

> it's urgently time to open the blinds, expose the truth about the US-led mayhem, and begin a new era in which US foreign policy becomes transparent, accountable, subject to the rule of law both domestic and international, and directed towards global peace rather than subversion of supposed enemies.[24]

Sachs retains a fundamental belief in the possibility, indeed necessity, of a positive peace. In other words, he seeks a retreat from the hyper-normalisation of the present towards a more normal future.

The security apparatus polices the Trumanite state. It routinely inflates the threat from enemies, and after the hiatus of the cold peace, Russia has once again become the designated 'other', the enemy against whom fire is directed. The 'global war on terror' after 9/11 was accompanied by clandestine warfare against nebulous forces, including extraordinary rendition, but from 2014 attention pivoted back towards state adversaries. The Russian threat to the West was revived. As Joe Lauria, the editor of *Consortium News*, argues,

> Trumped-up fear of Russia has served US ruling circles well for more than 70 years. The first three National Intelligence Estimates of the CIA from 1947 to 1949, reported no evidence of a Soviet threat, no infrastructure to support a sustained threat, and no evidence of a desire for confrontation with the United States.

The war scare of 1948 helped save the US aircraft industry, which had been in decline since the end of World War II. Threat inflation of the late 1940s was followed by the 1954 bomber gap and the 1957 missile gap, and then in 1975–76 CIA director George H. W. Bush approved a Team B, 'whose purpose was to inflate Soviet military strength'.[25] Team B, which included the historian Richard Pipes, reported numerous instances of Soviet malfeasance, including the creation of an enormous fleet of nuclear submarines and plans to invade the United States, none of which proved true. When their claims proved false, they claimed 'the absence of proof of Soviet wrong doings, was,

---

24 Sachs, 'How the CIA Destabilizes the World'.
25 Joe Lauria, 'Russian Imperialism', *Consortium News*, 13 February 2024, https://consortiumnews.com/2024/02/13/russian-imperialism/.

in itself, proof of Soviet wrong doings', taking into account Soviet behavioural patterns.[26] Today, we have Team B thinking on steroids. This is sustained by what former CIA analyst Ray McGovern has christened MICIMATT, the Military-Industrial-Congressional-Intelligence-Media-Academia-Think-Tank complex. The reflex of the Trumanite state is to escalate, to show 'resolve' and to send 'messages' to the adversary. This is a token not of strength but of weakness and the absence of a defined strategic appreciation of the necessary balance between diplomacy and coercion.

Truth is invariably the first casualty of war, but propaganda in the Russo-Ukrainian conflict is exceptionally intense. The former US diplomat Chas Freeman writes that

> While many hundreds of thousands of people have fought and died in Ukraine, the propaganda machines in Brussels, Kyiv, London, Moscow and Washington have worked overtime to ensure that we take passionate sides, believe what we want to believe, and condemn anyone who questions the narrative we have internalised. The consequences for all have been dire. For Ukraine, they have been catastrophic.[27]

The art of heresthetics, structuring political reality to your advantage, has been honed to perfection. William Riker, who coined the term, describes three general categories of heresthetics: agenda control, strategic voting and manipulating dimensions, and offered 12 examples of how leaders achieve their goals.[28] Cold war heresthetics are a world of their own, in which the three categories are deployed to shape hegemonic narratives. Manipulation includes disinformation, which is conceptually similar to propaganda but in certain respects less accurate. Propaganda traditionally means the dissemination of truth, as in the Vatican's Congregation for the Propagation of Faith (*Propaganda Fidei*), established by Pope Gregory XV in 1622, but in the twentieth century assumed its present association with the dissemination of falsehoods.[29] In current usage, disinformation is the deliberate and usually

---

26 Mark Lesseraux, '"Noble Lies": How the Neocons Hijacked US Politics and Subsequently Altered America's Trajectory', *Pressenza*, 27 August 2024, https://www.pressenza.com/2024/08/noble-lies-how-the-neocons-hijacked-us-politics-and-subsequently-altered-americas-trajectory/.
27 Chas W. Freeman Jr., 'The Propaganda that Damned Ukraine', *UnHerd*, 4 January 2024, https://unherd.com/2024/01/the-propaganda-that-damned-ukraine/.
28 William H. Riker, *The Art of Political Manipulation* (New Haven, Yale University Press, 1986).
29 David Welch, *Propaganda: Power and Persuasion* (London, British Library Publishing Division, 2013).

malicious diffusion of untruths, whereas misinformation is simply mistaken information. In practice, the counter-disinformation industry became a propaganda campaign in its own right and not, as it sold itself, a neutral effort to establish the truth.[30] Those most zealous in the pursuit of disinformation have themselves become the purveyors of falsehoods. The increasing inability, and indeed unwillingness, to distinguish truth from deception fosters a mistrust of political elites and scepticism about the efficacy of government.

The Anti-Disinformation Industry

The 'othering' of Russia draws on long-term patterns of 'Russophobia'. This first became pronounced when Russia became a major military power following the defeat of Napoleon's Grande Armée in 1812 and the entry of Russian forces into Paris in 1814. The Swiss scholar Guy Mettan traces Russophobia's deep historical roots, going all the way back to the Great Schism between the Catholic and Eastern Orthodox churches in 1054, which he argues is 'the historically conditioned peculiarity of the European mentality'.[31] Barbara Emerson also notes the cultural aspects of Anglo-Russian rivalry in the nineteenth century, which she calls 'the first cold war', with Russia condemned for failing to conform to the purported civilisational standards of the other European powers.[32] This long-standing view of Russia as backward and barbaric took on a more sharply delineated form after the suppression of the Polish uprising of 1830–31, which established a pattern for the demonisation of Russia similar to that provoked by the Ukraine conflict today. Although laden with profound cultural baggage, the nineteenth struggle described by Emerson, dubbed the 'Great Game' by Arthur Connolly (1807–42), was not a 'cold war' in the way it is defined in this book. It shares some features, including intense propaganda, mutual denigration and endemic militarised hostility in the borderlands, but the absence of the nuclear threat renders it qualitatively different.

Sergey Filatov identifies four dimensions to contemporary Russophobia: the historical and political component, in which Russia unyieldingly refuses to subordinate itself to Western hegemony; nature and resources, with Russia's enormous natural wealth eliciting envy; the cultural factor, in which

---

30 Tom Wyatt, 'Counter-Disinformation: The New Snake Oil', *Racket News*, 19 May 2023, https://www.racket.news/p/counter-disinformation-the-new-snake.
31 Guy Mettan, *Creating Russophobia: From the Great Religious Schism to Anti-Putin Hysteria* (Atlanta, Clarity Press, 2017).
32 Barbara Emerson, *The First Cold War: Anglo-Russian Relations in the 19th Century* (London, Hurst, 2024).

an enduring Russian 'spirit' persists across the various change of regimes, from Muscovy, Tsarist Imperial, Soviet and 'democratic'; and the spatial, with Russia's enormity looming prominently in every schoolroom map, a disturbing vastness coloured pink in Soviet cartography (also, coincidentally, the British imperial colour).[33] Contemporary Russophobia is compounded by the discomfort provoked by Russia's failure to conform to the neoliberal modernity prevalent in the Political West. During Cold War I, this could be ascribed to the country having been 'hijacked' by the Bolsheviks and the communist temptation. In Cold War II, there could be no such excuse. Russia's recalcitrance must be due to some genetic fault. How could any country not wish to emulate the glories of the West? There is an equivalent Sinophobia, although not so prevalent in Europe, although now growing. Driven by American concerns about the emergence of a genuine peer competitor for the first time in the modern era, there is a global pushback against Chinese influence. In April 2024, Biden signed the law forcing the Chinese company ByteDance to divest from TikTok or face a ban on the popular social media site.

There are no longer 'reds under the bed', but Russkiis skulking in dark corners. Russia has become the subject of a whole 'anti-disinformation' industry, with damaging consequences on international politics. This was notable in the 'Russiagate' allegations that accompanied Trump's first election to the US presidency. In an epochal break with post-war tradition, a major candidate repudiated the bipartisan foreign policy consensus, questioning the utility of NATO and the obligations of the US alliance system as a whole. His approach was not isolationist, on the interwar model, but mercantilist: economic rationality trumped ideological fervour. In Trump's view, US foreign policy should focus on what benefits the economy and is profitable, rather than perpetuating outmoded models of democratic internationalism and humanitarian interventionism. He was equally sceptical about the UN-based model of sovereign internationalism. Instead, he harked back to the American tradition of conservative internationalism, which stood in sharp contrast to the Wilsonian activist tradition. He was thus the first genuinely post-Cold War US president. He repeatedly argued that it made sense to 'get on' with Russia, a view advanced by Henry Kissinger, both in office in the 1970s and later. Trump's landmark speech at the Mayflower Hotel in Washington on 27 April 2016 argued that

> I believe an easing of tensions and improved relations with Russia – from a position of strength – is possible. [...] Common sense says this

---

33 Sergey Filatov, 'The Roots of Russophobia', *International Affairs* (Moscow), 15 February 2024, https://en.interaffairs.ru/article/the-roots-of-russophobia/.

cycle of hostility must end. Some say the Russians won't be reasonable. I intend to find out.[34]

He was then hit with a slew of allegations accusing him of somehow being in hoc to the Kremlin, of colluding with Putin, and maintaining backchannel communications with the adversary, much of which was summarised in the sleazy Christopher Steele dossier.[35] None of these allegations proved true, but the various investigations hobbled his administration and prevented any serious rapprochement with Russia. The Russiagate allegations intensified hostility to Moscow, exacerbated the cold war confrontation and drove Europe towards interstate war.

Russian responsibility for the leaking of the Democratic National Committee's internal communications, showing a bias towards Hillary Clinton's nomination as the Democratic presidential candidate against that of Bernie Sanders, has been questioned (although not all are convinced). The only demonstrable act of Russian intervention was in the communicative sphere. The Internet Research Agency based in St Petersburg and funded by Prigozhin (who later gained notoriety at the head of the Wagner group) used Twitter, Facebook and other platforms to 'sow discord' in American politics. Most of the messages had nothing to do with the election, many came out after the vote, and their impact was minimal. Brad Parscale, responsible for Trump's digital campaign, compared Russia's impact to 'three pieces of salt inside a giant salad bowl the size of Madison Square Garden and you're never going to taste it'. The Russians spent less than $10,000 over the same period that the Trump campaign spent $100 million.[36] The Russiagate case continues to reverberate and stands as a monument to the communicative wars of the postmodern era.

The Hunter Biden laptop story in 2020 is particularly disturbing. The report by Miranda Devine in the *New York Post* on 14 October was not only suppressed, but 'the establishment' banded together to rubbish the story, alleging that the whole business had the 'classic earmarks of a Russian information operation'. Antony Blinken, secretary of state in the Biden administration, is

---

34 'Transcript: Donald Trump's Foreign Policy Speech', *New York Times*, 27 April 2016, https://www.nytimes.com/2016/04/28/us/politics/transcript-trump-foreign-policy.html.

35 Sakwa, *Deception*. See also Oliver Boyd-Barrett and Stephen Marmura (eds), *Russiagate Revisited: The Aftermath of a Hoax* (London, Palgrave Macmillan, 2023).

36 Ian Schwartz, 'Trump Strategist Brad Parscale vs. PBS "Frontline" on Campaign Use of Facebook: "A Gift"', *RealClearPolitics*, 3 December 2018, https://www.realclearpolitics.com/video/2018/12/03/trump_strategist_brad_parscale_vs_pbs_frontline_on_campaigns_use_of_facebook.html.

suspected of organising the letter signed by 51 intelligence officials. A group condemning disinformation was guilty of concocting an audacious disinformation campaign themselves.[37] This was 'a smear campaign and a censorship campaign unparalleled in modern American history'.[38] Devine's story demonstrated that Joe Biden was personally involved in his family's influence peddling operations, threatening to become the 'October surprise' of the 2020 election. A coordinated operation closed down the story, and Biden smoothly entered the White House.[39] This is the exemplary case of organised and politically motivated censorship, reinforced by digital blacklisting. The Biden campaign also accused Russia of placing bounties on American soldiers in Afghanistan. Both accusations proved false, yet shaped the political atmosphere and reinforced cold war stereotypes. Communicative struggles were not confined to the domestic arena. By moulding narratives and disparaging opponents, foreign policy options were narrowed.

Putin in particular was demonised, accused of numerous political murders, although evidence for his direct involvement is patchy. In her study, Amy Knight admits that 'I do not claim to have definitive proof of the complicity of Putin and his allies in these crimes'.[40] This did not stop Biden, once installed in the White House, of undiplomatically condemning Putin as a 'killer'.[41] He later accused Putin of being directly complicit in Navalny's untimely death in February 2024, although American intelligence agencies concluded that Putin did not order Navalny's death.[42] Despite decades of service in the Senate foreign affairs committee, Biden proved remarkably obtuse about international affairs and a model of how diplomacy should not be conducted. The personal denigration of a leader with whom you have to do business is not the best way of getting results. Ukraine and Europe have paid the price.

---

37 Taibbi, 'Report on the Censorship-Industrial Complex'.

38 Aaron Maté, 'How 10 Years of US Meddling in Ukraine Undermined Democracy and Fueled War', *Real Clear Investigations*, 30 April 2024, https://www.aaronmate.net/p/how-10-years-of-us-meddling-in-ukraine.

39 Miranda Devine later wrote a book about the story, *Laptop from Hell: Hunter Biden, Big Tech, and the Dirty Secrets the President tried to Hide* (New York and Nashville, Post Hill Press, 2021).

40 Amy Knight, *Orders to Kill: The Putin Regime and Political Murder* (New York, Thomas Dunne Books, 2017).

41 Philip Bump, 'On the Novelty of Biden Calling Putin a Killer', *Washington Post*, 18 March 2021, https://www.washingtonpost.com/politics/2021/03/18/novelty-calling-killer-killer/.

42 Aruna Viswanatha et al., 'Putin Didn't Directly Order Alexei Navalny's February 2024 Death, US Spy Agencies Find', *Wall Street Journal*, 27 April 2024, https://www.wsj.com/world/russia/alexei-navalny-death-us-intelligence-71bc95b0.

Russia is the main target of the anti-disinformation industry, although China is coming up fast. Outlets such as Russia Today (including the RT TV station) and Sputnik are considered part of a multifaceted Kremlin campaign to exacerbate political divisions and polarisation ('sow discord') in the West and in former Soviet bloc states.[43] This is considered part of a historical pattern reaching back to Soviet period 'active measures'.[44] The EU sanctioned RT on 2 March 2022, suspending its broadcasts and content, forcing the company to close its offices in France and Germany (as well as in the UK). Where Russia's 'malign influence' cannot be demonstrated, 'Russian malign inspiration' is censured. This was the case with the Patriotic Union in Germany, a group which denies the legitimacy of the postwar settlement. Their attempts to contact Russian officials were rebuffed, and 'German prosecutors found no evidence that Russian diplomats or any other Russian stakeholders either instigated the actions of the Patriotic Union or voiced their support for the planned regime change'. Russia nevertheless is condemned: 'Today we know a lot about tactics, instruments and tools used by Russian pro-Kremlin actors to destabilise Western societies, drive wedges between European nations, and undermine democratic institutions'. Malign inspiration 'works when humans gain awareness of new possibilities in what they are doing or planning to do, but at the same time they are stimulated by external factors and events to explore those possibilities'.[45]

This sounds rather like how a pluralist democracy should work. In Cold War II, exploration of even legal alternatives is constrained, always in danger of falling into the ever-widening rubric of subversive 'disinformation'. The EU launched its EUvsDisinfo project in 2015 to counter Russian propaganda, but its methodology has been questioned.[46] Brussels also funded EU4FreeMedia to integrate 'Russian journalists in exile' into leading European publications. These expatriates were unlikely to take an unbiased view of developments in Russia (with some notable exceptions), thus amplifying anti-regime narratives. The EU's Digital Services Act (DSA) of 2023 rightly obliges Twitter/X and other platforms to remove illegal content, on the pain of hefty fines, but

---

43 Mitchell A. Orenstein, *The Lands in Between: Russia vs. the West and the New Politics of Hybrid War* (Cambridge, Cambridge University Press, 2019).
44 Thomas Rid, *Active Measures: The Secret History of Disinformation and Political Warfare* (London, Profile Books, 2020).
45 Anton Shekhovtsov, 'Russian Malign Inspiration and How to Counter It', *EU Observer*, 9 January 2024, https://euobserver.com/opinion/157891.
46 Stephen Hutchings and Vera Tolz, 'Covid-19 Disinformation: Two Short Reports on the Russian Dimension', 6 April 2020, https://reframingrussia.com/2020/04/06/covid-19-disinformation-two-short-reports-on-the-russian-dimension/.

when it comes to political issues, 'illegality' is a contested concept. This came to a head, for example, over whether Tucker Carlson's interview with Putin in February 2024 represents an example of Russia's 'information war' against the West.[47] His 'understanding' (*versteher*) approach to Russia has long drawn criticism, as had Oliver Stone's series of interviews with Putin broadcast in 2017.

A commentary noted 'The appeal of Russian authoritarianism for the American far right is considerable, and not just because of Trump's fealty to Putin. A common skin colour and shared hostility to feminism and gay rights counts for a lot'.[48] In fact, matters are more complicated than that. The systematic silencing of Russian voices in the West, with Russian media taken off the airwaves and print media blocked, or considering the Russian viewpoint even if one disagrees with it, is condemned as morally wrong and politically suspicious.[49] In the Ukraine war, the view that there is no alternative, with compromise or diplomacy tantamount to appeasement, generates an escalatory logic that breaks through one red line after another, with no end in sight other than the ultimate red line – the taboo on the use of nuclear weapons.

In the UK, the National Security Act of July 2023 superseded earlier secrecy legislation. It created a Foreign Influence Registration scheme, analogous to the US Foreign Agents Registration Act (FARA), originally introduced in 1938 but much-amended thereafter. The British act requires the registration of foreign influence in the political system and monitoring of the influence activities of foreign powers. It is not clear how the work of Israeli and US agencies in the UK will be registered. More immediately, critics fear that the activities of dissident citizens will be monitored, with their views and ideas labelled 'disinformation'.

This is the concern that motivated protests against the introduction of an equivalent law in Georgia in spring 2024. The law stipulates that if more than 20 per cent of the operating funds of an NGO (there are an astonishing 25,000 in a nation of only 3.7 million) originate from foreign sources, NGOs must publicly disclose the fact and the source of their funding. This is very different to the 2012 Russian foreign agent law and its later additions, which stifles the development of independent human rights and political NGOs. The EU denounced the Georgian law as undemocratic, although it expressed

---

[47] Lisa O'Carrollin, 'Tucker Carlson Interview with Putin to Test EU Law Regulating Tech Companies', *The Guardian*, 8 February 2024, https://www.theguardian.com/world/2024/feb/08/tucker-carlson-interview-with-putin-to-test-eu-law-regulating-tech-companies.

[48] Edward Helmore, 'Carlson Off the Reins', *The Guardian*, 21 March 2022, p. 9.

[49] A point made by Thomas Fazi, 'Inside the Russian Mind', 1 July 2024, https://www.thomasfazi.com/p/inside-the-russian-mind.

no such qualms over equivalent Western legislation.[50] Western support for the protestors, as one commentary notes, 'brings to the fore issues with how liberal internationalists react to democratic decision-making when it contrasts with their preferred policies'.[51] This is democratism at work, in which double standards are part of the operative order of the Political West.

A plethora of monitoring agencies have been created to render the media 'accountable'. Among the most notorious is the Disinformation Governance Board, headed for a brief period in 2022 by Nina Jankowicz, the author of a sensationalist book on the subject.[52] She tweeted that the Hunter Biden laptop story was somehow Russian disinformation. The Atlantic Council sponsored the Digital Forensic Laboratory, tasked with hunting down 'Russia's vast disinformation machine'.[53] Other bodies in what Michael Shellenberger calls the 'censorship-industrial complex' include the Stanford Internet Observatory, the London-based Global Disinformation Index (GDI) and the Aspen Institute.[54] The GDI was established in 2018 and operates a 'dynamic exclusion list' to disrupt 'the business model of online disinformation by starving offending publications of funding'. Financed by George Soros's Open Society Foundation, the GDI is also supported by the UK government through the FCDO, the EU, the German foreign office and a body called Disinfo Cloud, sponsored by the State Department. One of GDI's founders, Clare Melford, was open about how the definition of 'disinformation' broadened from 'deliberately false content' to 'adversarial

---

50 Paul Robinson, 'The West's Double Standards on Georgia's "Foreign Agents" Bill', *Canadian Dimension*, 3 May 2024, https://canadiandimension.com/articles/view/the-wests-double-standards-on-georgias-foreign-agents-bill; Almut Rochowanski and Sopiko Japaridze, 'Unrest in Georgia over the "Foreign Influence Transparency Law"', *LeftEast*, 3 May 2024, https://lefteast.org/unrest-georgia-foreign-influence-transparency-law/. On EU condemnation, see Vadim Nikitin, 'Georgia Dreaming: Is Another Colour Revolution about to Kick off', *The Nation*, 20 May 2024, https://www.thenation.com/article/world/georgia-dream-protests-ngo-color-revolution/.
51 Anthony J. Constantini, 'The Real Stakes of Georgia's Foreign Agent Law', *The American Conservative*, 17 May 2024, http://www.theamericanconservative.com/the-real-stakes-of-georgias-foreign-agent-law.
52 Nina Jankowicz, *How to Lose the Information War: Russia, Fake News, and the Future of Conflict* (London, I. B. Tauris, 2020).
53 Caitlin Johnstone, 'We're Being Trained to Worry about "Russian Propaganda" While Drowning in US Propaganda', *Medium*, 30 August 2022, https://caityjohnstone.medium.com/were-being-trained-to-worry-about-russian-propaganda-while-drowning-in-us-propaganda-60258abfb21d.
54 Martin Gurri, 'Disinformation Is the Word I Use When I Want You to Shut Up', *Discourse*, 30 March 2023, https://www.discoursemagazine.com/p/disinformation-is-the-word-i-use-when-i-want-you-to-shut-up.

narratives'. She argued that 'Something can be factually accurate but still extremely harmful'. When the online journal *UnHerd* was placed on the Index, its editor, Freddie Sayers, noted that what Melford's team might find offensive was not necessarily disinformation. He rightly stressed 'most of these issues are highly contentious and require robust, uncensored discussion to find solutions'.[55]

Still in the UK, the Centre for Countering Digital Hate (CCDH) is affiliated with the Labour Together think tank and 'has been a targeting mechanism deployed against Labour's left-populist faction in the same way that the Center for American Progress has been used by Clinton/Biden Democrats against the intramural challenge from Bernie Sanders'.[56] A lawsuit filed by Twitter/X accused the CCDH of producing bogus research about hate speech and disinformation on social media.[57] The 'UK Files' documented 'the relationship between Britain's leading "centrist" political faction and one of the most aggressive pro-censorship organisations in the Western media world, and offer insight into Labour's intramural campaign to label former Labour leader Jeremy Corbyn guilty of antisemitism'. Matt Taibbi hoped that 'Americans seeing irrefutable evidence of a Labour faction's cynical use of "anti-disinformation" against their own will help break the illusion that this is solely a right-wing issue'.[58] The investigative reporter Asa Winstanley convincingly demonstrates how shadowy movements linked to the Israeli embassy in London weaponised antisemitism to bring down the radical left and anti-war challenge from Corbyn.[59] Cold War I had distorted domestic politics, including social democratic politics, in Europe and most of the Anglosphere in various ways, many of which were insidious. Substantive debate about fundamental issues, including nuclear armaments and deployments, were suppressed or distorted. Today,

---

55 Freddie Sayers, 'Inside the Disinformation Industry: A government-Sponsored Agency Is Censoring Journalism', *UnHerd*, 17 April 2024, https://unherd.com/2024/04/inside-the-disinformation-industry/.
56 Matt Taibbi, 'Editor's Note: On "UK Files, Part 2"', *Racket News*, 31 January 2024, https://www.racket.news/p/editors-note-on-uk-files-part-2.
57 Paul Holden, 'The "UK Files": A History of the Center for Countering Digital Hate', *Racket News*, 14 November 2023, https://www.racket.news/p/the-uk-files-a-history-of-the-center.
58 Matt Taibbi, '"UK Files" Reports Show: Both Left and Right Can be Targets of Censors', *Racket News*, 14 November 2023, https://www.racket.news/p/uk-files-reports-show-both-left-and.
59 Asa Winstanley, *Weaponising Anti-Semitism: How the Israeli Lobby Brought Down Jeremy Corbyn* (New York, OR Books, 2023).

Cold War II once again brings cold war practices into the heart of social and political life.

Communicative Conflicts

Populations are drawn into what the veteran journalist John Pilger calls the 'submissive void'. The controversial documentary maker Leni Riefenstahl describes this as a public receptive to having their perceptions moulded by official narratives.[60] Despite the development of so-called 'information societies' in an era of multiple news sources, Pilger argued that 'brainwashing is insidious and relentless, and perception is filtered according to the needs and lies of state and corporate power'. He observed that nine of the top ten media companies are based in the United States, including Google, Twitter/X and Facebook. This is the United States, he notes, that

> In my lifetime [...] has overthrown or attempted to overthrow more than 50 governments, mostly democracies. It has interfered in democratic elections in 30 countries. It has dropped bombs on the people of 30 countries, most of them poor and defenceless. It has attempted to murder the leaders of 50 countries. It has fought to suppress liberation movements in 20 countries.

Despite this pernicious record, 'The extent and scale of this carnage is largely unreported, unrecognised; and those responsible continue to dominate Anglo-American political life'.[61] He praised the work of an 'inspirational samizdat': Robert Parry's *Consortium News*, Max Blumenthal's *Grayzone*, *MintPress News*, *CounterPunch*, *Declassified UK*, *Common Dreams* and many more. He also recognised the brave reporting of journalists such as Chris Hedges, Patrick Lawrence, Jonathan Cook, Diana Johnstone and Caitlin Johnstone, to which we may add Aaron Maté, Matt Taibbi, James Carden, Glenn Greenwald, Anatol Lieven, Ted Snider, Seymour Hersh and many more, whose work informs this book. The Quincy Institute for Responsible Statecraft, founded in 2019, should be specifically acknowledged as providing an ethically informed critical realist perspective on foreign policy issues. Mention should

---

60 Space does not allow this point to be developed, but the warning is clear: no society is immune from a frenzy of the type that seized Nazi Germany.
61 John Pilger, 'Silencing the Lambs: How Propaganda Works', Trondheim World Festival, 7 September 2022, *Consortium News*, 8 January 2024, https://consortiumnews.com/2024/01/08/john-pilger-silencing-the-lambs-how-propaganda-works-2/. Pilger died on 30 December 2023 at the age of 84, working indefatigably to the end.

also be made of the Institute for Policy Studies, established in 1963, which describes itself as a 'progressive organization dedicated to building a more equitable, ecologically sustainable, and peaceful society'.

In the United States, there is also an informational ecosystem associated with traditional conservatives, notably Dmitry K. Simes, Patrick Buchanan, Scott Ritter (a former UN weapons inspector) and Colonel Douglas McGregor, who provide some of the most perceptive analysis of the Russo-Ukrainian war, along with Ray McGovern and others in the Veteran Intelligence Professionals for Sanity group. They repudiate neoconservative militarism and neoliberal crusading. For them, the United States should become a 'normal' great power and get its own house in order before imposing its values on others. They stand in the hallowed American tradition of conservative internationalism. Reagan's UN representative, Jeane Kirpatrick, at the end of Cold War I called for US foreign policy to become 'normal', to lose its 'exceptionalist' interventionist mentality and obsession with hegemony.[62] In other words, Kirkpatrick opposed the crusading zeal of the neoconservatives and their destructive obsession with the assertion of American primacy and the liberal averment of democratic internationalism.

Not surprisingly, many of these individuals came into the crosshairs of the US security establishment. As part of a broad criminal investigation of Americans who work with Russian state television, Ritter's house was subject to a day-long search by the FBI on 7 August 2024.[63] Simes, who emigrated from the Soviet Union in 1973 and went on to work with Richard Nixon, was subject to a similar search on 13 August. Simes moved back to Russia in October 2022 and co-hosts *The Great Game*, an international affairs discussion programme on Russian TV.[64] He and his wife were later charged with money laundering and sanctions violations in relation to his Russian TV work. The former Democrat Representative for Hawaii, Tulsi Gabbard, one of the most eloquent critics of the Ukraine war, became subject to surveillance as part of the Transport Security Administration's 'Quiet Skies' programme (costing some $1bn annually), including being followed by air marshals every time

---

62 William S. Smith, 'Jeane J. Kirkpatrick: 30 Years Unheeded', *The National Interest*, 13 June 2020, https://nationalinterest.org/feature/jeane-j-kirkpatrick-30-years-unheeded-162667.

63 For his perspective, see Scott Ritter, 'Russia Has Never Tried to Dictate any Narrative to Me, Unlike the West', *RT.com*, 19 August 2024, https://www.rt.com/news/602809-scott-ritter-rt-contribution-russophobia/.

64 Steven Lee Myers and Julian E. Barnes, 'US Investigating Americans Who Worked with Russian State Television', *New York Times*, 22 August 2024, https://www.nytimes.com/2024/08/21/technology/us-fbi-russia-election-disinformation.html.

she boards a plane.[65] She was nominated by Trump to become Director of National Intelligence in his second administration. In the UK, the independent journalist and critic of Israeli policy, Richard Medhurst, was arrested hours after criticising the country's anti-terror laws.[66]

The scale of media manipulation by disinformation campaigners and the authorities is occasionally exposed. The Twitter Files revelations were made possible by Elon Musk's purchase of Twitter (which he renamed X) and his bizarre, although characteristic, decision to act as the whistleblower on his own newly acquired company. His decision to buy the company in the first place was prompted by disenchantment with the legacy press (dismissively described as the MSM). The Twitter Files investigators soon discovered a startling series of information misdemeanours.[67] A shocking level of collusion between US government officials and social media companies was exposed. The basic story is that Twitter had surreptitiously teamed up with the FBI and the Department of Homeland Security's (DHS) Cybersecurity and Infrastructure Security Agency (CISA) to combat what was labelled misinformation or disinformation, including studies of Russian bot activity.

They identified the censorship–industrial complex, mentioned earlier, that inferred Russian activity based on algorithmic models that were notoriously unreliable. Above all, the Hunter Biden laptop story in 2020, which may have damaged Joe Biden's electoral prospects, was suppressed. The digital visibility of the left-leaning Green candidate in that election, Jill Stein, was systematically de-amplified. They exposed the Hamilton 68 fiasco, a register hosted by the Alliance for Securing Democracy (ASD) of 600 purported Twitter/X accounts linked to 'Russian influence activities'.[68] In fact, the list had been manipulated not to track Russians but US citizens.

Not deterred, the ASD later developed the Hamilton 2.0 Dashboard to track 'narratives and topics promoted by Russian, Chinese, and Iranian

---

65 James Bovard, 'Gabbard Episode Shows the Surveillance State Strong and Stupid as Ever', *The American Conservative*, 23 August 2024, https://www.theamericanconservative.com/gabbard-episode-shows-the-surveillance-state-strong-and-stupid-as-ever/.
66 Brett Wilkins, '"Can't Make This Up": Journalist Arrested Under UK Anti-Terror Law Hours After Criticising It', *Common Dreams*, 21 August 2024, https://www.commondreams.org/news/richard-medhurst.
67 The chosen investigators included Bari Weiss, Michael Schellenberger and Matt Taibbi with notable contributions by Sue Schmidt, Emily Bivens, Aaron Maté, Matt Orfalea and many others. Most were independent contributors on Substack. The team at Racket News, including the site manager Bivens, provided significant support to the investigatory team.
68 J. M. Berger, 'The Methodology of the Hamilton 68 Dashboard', *ASD*, Brief No. 001, August 2017, https://securingdemocracy.gmfus.org/wp-content/uploads/2018/06/ASD-Policy-Brief-Latest-edited.pdf.

government officials and state-backed media on Telegram, YouTube, Instagram and state-sponsored news websites'.[69] On the eve of the 2024 European Parliament elections, Musk revealed that the EU had offered him 'an illegal secret deal'. If the platform agreed secretly to censor online speech, then the EC would not fine it for alleged violations of content moderations rules of its recently adopted DSA. Twitter/X refused, but other major platforms accepted the deal.[70] In September 2024, Twitter/X was banned in Brazil over disinformation issues and battles with the Lula da Silva government and Musk's support for the former right-wing president, Jair Bolsonaro. In this line, the founder of Telegram, Pavel Durov, was arrested as he entered France in August 2024, accused of failing to moderate criminal activity on the platform. Such activities included child sexual abuse, drug trafficking, fraud, money laundering and enabling terrorism. Telegram has nearly a billion users worldwide and became an important channel for both the Russian and Ukrainian militaries in the war. Telegram allows group chats of up to 200,000 people, compared to WhatsApp's maximum of a thousand. It is widely used by Russian officials, with the Kremlin condemning Durov's arrest as a threat to 'freedom of communication'. Roskomnadzor (the state communications regulatory agency) tried to close the network in 2018, but gave up after two years.

Durov himself left Russia in 2014 after selling his Facebook equivalent VKontakte network, which he established in 2006, to Kremlin-friendly buyers after refusing to share Ukrainian user data. Since then he has lived in Dubai, where Telegram is based. It reportedly has only 50 staff, mostly developers, whereas Meta, Facebook's parent company, has about 40,000 employed in its safety and security teams alone.[71] Telegram insists that it observes all EU laws, including the DSA. It argues that 'It is absurd to claim that a platform or its owner are responsible for abuse of that platform'.[72] Britain's Online Safety Act, passed in October 2023 after half a decade of controversy, obliges platforms to take proactive measures to protect users from illegal and harmful content

---

69 German Marshall Fund of the US, *ASD*, 'Hamilton 2.0 Dashboard', https://securing-democracy.gmfus.org/hamilton-dashboard/.
70 Thomas Fazi, 'Inside the EU's War on Free Speech: Elon Musk Can't Win this Battle', *UnHerd*, 20 July 2024, https://unherd.com/2024/08/inside-the-eus-war-on-free-speech/.
71 'The Arrest of "Russia's Mark Zuckerberg" Rattles Social Media', *The Economist*, 27 August 2024, https://www.economist.com/business/2024/08/27/the-arrest-of-telegrams-founder-rattles-social-media.
72 Adrienne Klasa, 'French Extend Detention of Telegram Chief', *Financial Times*, 28 August 2024, p. 10.

such as hate speech and incitement to violence. Much of the anti-immigrant violence following the killing of three children in Southport in August 2024 was organised via social media (above all Telegram). The tension between free speech and the suppression of harmful content is one of the major issues of our day and, as argued above, has become entwined in Cold War II geopolitical contestation as well as 'populist' challenges to liberal hegemony.

Elon Musk disbanded the moderation team when he took over, since the Twitter Files revealed that the company usually acceded to government requests to censor material. Musk warned that if the EU tried to pursue enforcement action based on the DSA, he would take it to court. Already, in May 2023 Musk had withdrawn from the EU's *Code of Practice on Disinformation*, which had begun as a voluntary code of conduct but had been made compulsory by the DSA. Thus, Musk emerged as the champion of free speech, but it was unlikely that he could win the battle against what he perceived as censorship but which government officials consider essential safeguarding measures. Although Musk complied with most government requests to take down material, Twitter/X remains one of the only platforms, along with Telegram, where information is allowed to flow freely. Thomas Fazi argues that the global attack on free speech reflects 'the structural decay of liberal-democratic institutions [...] micromanaging the public conversation taking place on social media platforms [...] has come to be seen as an imperative for keeping the status quo safe from the threat of democracy'.

The 'censorship-industrial complex' emerged in the second half of the 2010s, when the West was rocked by a 'populist' insurgency against globalisation and the neoliberal order. This is compounded by the growing militarisation of geopolitical contestation, requiring 'an even more compliant populace given its political and economic consequences'. Intensifying confrontation with Russia over Ukraine prompted NATO to develop its 'hybrid or cognitive warfare doctrine, which conceptualises the management of Western public opinion as an integral part of warfare'. Fazi quotes NATO's general secretary, Jens Stoltenberg's, statement in 2019 that 'Nato must remain prepared for both conventional and hybrid threats: from tanks to tweets'.[73]

The information policing industry suppresses not only the 'malign influence' allegedly generated by state actors, above all Russia, China and Iran, but in the context of the Trumpian disruption, the 'contagion' of mass movements, typically labelled populist. As noted, Andrew Lowenthal points out that anti-disinformation campaigns describe language as a kind of disease.[74]

---

73 Fazi, 'Inside the EU's War on Free Speech'.
74 Cited by Taibbi, 'Report on the Censorship-Industrial Complex'.

Anti-disinformation campaigns are ultimately about shaping the narrative and suppressing dissident perspectives that challenge mainstream views. Free discussion in the public sphere is constrained, and ultimately policymaking itself is impaired. When groupthink predominates and people are afraid to challenge received wisdom, the quality of decision-making inevitably deteriorates. Matt Taibbi notes that faced by the 'disease' of dangerous political ideas, defenders of orthodoxy stress the importance of 'banding together'.[75]

The Political West is forever vigilant against attempts to drive 'wedges' between allies and bloc unity is fiercely policed, so in domestic affairs the founder of Bellingcat, Eliot Higgins, argues that 'rivalry between media titles is a thing of the past. The future is collaboration, the hunt for evidence a shared endeavour, the truth out there if we wish to discover it'.[76] Bellingcat examined Russian activity, demonstrating that the Buk missile that downed Malaysia Airlines MH17 in July 2014, with the loss of all 298 passengers and crew on board, came from Russia, as well as exposing the identities of the would-be assassins of Sergei and Julia Skripal in Salisbury in March 2018 and of Alexei Navalny in August 2020. Media rivalry would appear to be an essential feature of an open and democratic society, but in Cold War II the 'emergency' imperatives of national security tend towards confirmation bias.

The scale of media manipulation was exposed by House Judiciary Committee report of July 2023. It revealed that the FBI routinely colluded with Ukraine's spy agency to shape reports of battlefield developments, exaggerating successes while ignoring failures. The FBI 'routinely relayed these lists [of accounts] to the relevant social media platforms' and sought the suppression of negative information. The House report noted that 'authentic accounts of Americans, including a verified US State Department account and those belonging to American journalists, were ensnared in the censorship effort and flagged for social media companies to take down'. Taibbi also reveals how the CIA pressured Twitter, calling for the suppression of 'long lists of newspapers, tweets or YouTube videos guilty of "anti-Ukraine narratives"'.[77] These efforts were not enough for Ukrainian president Volodymyr Zelensky. In January 2024, he lamented that

---

75 Taibbi, 'Report on the Censorship-Industrial Complex'.
76 In Luke Harding, 'We are Bellingcat by Eliot Higgins Review – the Reinvention of Reporting for the Internet Age', *The Guardian*, 1 February 2021, https://www.theguardian.com/books/2021/feb/01/we-are-bellingcat-by-eliot-higgins-review-the-reinvention-of-reporting-for-the-internet-age.
77 Jim Bovard, 'Truth Is the Biggest Threat to DC "Democracy"', *The Libertarian Institute*, 18 December 2023, https://libertarianinstitute.org/articles/truth-is-the-biggest-threat-to-dc-democracy/.

> Today, unfortunately, Russia controls a large percentage of the information space. And I'm not talking about Ukraine here, but about social media everywhere in the civilised world: Europe, the United States, the UK, the African continent and Latin America. Russia invests a lot of money in various media in other countries, as well as in social networks.

'Russian narratives' were presented as reality, hence in his view 'one of the most difficult challenges today is to combat Russian disinformation in the world'.[78] He implicitly conceded that Russia was winning the argument across the 'civilised world', although he signally failed to mention Asia – where the major countries (except Japan) refused to adopt the West's anti-Russia sanctions.

The Twitter Files exposed aspects of the anti-disinformation universe that had previously been hidden, including the mechanisms of US government censorship and deamplification. Later revelations revealed the more offensive tactics of an ostensibly volunteer group called the Cyber-Threat Intelligence League (CTIL), initially deployed against anti-vaccine movements, ranging from the use of burner phones, the creation of fake identities, trolling operations and sockpuppet accounts to the infiltration of domestic political groups. The report revealed shocking details about the censorship–industrial complex, describing the development of contemporary digital censorship programmes and the role of military and intelligence agencies, including partnerships with civil society organisations and commercial media. In 2020, CISA created the Election Integrity Partnership with the Stanford Internet Observatory and other government contractors, which urged Twitter, Facebook and other social media platforms to monitor posts by citizens and state officials alike.[79] These were in effect state-sponsored censorship programmes, which also engaged in 'offensive' information operations.

In October 2023, one of the delisted organisations, the liberal anti-establishment investigative website, *Consortium News*, filed a legal suit against the United States and the Pentagon-funded Newsguard Industries (one of the contractors in blacklisting operations). The case described a state-funded

---

78 Society and Defence conference, Sweden, 7 January 2024, reported by Andrei Korybko, 'Zelensky Demanded that Intelligence Agencies Censor the Media to Fight "Russian Disinformation"', *Substack*, 8 January 2024, https://korybko.substack.com/p/zelensky-demanded-that-intelligence.
79 Michael Shellenberger, Alexandra Gutentag and Matt Taibbi, 'CTIL Files #1: US and UK Military Contractors Created Sweeping Plan for Global Censorship in 2018, New Documents Show', *Public*, 28 November 2023, https://public.substack.com/p/ctil-files.

effort to defame 'media organisations that oppose or dissent from American foreign and defence policy'. In a mirror action, the conservative news outlets, *The Federalist* and *The Daily Wire* (joined by the State of Texas), took on the State Department's Global Engagement Centre (GEC) and the UK's Global Disinformation Index, which curates the rather sinister Dynamic Exclusion List of alleged reprehensible sites. The GEC was established in 2016 to counter foreign propaganda, but it was alleged to have used taxpayer funds to counter domestically generated 'disinformation', something previously prohibited by Congress. The Smith-Mundt Act of January 1948 prohibits 'the US government from propagandising its own citizens at taxpayer expense', but Obama 'reformed' the law in 2012 to allow the creation of the GEC. Both the GEC and GDI stand accused of undermining domestic free speech by engaging in 'censorship enterprises' by blacklisting 'risky' news outlets. These included not just the two that brought the case but also *RealClearPolitics*, *The American Conservative*, the *New York Post*, the *Federalist*, the *American Spectator* and many more.

The GEC is headquartered in the State Department and enjoys a budget of $61m and a staff of 125 to 'counter disinformation from Russia, China, Iran and terrorist organizations', as the *Washington Post* put it in an editorial arguing against defunding.[80] *The Federalist* sought to stop 'one of the most audacious, manipulative, secretive, and gravest abuses of power and infringements of the First Amendment rights by the federal government in American history'. In its view, the State Department was using a counter-terrorism centre, created to stave off foreign 'disinformation', to prevent Americans from writing, sharing and hearing views disputing those of government officials.[81] The *Daily Wire* added that

> The Biden administration is illegally funding organizations with the stated goal of financially crippling media outlets whose coverage does not walk in lockstep with the government's ideological agenda. […]

---

80 Editorial, 'Don't Defund the Fight Against Russia and China's Disinformation', *Washington Post*, 20 March 2024, https://www.washingtonpost.com/opinions/2024/03/19/house-republicans-disinformation-global-engagement-center/.

81 Joy Pullmann, 'State of Texas Joins The Federalist, Daily Wire in Suing the Federal Censorship-Industrial Complex', *The Federalist*, 6 December 2023, https://thefederalist.com/2023/12/06/state-of-texas-joins-the-federalist-daily-wire-in-suing-the-federal-censorship-industrial-complex/. For the Eastern District of Texas official documentation, see https://dw-wp-production.imgix.net/2023/12/DailyWire-v-State-final.pdf.

we're suing for our rights, all news organizations' rights, and the constitutional guarantee of a free press that all Americans deserve.[82]

The case joined the pending US Supreme court case *Missouri v. Biden* (also known as *Murthy v. Missouri*), charging that government officials modified the content moderation and user policies of social media monopolies by threatening to destroy their business models. The plaintiffs sought to prohibit government officials from contacting social media companies to remove posts considered 'misinformation'. They allege that the GEC deployed an astonishing 365 different tools for purging unfavourable information, as well as investing millions in devising multiple internet disinformation 'tools'. It then shared this expertise with favoured media outlets, academics and government agencies, as well as marketing these government-funded technologies to Silicon Valley tech giants such as Facebook, Twitter/X and LinkedIn.[83] The top ten 'riskiest' sites included the *New York Post*, which had published material on Hunter Biden's laptop, only to have the story traduced by a posse of actual and former intelligence agents. In fact, as we have seen, the *Post*'s reporting was accurate, and it was the ostensibly trustworthy media outlets, such as NPR and the Huffington Post, which misreported the Russiagate Trump–Russia collusion allegations and asserted that the laptop story was Russian disinformation. In June 2024, the Supreme Court ruled against Missouri in the social media case.[84]

Taibbi delicately notes that it is not 'factuality and reliability' that are the relevant metric in the work of the anti-disinformation industry. They measure 'something that has far more to do with where the outlets are oriented in relation to official narratives'. The State Department allocates some $250mn annually to the effort, even though the Smith–Mundt Act bars agencies like the State Department from engaging in domestic propaganda. A related issue is why the funds are not simply directed towards the generation of content favourable to official positions such as *Voice of America*. In fact, allocations to Cold War agencies such as Radio Free Europe/Radio Liberty have been greatly increased. The budget of its parent agency, the US Agency for Global Media, reached an astonishing $840 million in 2023, compared to RT's

---

82 Anastasia Kaliabakos, 'Conservative Media Outlets Are Beating Back the State Department', *The American Conservative*, 9 May 2024, https://www.theamericanconservative.com/conservative-media-outlets-are-beating-back-the-state-department/.
83 Pullmann, 'State of Texas'.
84 Mason Letteau Stallings, 'Supreme Court Rules against Missouri in Social Media Case', *The American Conservative*, 26 June 2024, https://www.theamericanconservative.com/supreme-court-rules-against-missouri-in-social-media-case/.

relatively miserly budget of $288 million. Despite generous budgets, Taibbi argues that it is an

> increasingly obvious fact that government propaganda efforts are not trusted. Worse, traditional legacy organisations like *The New York Times* and the *Washington Post* are seen now as transparent vehicles for official propaganda, which is leading to significant loss of trust for them.[85]

They serve to disseminate intelligence agency leaks. He also mentions the Orwellian concept of 'malinformation', defined by the DHS's CISA as information 'based on fact, but used out of context to mislead, harm, or manipulate'.[86] In other words, material that is both true and wrong – that is, an inconvenient truth.[87]

A classic case of malinformation is when Andrea Kendall-Taylor, a former senior US intelligence official, told PBS that although it was true that the battle lines in Ukraine had not changed much in recent months, the 'narrative of a stalemate is wrong and unproductive'. Instead, the 'Ukraine will win' narrative was asserted, irrespective of the actual situation. As Taibbi notes,

> The war in Ukraine is making history, not just on the battlefield, but in the annals of propaganda. It is the first global news event in which audiences have been told outright that the narrative must be preserved as a strategic imperative – in this case, 'Ukraine Will Win' – no matter what contrasting truths pop up.[88]

Not surprisingly, in his interview with Tucker Carlson in February 2024, Putin lamented that 'In the war of propaganda, it is very difficult to defeat the United States'.[89] Critical independent outlets are denounced. Established in 2017, *Substack* swiftly became one of the most important platforms for independent media and hence became the target of attack. *The Atlantic* journal in November 2023 argued that 'Substack has a Nazi problem', along with the

---

85 Matt Taibbi, 'Sue the Bastards: Federalist, Daily Wire Take the State Department to Court', *Scheerpost*, 6 December 2023, https://scheerpost.com/2023/12/06/matt-taibbi-sue-the-bastards-federalist-daily-wire-take-the-state-department-to-court/.
86 Matt Taibbi, 'FOIA Exclusive: Did Pharma Companies Help Plan "Virality Project" Censorship Program?', *Racket News*, 11 December 2023, https://www.racket.news/p/foia-exclusive-did-pharma-companies.
87 Matt Taibbi, 'Not a Nothingburger: My Statement to Congress on Censorship', *Racket News*, 2 December 2023, https://www.racket.news/p/not-a-nothingburger-my-statement.
88 Matt Orfalea and Matt Taibbi, 'Big Brother – War Is Good', *Racket News*, 22 February 2024, https://www.racket.news/p/big-brother-war-is-good.
89 Vladimir Putin, 'Interview to Tucker Carlson', *Kremlin.ru*, 9 February 2024, http://en.kremlin.ru/events/president/transcripts/73411.

presence of white supremacists on the platform. The report prompted some of its users to defect to rival platforms, such as *Buttondown*. Instead of stressing that it was a service and not a publisher, *Substack* entered the political fray. Its response only exacerbated the crisis when it argued that the best way to challenge noxious ideas is through scrutiny, reserving bans only for pornography and incitements to violence. As one commentator notes, 'There is no good reason why *Substack* should be making political judgments about how to use its space any more than, say, a postal service does'.[90]

Cold war struggles are mediated through the efforts of public relations (PR) campaigns. Moscow hired a number of lobbying companies to present its case to Western audiences, although the efficacy of this work can be questioned. Lobbyists hired by Moscow and Kiev battled it out in the streets of Washington.[91] Once the war began, the PR companies hurried to sever their links with Russia, leaving the field open to Ukraine to dominate the informational space. In the first two years of the war, 46 firms and individuals had been registered under FARA to represent Ukrainian interests, including some of the major companies in the business, such as Hill & Knowlton. They received nearly $13 million from Ukrainian clients and managed some 14,000 political activities on their behalf. They lobbied for continued American support for the war effort, with some companies working pro bono for the cause.[92] Other countries active in Washington include Saudi Arabia, which spent over $70 million on lobbying efforts between 2022 and 2023. Israel, of course, has long enjoyed a dominating presence and its efforts have persistently shaped US policies in the Middle East. As noted, Labour Party leader Jeremy Corbyn came under particularly severe attack. His views are indistinguishable from long-term British policy, which supports a two-state solution and recognises the Palestinian Authority. The difference is that he actively campaigns for the creation of a Palestinian state and opposes Israel's efforts to obstruct it.[93] The distorting influence of the American Israel Public Action Committee has been the subject of forensic analysis.[94] Criticism of Israeli government policy or anti-Zionism is too easily framed as antisemitism.[95]

---

90 Stephen Bush, 'Substack Has Offered Exactly the Wrong Response to Its "Nazi Problem"', *Financial Times*, 9 January 2024, https://www.ft.com/content/648ec2c0-d71b-4dc6-af15-56fedc54eb2d.
91 Ben Freeman, 'The Lobbying Battle Before the War: Russian and Ukrainian Influence in the US', *Quincy Brief*, No. 26, July 2022, https://quincyinst.org/wp-content/uploads/2022/07/QUINCY-BRIEF-NO.-26-July-2022-FREEMAN-5.pdf.
92 Ben Freeman, 'The Ukraine Lobby Two Years into the War', *Responsible Statecraft*, 22 February 2024, https://responsiblestatecraft.org/ukraine-lobby/.
93 Ilan Pappe, *Lobbying for Zionism on Both Sides of the Atlantic* (London, Oneworld, 2024).
94 John J. Mearsheimer and Stephen M. Walt, *The Israel Lobby and US Foreign Policy* (London, Penguin, 2008).
95 For example, *The Guardian* sacked their long-standing cartoonist Steve Bell for a caricature completed on 9 October 2023, representing Gaza on Netanyahu's stomach

The work of think tanks deserves special mention. In Washington, London and elsewhere, there is an extensive ecosystem of interlocked institutions advocating the intensification of militarism and cold war-style ideological conflict. Many are funded by the military–industrial complex and thus organically promote the Trumanite state. Their job, according to a recent study by Glenn Diesen, is to manufacture consent for the policies of their paymasters, the weapons manufactures, energy companies, oil-rich sheikdoms, oligarchs and state agencies. Diesen notes that one of their achievements is to convince the population that propaganda is confined to authoritarian states and that the free market ensures a pluralism of views.[96] The Atlantic Council, considered the public policy arm of the military–industrial complex, has been notably hawkish vis-à-vis Russia, long fuelling the proxy war between Russia and the Political West. Its associates edit *The Daily Beast*, a virulently anti-Russian outlet, and manage the neo-McCarthyite website PropOrNot, devoted to exposing alleged Russian propaganda and its witting or unwitting agents. PropOrNot published a list of 200 websites that allegedly were 'routine peddlers of Russian propaganda', including *WikiLeaks* and *Antiwar.com*. Even the libertarian Ron Paul Institute was condemned by the site, as well as a range of left-wing and anti-war organisations. The Center for a New American Security (CNAS), which counted Victoria Nuland, a former adviser to Dick Cheney and an architect of Washington's Ukraine policy, as a former CEO. Michèle Flournoy, CNAS's founder and a board member of defence contractor Booz Allen Hamilton, as undersecretary for defence in the Obama administration shaped policy on Afghanistan and helped convince Obama to overthrow Muammar Gaddafi in Libya in 2011. With Biden's election, CNAS alumni flocked to staff foreign policy positions in the new administration, and in particular the team around vice-president Kamala Harris. Not surprisingly, calls for an end to hostilities, a review of US foreign policy priorities or some new balance in Transatlantic relations are denounced as Kremlin 'talking points'. The combined effect was to ratchet up tension, with no mechanism for de-escalation in sight. The second Trump presidency, however, once again suggested a different agenda, but a break with the Trumanite consensus would represent a foreign policy revolution.

---

with the words 'Residents of Gaza, get out now', an explicit reference to David Levine's depiction of Lyndon Johnson in 1966, with his stomach scar showing a map of Vietnam. Bell, who had been drawing for *The Guardian* since 1981, was accused of antisemitism.

96 Glenn Diesen, *The Think Tank Racket: Managing the Information War with Russia* (Atlanta, Clarity Press, 2023).

Chapter 7

WHY THIS COLD WAR IS DIFFERENT

Postcommunism as a condition is not restricted to the former communist states but affects the rest of the world.[1] The long after-life of the revolutionary socialist challenge continues to shape Western polities. Even after the dissolution of the communist order and the disintegration of the Soviet Union in 1989–91, the instruments and practices devised to counter the communist and Soviet threat not only survived but radicalised. The Political West, formed in and shaped by cold war, lives on in the form of NATO and the entirety of the cold war security arrangements, as well as the ideological apparatus and the military–industrial complex of the Trumanite state. Nevertheless, the collapse of communism unravelled the consensus focused on Cold War imperatives and opened up the terrain to new forms of contestation. Class politics gave way to culture wars and technocratic 'third way' depoliticised governance practices. In international affairs, the cold peace lasted a bare 25 years before full-scale cold war was reignited with Russia in 2014 (over Ukraine) and with China in 2018 (trade war). The notion of cold war is misleading if it simply suggests a rehash of the earlier conflict, but my argument is that cold war entails a certain style of international politics in the nuclear age, a distinctive culture, based on an enduring pattern of hostility between consistently aligned groups of protagonists, contesting not only militarily but also through economic and ideational antagonisms. This in turn has profound domestic effects, reproducing patterns of control, information management and imposed consensus on the key issues of the day. Cold war binaries are restored, in which one side claims to be on the right side of history and to speak the truth while the adversary is historically anachronistic and spews only falsehoods and 'disinformation'.

---

1 Richard Sakwa, *Postcommunism* (Buckingham and Philadelphia, Open University Press, 1999).

Wars of Reality

Cold War II is more amorphous but no less dangerous and pervasive than the first. The regimes of truth established by classical concepts of liberalism and socialism, 'based on a belief in the limitless power and normative value of the mind', have dissolved.[2] In the absence of clearcut ideological divisions and the erosion of the civic culture of high modernity, the distinction between truth and falsehood breaks down. Mediatised narratives and the culture of the spectacle themselves became the terrain of contestation.[3] As Hannah Arendt famously observed,

> The ideal subject of totalitarian rule is not the convinced Nazi or committed Communist, but for people for whom the distinction between facts and fiction (i.e., the reality of experience) and the distinction between true and false (i.e., the standards of thought) no longer exist.[4]

She also notes that 'ideological thinking becomes emancipated from the reality that we perceive with our five senses, and insists on a "truer" reality concealed behind all perceptible things [...]'.[5]

Outside of the Political West, countries draw on earlier representations of the high modernity of the West and appeal to the impartiality of the Charter system to sustain neo-revisionist positions. Russia positioned itself as the leader of the traditionalist and anti-colonial camp, China as the bearer of a more cooperative model of peace and development, and India, as a non-aligned mature actor intent on development and defence of national sovereignty. The Political West regressed to a more reactive, dogmatic and militarised ethos, concerned with little beyond preservation of its accustomed hegemony. Having lost a sense of the future, it can only return to the past.[6] The 'American Dream' gave way to the Chinese Dream.[7] Meanwhile, the Global South, or the World Majority as it is increasingly termed, has more important things

---

2 Ivan Timofeev, 'In 2022, the World as We Knew It Ended', *RT.com*, 5 January 2023, https://www.rt.com/russia/569440-the-end-of-the-end-of-the-history/.
3 Guy Debord, *Society of the Spectacle* (London, Rebel Press, 1994), first published in 1967, offered a prescient analysis of the emerging void in political traction. Jean Baudrillard then explored the absences of the postmodern condition in his 1981 study of simulacra, *Simulacra and Simulation* (Ann Arbor, University of Michigan Press, 1994).
4 Hannah Arendt, *The Origins of Totalitarianism* (San Diego, Harcourt, 1968), p. 474.
5 Arendt, *The Origins of Totalitarianism*, p. 470.
6 Richard Sakwa, 'Living in the Void: The End of the Revolution and the Politics of Krisis', *International Political Anthropology*, Vol. 17, No. 1, 2024, pp. 63–80.
7 On the former, see David Leonhardt, *Ours Was the Shining Future: The Story of the American Dream* (New York, Random House, 2023).

to do than fight a cold war. Anti-hegemonic counter-movements are not virtuous simply by opposing the disruptive and destructive behaviour of their protagonist. Unless they can demonstrate genuine commitment to Charter principles, they simply become counter-hegemonic – reproducing the same pattern of international politics, only from the opposite pole, rather than anti-hegemonic, challenging the logic of hegemony in its entirety. This is made all the harder as the competing core alignments, representing rival conceptions of world order and the good life, assume more delineated geopolitical forms. There is no escape from cold war.

An ontological conflict is about the very essence of being. The concept of ontological security focuses on what motivates states rather than concentrating on outcomes. In establishing the theory, Jennifer Mitzen argues that 'in addition to physical security and economic prosperity, states also seek ontological security, or security of the self'.[8] This becomes bound up with contesting appreciations of political reality. The harshness of the battle lines in Cold War II is derived in part from the struggle between universalist and particularist approaches. Russia and China advance perspectives that reflect their historically contingent development and geographical position, although they insist on their allegiance to the universal principles enshrined in the Charter system. Their critics rightly point out that they too often fail to live up to their professed commitments. Great power considerations externally and regime perpetuation domestically shape their policies as much as they do elsewhere, yet defence of the principle of sovereign internationalism (Westphalia plus as defined earlier) in an anarchic world of competing states is the only sustainable framework for a manageable international politics. By contrast, the United States and its allies in the Political West believe that their experience is of universal validity, which in recent years has been refracted through the 'rules-based order'. The 'Bush doctrine' of the early 2000s argued that America's mission was to spread democracy, if necessary – like the French Revolution – at the point of a bayonet. Democratic internationalism effectively claims to know what is in the best interests of other states more than the states themselves. This may indeed sometimes be the case, but intervention is only legitimate when conducted with the sanction of the UN. Illicit interventions call into question the legitimacy of other systems. There can hardly be a meeting of minds when the perspectives are so different.

The dividing line is as much cultural as ideological. As one critic puts it, 'the world is not reducible to the American experience of it'. US advocacy of

---

8 Jennifer Mitzen, 'Ontological Security in World Politics: State Identity and the Security Dilemma', *European Journal of International Relations*, Vol. 12, No. 3, 2006, p. 341.

ideological postulates, such as 'democracy', 'freedom' and 'human rights' are advanced

> not as elements of rational, responsible and limited responses to the task of securing better government in different parts of the world but as a magical formula, an incantation, a gnosis, as contemptuous of material reality in all its historicity and maddening local particularity as the irrational, esoteric religions of old.[9]

Like the universalism of the Roman Catholic church, this exceptionalist ideology has become a new religion of politics, a culture that asserts a revealed truth rather than political postulates to be debated and tailored to local needs. This political theology then shapes reality, including the information coming to leaders. In Cold War I, 'intelligence' at least aspired to provide relatively accurate information about how the other side viewed the world and informed assessments (although with plenty of Team B type failures, as well as gross over-estimates of Soviet economic growth), but in Cold War II the intelligence community and the associated media and think tank penumbra condemn the very notion of understanding. This is forcefully in evidence in the Russiagate scandal. Hence, the risible term *Putinversteher* – Putin-understander, and the even more preposterous *Russlandversteher*. The absence of understanding is hardly to be commended. Arguments and positions are reduced to their alleged source ('Kremlin propaganda' and the like) and not on their intrinsic merits. Bergman puts it well when he argues:

> to observe some of the same things as Russian propaganda does not logically mean that therefore it is untrue. Much of the propaganda by any country is factually correct. It is anti-scholarly to in effect take the position that if Russia or any other country says something, that scholars cannot say the same because that would be propaganda or supporting propaganda. By the same token, we would not be able to agree with anything Western governments say, because that would also be supporting propaganda? Or do Western governments not do propaganda?[10]

Such reductivist thinking reduces the ability of a political community to process information in a rational manner and on that basis to devise policy. According to Wilhelm Dilthey, this is the essential principle of hermeneutics:

---

9 Matthew J. Dal Santo, 'The Putin Interview', *Landmarks: A Journal of International Dialogue*, 13 February 2024, https://landmarksmag.substack.com/p/a-symposium-on-tucker-carlsons-controversial.
10 Bergman, 'Confronting Censorship'.

'Action everywhere presupposes the understanding of other persons [...] The historical consciousness developed on this basis has enabled modern man to hold the entire past of humanity present within himself.'[11]

Instead of understanding the Russo-Ukrainian war through the lens of hermeneutics, it has been interpreted through the prism of securitisation. All sides describe it as existential. For Ukrainian nationalists, it is a struggle for the country's existence as a polity integrated into the Political West. The war is presented as a struggle of civilisation against barbarism, with Ukraine the bulwark holding back the Eastern hordes. Russia presented the war as an existential struggle for security, but also for civilisational identity and traditional ties between the Eastern Slavic peoples and the Russian Orthodox communality, broadly defined as the *Russkii mir*. The Political West insisted that the rules-based order was at stake in Ukraine, and if it lost then the foundations of international law would crumble. Authoritarian leaders elsewhere would be encouraged to disobey the rules. China would invade Taiwan, and the 'rules-based order' globally would lose credibility and ultimately disintegrate – a revived version of the discredited 'domino' theory. The perception that US 'credibility' was on the line in Southeast Asia in 1964 tipped the country into war in Vietnam, despite warnings from the outstanding diplomat George W. Ball that Washington was in danger of 'becoming the puppet of our puppet'. The reference then was to Saigon, raising the question of who today can issue similar warnings regarding Kiev, Warsaw or any number of other embittered East European capitals, not to mention Jerusalem.[12]

Ontological insecurities arise from the respective strategic cultures, reflecting longstanding identities, representations of international affairs and assessments of the security environment. Honour and status are crucial, becoming more salient when fundamental issues of security are at stake.[13] Russia's refusal to accept a subaltern position in a geopolitical order dominated by Washington and advocacy of multipolarity was perceived as provocative and threatening to the US-led political order. The Political West refused to recognise Russia's self-evaluation of its status in world affairs, generating mistrust and ultimately conflict. The corralling of Ukraine's multiple identities and foreign policy concerns into a single pro-Western channel alienated

---

11 Wilhelm Dilthey, *Selected Works, Volume 4: Hermeneutics and the Study of History* (Princeton, Princeton University Press, 1996), p. 235.

12 James W. Carden, 'Where Is Joe Biden's "Devil's Advocate"?', *The American Conservative*, 18 March 2024, https://www.theamericanconservative.com/where-is-bidens-devils-advocate/.

13 Cf. Andrei P. Tsygankov, *Russia and the West from Alexander to Putin: Honor in International Relations* (Cambridge, Cambridge University Press, 2012).

constituencies within the country, which sought external backers for their particular vision of how the polity should be shaped.

Underlying Cold War II are contrasting understandings of reality. One of the main exponents of the idea that each civilisation has its own idea of truth and that no culture (drawing on the philosophy of Martin Heidegger) 'was objectively better than another' is Alexander Dugin. As a recent study puts it, he draws on anthropological and Traditionalist thinking to argue that 'In a world of difference, no society would claim to know "the truth" for anyone but themselves. The opposite claim, that an objective reality exists beyond culture, was nothing but a Trojan horse for epistemological colonialism.' The geopolitical conclusion is clear:

> If one culture claimed to have accessed knowledge that wasn't specific to them but was instead true for everybody, it was then justified in invading and erasing the thinking of others, taking what once was a world with a vast array of knowledge systems and replacing it with one. And it so happens that the culture bringing this scourge of epistemological uniformity on the world is – surprise – the modern West with its scientific method.[14]

Dugin is a highly controversial figure, with critics considering him an exponent of neo-fascist ideas. It is perhaps better to view him as a proponent of radical right-wing communitarianism, the philosophical family to which fascism belongs.[15]

The Rubin's vase metaphor came into its own as the Ukraine crisis unfurled in 2014, marking the beginning of an internationalised civil war and a new cold war. Cultural 'othering' was intensified, reflecting very different understandings of political reality. In a phone call with Obama, German chancellor Angela Merkel talked of Putin living 'in another reality'.[16] Putin's rationality was questioned, even raising doubts about his sanity. The US secretary of state John Kerry was at a complete loss to understand what motivated Putin: 'You almost feel that he's creating his own reality, and his own sort of world, divorced from a lot of what's real on the ground for all those

---

14 Benjamin R. Teitelbaum, *War for Eternity: The Return of Traditionalism and the Rise of the Populist Right* (London, Penguin, 2021), p. 232.
15 Suslov, *Putinism*, pp. 64, 67 and *passim*.
16 Peter Baker, '3 Presidents and a Riddle Named Putin', *New York Times*, 23 March 2014, https://www.nytimes.com/2014/03/24/world/europe/3-presidents-and-a-riddle-named-putin.html.

people, including people in his own country.'¹⁷ The sentiment is reciprocated by Russian commentators. The asymmetrical end of Cold War I was refracted in incommensurate understandings of the character of European security and international politics. Russian security concerns did not fit into the Political West's mental picture of the world, while the Russian leadership simply could not understand why their concerns were treated with such disdain. The only answer was malevolence, the attempt to defeat Russia, like so many previous adversaries – Swedes, Poles, French and Germans (repeatedly). In the fog of mutual incomprehension, the West's response was to personalise the issue. Kerry went on to argue that the Ukraine crisis was 'obviously very personally driven in ways that I think are uniquely inappropriate to 21st century leadership'. He argued,

> It's an amazing display of a kind of personal reaction to something that just doesn't fit into the lessons learned for the last 60 years or 70 years. It's so divorced that it leaves you feeling badly for the consequences. I think the Russian people are going to pay a price for this. It's unfortunate for the Russian people, who clearly don't fit into the costs that are being attached to this, because it appears to be so personal to President Putin.¹⁸

The idea that Russia's actions in Crimea were a response to a genuine security threat simply does not factor into this kind of analysis. Challenges to hyper-normality are perceived as not only irrational but also deviant. In reality, the loss of the Sevastopol Naval Base would have represented Russia's worst irrecoverable defeat in a thousand years. Kerry's implicit appeal to the norms of the Charter International System sounded hollow, since it was precisely the Political West's appropriation and selective application of those norms that riled Moscow.

This is the context in which the notion of 'cognitive war', the struggle over meanings and interpretations, gained currency. In NATO's usage, it encompasses all the elements of information warfare, including psychological and neurological dimensions, to generate complex platforms for military action. In response, the Russian chief of the general staff, Valery Gerasimov, argued that 'Moral-psychological-cognitive-informational struggle' is central

---

17 Gerald F. Seib, 'Kerry Sees Ukraine Crisis as Uniquely Putin's', *Wall Street Journal*, 29 April 2014, https://www.wsj.com/articles/SB10001424052702304163604579530 141321140198.
18 Seib, 'Kerry Sees Ukraine Crisis as Uniquely Putin's'.

to contemporary conflicts.[19] Gerasimov was responding to Western 'hybrid warfare', but it was interpreted as a new Russian doctrine of military affairs. The notion of hybrid warfare is notoriously ill-defined, since war has always combined military, political and psychological elements.

The election of the comedian Volodymyr Zelensky to the Ukrainian presidency in April 2019, and shortly afterwards the overwhelming victory of his hastily formed Servant of the People party in parliamentary elections, merged fiction and reality. The TV show *Servant of the People* portrayed how through a series of accidents an ordinary teacher was elevated to the presidency to root out corruption and forge a better Ukraine. Zelensky's official platform ran to only 1,601 words, but the 51 episodes of the TV show acted as his real manifesto, with all of the elisions and ambiguities inherent in the medium.[20] Zelensky went on to pursue radical neoliberal policies, including the privatisation of land and state property, the weakening of labour and welfare legislation, and steep increases in the price of utilities. His populist constitution of 'the people' was untethered from a specific social or ideological base and instead appealed to an abstract Western-oriented progressive ideology. The growing domestic opposition was condemned as a residue of the Soviet past, not worthy of the remaining part of the political community, hence justifying repression. Neoliberal authoritarianism and radical nationalist mobilisation eroded the legitimacy of political opposition, and with it the 'excesses' of democracy and the very idea of 'the political' – agonistic contestation over matters of concern to the community.[21] This sharply polarised, militarised and 'monist' perspective was then projected onto international affairs, even though Zelensky's original popularity had been derived from his promise of peace.

The ontological impasse was complete, further degrading the possibility of diplomatic solutions. The Political West and Russia lived in parallel worlds, failing to see the common reality that united them. Old tropes about Russia as inherently expansionist and imperialist were revived, accompanied by cold war containment strategies. The ideology of Putinism (if there is such a thing) is charged with 'providing the elites and the population with a cognitive prism, whose ability to convey an accurate picture of reality is considerably impaired'.[22] America in turn was portrayed as a rogue state sowing conflict and discord globally. The Washington elite was increasingly portrayed as out

---

19 Valerii Gerasimov, 'Tsennost' nauki i predvidenii', *Voenno-promyshlennyi kur'er*, No. 8, 27 February 2013, http://vpk-news.ru/articles/14632.
20 The contradictions are brilliantly dissected by Olga Baysha, *Democracy, Populism, and Neoliberalism in Ukraine* (London and New York, Routledge, 2022).
21 Baysha, *Democracy, Populism, and Neoliberalism in Ukraine*, pp. 4–5.
22 Suslov, *Putinism*, p. 277.

of touch with reality, suffering from 'hegemonitis' – having wielded unchallenged power for too long.[23] This came to a head over US policy in Palestine. As one commentary notes, 'Biden has built an alternative reality, running parallel to real events in Gaza'.[24] The observation applies not only to Gaza. All parties came to believe that the other side could not be trusted and would not change their positions unless forced to do so. Deaf to the concerns of the other, the only response was to bring the other side to its knees. The logic is escalatory, edging the world towards a global conflict.

Separate realities become partial realities, with distinct regimes of untruth. Each is reinforced and presented as the only reality, creating a disjuncture that repudiates the very possibility of a universal truth and on that basis compromise. David Bromwich comments:

> The greater the improbability of an official explanation, the more pressing is the need to shore it up with unchecked reiterations, confirmations, enhancements. So the kingdom of untruth expands, without boundary or restraint. An officially sanctioned account of this or that event is affirmed by bureaucratic oversight and announced to the populace by a cooperative press and media. A consensus is thereby established that floats free of any concern with veracity.[25]

The wars in Ukraine and Palestine were internalised and presented as hyper-normal to an extraordinary and surprising degree. Arta Moeini observes that 'both the ruling classes and the civilian populations across the world' perceived 'far-off external conflict in existential terms and put themselves at the centre of it as a messianic protagonist'. This is because of the 'profound crisis of meaning and legitimacy exacerbated by the identarian turn taken by both the Left and the Right since the Sixties, and the complete politicisation of all aspects of life in late or hyper-modernity'. With the boundaries between the personal and the political eroded, identity-based existence has 'become a poor man's substitute for the deep-rooted and embodied meaning that was previously derived from communal, traditional life and held in common within a culture'.

Distant conflicts become an opportunity for catharsis, offering 'the fleeting possibility of escaping the existential angst of an atomised life lived

---

23 Tarik Cyril Amar, 'Bullshit Blowback', 19 May 2024, https://tarikcyrilamar.substack.com/p/bullshit-blowback.
24 Bruno Maçães, 'Joe Biden's Understanding of the Israel-Hamas War Is Based on Myth and Fantasy', *New Statesman*, 17–23 May 2024, p. 31.
25 Quoted by James W. Carden, 'The Ukraine War Runs on Prevarication', *The American Conservative*, 17 February 2024, https://www.theamericanconservative.com/the-ukraine-war-runs-on-lies/.

under the automatism of modernity, and for feeling a sense of unity, purity and spiritual community forged in the virtual fires of war'. While the global masses seek transcendence, the ruling classes internalise and instrumentalise these sentiments 'to buttress and justify their political regimes'. The ontological insecurity of civilian populations stems from the search for meaning and permanence, 'the ruling classes suffer from an additional insecurity that is rooted in the need to legitimise their power (even to themselves) in a world where all institutional authority is increasingly doubted'. Hence, Israel and Ukraine are removed from their actual contexts and transformed into 'ideological proxies by different foreign actors. Ukraine thus becomes existential to the United States, even though the fate of Ukraine will never have a decisive impact on America's national interest or the collective interest of Americans.'[26]

The anti-understanding bias results in the foreshortening of perspectives and the removal of context. Evil actors spring into action fully-fledged, with no analysis of what provoked them in the first place. Russia invaded Ukraine in February 2022 because Putin is evil and hates democracy, and Hamas's savage attack on Israel on 7 October 2023 had nothing to do with 70 years of displacement and oppression. This is the 'Marvelisation' of politics, from Marvel Comics.[27] Caitlin Johnstone powerfully argues that

> enemies of the empire are portrayed the same way that the children's cartoon show Captain Planet portrayed its villains, cackling evilly about how they're going to dump toxic waste into the ocean for no reason other than to hurt the environment.[28]

In this anti-hermeneutical universe, there is no beginning or end, context or comparison, just an endless present.[29]

---

26 Arta Moeini, 'Gaza, Ukraine and Our Quest for Catharsis', *UnHerd*, 4 November 2023, https://unherd.com/2023/11/gaza-ukraine-and-our-quest-for-catharsis/.
27 Cf. Jean Baudrillard, *The Intelligence of Evil* (New York, Berg, 2005).
28 Caitlin Johnstone, 'Turns Out "Israel Has a Right to Defend Itself" Meant "Israel Has a Right to Commit Genocide"', *Substack*, 15 January 2024, https://caityjohnstone.medium.com/turns-out-israel-has-a-right-to-defend-itself-meant-israel-has-a-right-to-commit-genocide-dc8a544deff0.
29 For an impressionistic account, devoid of political analysis or context, see Peter Pomerantsev, *Nothing Is True and Everything Is Possible: Adventures in Modern Russia* (London, Faber, 2015).

Decolonial Polarisation

In Cold War I, hostility was largely directed towards the Soviet regime in the Kremlin and communism in general, while the Russian and other peoples were often considered victims as much as perpetrators. This is very different in Cold War II, in which the entirety of peoples are demonised. President Kennedy argued the opposite, insisting that peace 'requires respect of the other party, a fair and generous appraisal of the other's interests and worth'.[30] His call for empathy did not necessarily entail sympathy for the protagonist, but it demanded understanding and pluralism. In Cold War II, the culture of respect for the adversary is long gone. This explains why little attempt has been made to distinguish between sanctions directed at changing state policy and those inflicted on the people as a whole. Collective punishment is the response to perceived collective guilt. There were even calls to punish Russian citizens living in the UK who allegedly supported Putin.[31] Collective punishment is always morally dubious, but there is remarkably little debate when applied to Russia. The underlying premiss appears to be that given sufficient pressure, the Russian people will rise up to overthrow what is considered a tyrannical regime. The evidence points the other way. Collective punishment only hardens attitudes, stiffens resolve and increases support for Putin and the leadership as a whole – the classic 'rally round the flag' effect.[32]

More sophisticated analysis points to the way that the Russian system is 'co-constituted' by the people and the state.[33] Complex interactions between the state and society involve the delivery of public goods, such as individual security, timely pension and wage payments, improved infrastructure, rising (although uneven) living standards and much more, as well as the intangible benefit derived from pride of being part of a great power with an influential and distinctive voice in international affairs. This is the ill-defined yet dynamic 'social contract' with the state, in return for which citizens give their service and loyalty. The state in turn is responsive to public concerns, and when it oversteps the mark – as with the 'monetisation' of social benefits in

---

30 Sachs, *To Move the World*, p. 80.
31 A list of 90 names was sent to the prime minister by the former KGB agent and associate of Alexander Litvinenko, Andrei Sidelnikov, the head of the campaign group Speak Up!, who ran the Revenge project collecting the names and advocating the confiscation of assets. David Batty, 'Campaigner Calls on PM to Freeze Assets of Thousands of Russians in Britain', *The Guardian*, 21 March 2024, p. 11.
32 As evidenced, for example, by Levada Centre surveys reported by Volkov and Kolesnikov, 'Alternate Reality'.
33 Samuel A. Greene and Graeme B. Robertson, *Putin v. the People: The Perilous Politics of a Divided Russia* (New Haven, Yale University Press, 2019).

2006, the pension reform in 2018 and the repeated inappropriate siting of landfill waste tips – protest ensues. The Kremlin closely monitors the popular pulse (it even has its own sociological service) and shapes policy in that light. It also seeks to shape the cultural landscape.

At the heart of this is memory of the Soviet victory in World War II, which became increasingly sacralised. In memory politics, the past arcs over the present, revising everything in its light while imbuing the present with the sense of an unfinished and continuing past. Wars over memory become conflicts over reality. It has become a criminal offence to question the basic tenets of the official version of history. The counterpart of this is an increasingly strident 'revisionist' historiography in the heartlands of the Political West. In January 2006, the Parliamentary Assembly of the Council of Europe (PACE) adopted a resolution on 'The Need for International Condemnation of Crimes of Totalitarian Communist Regimes', condemning the crimes committed by 'the totalitarian communist regimes'.[34] The European Parliament (EP) in September 2008 established 23 August (the anniversary of the Molotov–Ribbentrop Pact of 1939) as the 'European Day of Remembrance for Victims of Stalinism and Nazism'.[35] The 2009 EP resolution 'On European Conscience and Totalitarianism', and the resolution adopted by PACE called 'Divided Europe Reunited: Promoting Human Rights and Civil Liberties in the OSCE Region in the 21st Century', branded Nazism and Stalinism as equivalent totalitarian regimes. The two were held equally responsible for provoking World War II and for the crimes against humanity of those years.[36] On the 80th anniversary of the start of World War II, the EP returned to the issue on 17 September 2019 when it passed a resolution arguing that 'although the crimes of the Nazi regime were evaluated and punished by means of the Nuremberg trials, there is still an urgent need to raise awareness and carry out moral and legal assessments of the crimes of communist dictatorships'.[37] This had long been the view of East European postcommunist elites, but the

---

34 'The Need for International Condemnation of Crimes of Totalitarian Communist Regimes', PACE, 25 January 2006, http://assembly.coe.int/nw/xml/xref/xref-xml-2html-en.asp?fileid=17403&lang=en.
35 'Proclamation of 23 August as European Day of Remembrance for Victims of Stalinism and Nazism', European Parliament, 23 September 2008, https://www.europarl.europa.eu/doceo/document/TA-6-2008-0439_EN.html.
36 Igor Torbakov, 'History, Memory and National Identity: Understanding the Politics of History and Memory Wars in Post-Soviet Lands', *Demokratizatsiya*, Vol. 19, No. 3, 2011, pp. 209–32.
37 European Parliament, 'Motion for a Resolution', 17 September 2019, https://www.europarl.europa.eu/doceo/document/B-9-2019-0098_en.html.

'new Europe' view now shapes West European 'old Europe' perspectives. The Soviet Union is effectively held equally responsible for starting the war. This ignores the larger problem of creating a collective security regime in Eastern Europe in the 1930s, and the West's appeasement policy that from Moscow's perspective was a strategy intended to turn Hitler eastwards.

Political equivalence is at the heart of Yale historian Timothy Snyder's comparative analysis of Nazi Germany and Stalin's Soviet Union in the 'bloodlands' in the centre of Europe.[38] Snyder's work transformed the politics of memory, above all by delegitimising the Soviet Union and its overwhelming contribution to Hitler's defeat, and hence enjoys enormous popularity among Western elites. However, his methodology is deeply flawed, with no convincing model to explain the 'bloodlands' in Eastern Europe from 1930, his arbitrarily chosen start date. German and Soviet actions are juxtaposed rather than causally connected.[39] Moscow considers this a shameful repudiation of the common endeavour against Nazi Germany. Such historical revisionism reinforces Russia's alienation from the Political West. Unmediated NATO enlargement excluded Russia from the post-Cold War European security order, and it is now being expunged from shared collective memory of the common victory over Nazi Germany. Anatol Lieven notes that

> the memory of these [Stalinist] crimes was weaponized by forces in the West and in Eastern Europe to serve their anti-Russian agendas. In particular, the attempt to equate Soviet and Nazi crimes and blame the Soviet ones on Russia and the Russian people caused widespread national outrage, especially given that so many of the victims of communism were Russians, and so many of the perpetrators (including Stalin himself) were non-Russians.[40]

Revisionist perspectives on European history divide the continent and delegitimate pan-continental aspirations. The rewriting of twentieth-century history stokes conflicts in the twenty-first century.

---

38 Timothy Snyder, 'Hitler vs. Stalin: Who Was Worse?', *New York Review of Books*, 27 January 2011, https://www.nybooks.com/online/2011/01/27/hitler-vs-stalin-who-was-worse/; drawing on his *Bloodlands: Europe between Hitler and Stalin* (London, Vintage, 2011).
39 As argued by Tom Lawson, 'Bloodlands: Europe Between Hitler and Stalin', *Reviews in History*, December 2016, https://reviews.history.ac.uk/review/2036.
40 Anatol Lieven, 'To Seek Peace in Ukraine, Remember the End of the Cold War', *The Nation*, 22 February 2024, https://www.thenation.com/article/world/ukraine-us-russia-gorbachev/.

This is evident in decolonisation discourse, which is now turned against Russia to delegitimate its very existence as a state and cultural entity. In 1991, the 15 union republics separated from the defunct Soviet Union. Russia assumed the privileges (including a permanent seat on the UN Security Council) and obligations (the national debt) as the continuer state. It occupies 77 per cent of the former USSR across 11 time zones and is home to at least 196 distinct nationalities, some 146 of which are autochthonous peoples. The concept of 'decolonisation' comes from the Cold War I armoury, applied to the so-called 'captive peoples' in the Soviet orbit. In June 2022, the US government-funded Helsinki Commission (the Commission on Security and Cooperation in Europe) launched a programme on 'decolonising Russia'. The basic idea, as Diesen puts it, was that 'Russia is not a country, but an empire that the US must break up by supporting separatist movements within the country'.[41] Postcolonialism as an academic exploration initially focused on hybrid literatures emerging out of the experience of colonialism, but has now broadened into an all-encompassing view of post-imperial relations. Decoloniality is rather different, focusing on the deeper processes of colonialism and how colonial practices are reproduced in post-colonial settings. In postcommunist Europe, the concepts arguably have been misappropriated and are applied instrumentally. History and memory politics have been politicised and feed into cold war narratives. Amidst calls to 'decolonise' everything, including academic curriculums, history and area studies, the Soviet Union is characterised as an imperial and colonial endeavour. Russocentrism is condemned in favour of emphasis on the other North Eurasian (post-Soviet) nation-states and their earlier histories. The ideology of decolonisation includes calls to 'decentre' East European studies. The focus shifts from the Russian metropolis towards the formerly subaltern nations, both within Russia and in the larger 'post-Soviet' and 'postcommunist' neighbourhood. For some, this represents little more than the extension of American 'cancel culture', an expression of a peculiar type of Anglo-Saxon 'wokeness', to a region which at the best of times was little understood.

The 'derussification' campaign in Ukraine intensifies the longstanding 'decommunisation' programme and seeks to extirpate all elements of the peoples' thousand years of shared history. The nationalist struggle to negate Russia extends to the global stage. The 'Ukrainisation' of the Political West's public sphere has long been in train, but after 2022 assumed radical forms. Engagement with all aspects of Russian life, economy and culture is cancelled. Early in the war, an unprecedented cultural and sporting boycott of

---

41 Diesen, *The Ukraine War*, p. 236.

Russia was imposed. The opera soprano Anna Netrebko and the conductor Valery Gergiev came under intense pressure to condemn Putin and the war. The Metropolitan Opera in New York severed its connection with Netrebko. Russian tennis players were banned from Wimbledon. Collaborative educational projects, art exhibitions and citizen diplomacy endeavours all came to an end. The IELTS international English language assessment system cancelled all examinations in Russia. Concerts featuring Russian music were dropped. The closure of the 850 McDonald's restaurants and 130 Starbucks coffee shops in Russia was deigned to impede the war effort.[42] Even the *Washington Post* was moved to note that 'something more powerful than a boycott may be forming, which is the growing sense that Russia may indeed be exceptional among nations, and uniquely toxic'.[43] That certainly was the Ukrainian nationalist view, but not necessarily one that the West should share. Alarmingly, Western policy towards Russia was increasingly made in Kiev and not in the West.

The war in Ukraine is devastating, but far from unique. The illegal Anglo-American invasion of Iraq in 2003 caused at least 300,000 direct deaths, the United States may have killed up to 40,000 civilians when it freed Mosul from Islamic State in 2017, the Anglo-Saxon powers armed Saudi Arabia in its murderous war on the Houthis in Yemen from 2015, and the United States continued to arm Israel throughout its war on Gaza following the horrendous Hamas attack of 7 October 2023. Why were sanctions not imposed on the Anglo-Saxon world, or its leaders designated pariahs? The question of course is rhetorical. It reflects the systemic application of double standards, as described earlier. A commentary notes,

> It is profoundly ironic that those who react to the war in Ukraine by aggressively or indiscriminately cancelling or restricting artists and

---

42 For a critique, see Maxim D. Shrayer, 'Punishing All Things Russian for Putin's Crimes: The Moral and Historical Illiteracy of Boycotting Russian Identity and Culture', *Tablet*, 4 April 2022, https://www.tabletmag.com/sections/news/articles/punishing-all-things-russian-for-putins-crimes.

43 Philip Kennicott, 'Ukraine Wants a Boycott of Russian Culture', *Washington Post*, 15 December 2022, https://www.washingtonpost.com/arts-entertainment/2022/12/14/ukraine-culture-boycott/. See also, for example, Oleksandr Tkachenko, 'As Ukraine's Culture Minister, I'm Asking You to Boycott Tchaikovsky Until This War Is Over', *The Guardian*, 7 December 2022, https://www.theguardian.com/commentisfree/2022/dec/07/ukraine-culture-minister-boycott-tchaikovsky-war-russia-kremlin.

artistic works simply for being Russian are reflecting the same kind of nationalist thinking driving the Russian invasion in the first place.[44]

The success of the cancel campaign only serves to confirm Moscow in its view that it faces an existential threat from Ukraine and its Western backers.

The Russo-Ukrainian war is a civil war within the single East Slavic and Orthodox civilisation. This does not mean endorsing Putin's view that Belarusians, Russians and Ukrainians are ultimately 'one people', let alone that they should belong to a single state. But it does identify civilisational commonality. This is reflected in numerous similarities in the way of life of the respective peoples and shared cultural experiences. For example, the TV serial *Slovo patsana: Krov na asfalte* ('The Lad's Word: Blood on Tarmac'), a story set in Kazan in 1989 as the Soviet Union disintegrated. Teenage street gangs run riot across the city, engaging in street fights that only end when there is 'blood on the asphalt'. The series proved extremely popular in Ukraine, provoking heated condemnation by officials intent on extirpating the Russian language. They condemned the film as 'Russian psychological warfare'. By contrast, according to the film director and critic Andriy Alferov, the programme reflected the 'shared Soviet past – the one Ukraine is trying to forget [...] We all came from Soviet Ukraine'. He argued that

> We accuse Russia of living in the past and that people there exalt Stalin as a miracle alongside Czar Nicholas II. But our heads are also turned to the past. We made up a story for ourselves that we were a colony, even though we were full partners in the creation of the Russian Empire and the Soviet Union. We have to acknowledge that.[45]

There can be few more resonant statements of the hybridity of the 'postcolonial' condition, and a repudiation of the decolonial perspective that Ukraine had been a Russian colony on the classic imperial model. In fact, Russian and Ukrainian state development had long been entangled, and their very closeness is the source of much of the bitterness generated in the post-Soviet years.

Much of the accompanying rhetoric is exaggerated, but the reinvigorated interest in national and sub-national peoples and histories is welcome.

---

44 Kevin M. F. Platt, 'The Profound Irony of Cancelling Everything Russian', *New York Times*, 25 April 2024, https://www.nytimes.com/2022/04/22/opinion/russian-artists-culture-boycotts.html.

45 Liza Rozovsky, 'Smash Hit Soviet-era Show Unites Viewers in Russia and Ukraine', *Haaretz*, 14 January 2024, https://www.haaretz.com/life/television/2024-01-14/ty-article-magazine/.premium/the-russian-bridgerton-but-with-soviet-despair-instead-of-sex-and-corsets/0000018c-fe43-d832-a59d-fef789540000.

However, decolonial narratives distort history as much as imperial narratives had done earlier. The Soviet Union was a complex political formation that for much of its history nurtured state building and in certain periods even nation building.[46] Soviet nations provided the framework for the socialist modernisation project.[47] Today, Russia remains a patchwork of nations and peoples, and the polycultural constitutional settlement after 1991 provides a relatively tolerant framework for civic inclusion. 'Polyculturalism' is the term used to describe the civilisational inclusion of autochthonous peoples, whereas 'multiculturalism' describes the adaptation of a dominant culture to the influx of non-native immigration. Ethnic Russians comprise some 80 per cent of the population, but the regime is careful to constrain ethnic Russian nationalism. The fragile balance in inter-ethnic relations is maintained by the regime through compromises and derogations, which in some cases (as in Ramzan Kadyrov's Chechnya) run directly counter to constitutional provisions. The regime argues that the decolonial destruction of Russia and its disintegration into a patchwork of 'postcolonial' states would have incalculable but dangerous consequences for society and humanity. These fears are well-grounded.

Decentring Democracy

The cultural focus of the decolonisation narrative marginalises material or security concerns and amplifies cold war moralistic 'evil empire' tropes. Instead of providing complexity and sophistication, analysis becomes simplistic and reductionist – the battle of good and evil, brave small nations against imperial overlordship and cultural liberation vs colonial oppression. The post-Soviet decolonisation endeavour is disturbingly silent about other hegemonies and imperial dominations. The manifold elisions and suppressions of the postcommunist syndrome fuel cold war narratives in a no less obscurantist and primitive manner as in the original cold war. The crucial contribution of early postcolonial studies, namely the emphasis on hybridity, the irreversible mix of development and exploitation and the imbrication of colonialist and colonised, is lost.[48] Orientalist and essentialist representations

---

46 See, for example, Terry Martin, *The Affirmative Action Empire: Nations and Nationalism in the Soviet Union, 1923–1939* (Ithaca and London, Cornell University Press, 2001) and Ronald Grigor Suny, *A State of Nations: Empire and Nation-Making in the Age of Lenin and Stalin* (Oxford, Oxford University Press, 2002).
47 For an example, see Artemy Kalinovsky, *Laboratory of Socialist Development: Cold War Politics and Decolonization in Tajikistan* (Ithaca, Cornell University Press, 2018).
48 For a subtle study of the issue, see Kevin M. F. Platt, *Border Conditions: Russian-Speaking Latvians Between World Orders* (DeKalb, Northern Illinois University Press, 2024).

of national histories come to the fore. The Russian oppositionist Leonid Ragozhin rather tartly notes,

> What used to be the main theme of anti-Western Soviet propaganda back in the 20th century is now a favourite toy of hawkish Atlanticists, pro-Ukraine activists and East European ethnonationalists. Talking about the decolonization of Russia (and Russia alone – one hardly hears about returning Tennessee to the Cherokees) has become the surest way of attracting the attention of institutions that fund scientific research and political activism.[49]

The Manichean division of the world into good and evil powers, democracies and autocracies, is inherently anti-democratic and anti-pluralist. Old propaganda techniques are revived to fight the new cold war.[50] Once again, troubling questions are raised about the extent to which attempts to defend democracy from subversion undermine the freedom which make democracy viable. Democratism is an intrinsic part of democracy itself,[51] but is dangerously amplified by geopolitical concerns. The division between a more 'advanced' Political West against 'retrograde' states reaches deep into societies themselves and reflects the 500 years of Western civilizational dominance. The geopolitical imperative for domestic political outcomes to align with the perceived interests of the Political West has spawned a range of intimidatory and disciplinary mechanisms, including 'colour' regime change operations. Their current sophistication and 'normalisation' make Kissinger's machinations (although they were many and varied, including the overthrow of Salvador Allende in Chile in September 1973) in Cold War I look crude and amateurish. In domestic affairs, deviants are shepherded back into the fold or suppressed. A letter to Biden drafted by 30 members of the Progressive Caucus in Congress on 24 October 2022 advanced the rather modest end eminently sensible proposal that the Ukraine war must end in a 'negotiated settlement'. This sparked a ferocious backlash. It was condemned as dishonouring the Ukrainian people's heroic struggle and 'an olive branch to a war criminal'. A day later, the so-called progressives withdrew the letter. A commentary notes 'They retracted it because a new Cold War atmosphere

---

49 Leonid Ragozhin, 'The Controversy of the Decolonization Discourse', *Russia.Post*, 17 January 2024, https://www.russiapost.info/society/decolonization.
50 Alan MacLeod, 'An Intellectual No-Fly Zone: Online Censorship of Ukraine Dissent Is Becoming the New Norm', *MintPress News*, 25 April 2022, https://www.mintpress-news.com/online-censorship-ukraine-russa-google-facebook-twitter/280304/.
51 This is the implication of Finley's *The Ideology of Democratism*.

now pervades Washington', warning that progressives would also be beaten into silence and 'acquiesce to America's increasingly confrontational policy towards China'.[52] The anti-disinformation industry polices the permitted bounds of public discourse.

Communist eschatology focused on 'building socialism', a future-oriented project, whereas in the postcommunist era this shifted towards a spatial representation of modernisation and development. In Georgia, the EU 'represents the promise of salvation after years of unjust suffering and sacrifice [...] recognizing Georgia as an inherently "European" nation'.[53] In Ukraine, this divisive political imaginary had profound domestic consequences. An idealised Europe was contrasted with Russian despotism and authoritarianism. The self-declared progressive forces, combining liberal and nationalist trends, aligned with the Political West and closed down political space for a more inclusive and democratic discussion about the fate of the community. The hegemonic status of Ukraine's 'European' destiny stigmatised constituencies who sought to maintain cultural and economic ties with Russia as ultimately not part of the genuine 'Ukrainian' community. These views were considered not normal contradictions to be resolved politically, but alien ideas to be destroyed. Olga Baysha argues that in this case and in Russia '"progressive" articulations [...] ended up undermining the basis of the democratic public sphere through the closure of democratic space'.[54] Reframing political contestation as civilisational struggle transforms democracy into democratism, where 'right' decisions are imposed and alternatives emerging out of democracy itself are suppressed. Political representation thereby becomes symbolic rather than substantive. Liberal democracy mutates into 'liberal authoritarianism', the imposition of an ideological consensus based on liberal values while stripping liberalism of its pluralist dimensions.[55]

Cold War I was overtly ideological, with overlays of cultural and normative contestation, while the second is more profoundly civilisational. The struggle is as much about definitions of what it means to be civilised as about

---

52 Peter Beinart, 'Washington's New Cold War Cancel Culture', *New York Times*, 4 November 2022, https://www.nytimes.com/2022/11/04/opinion/ukraine-congress-progressives-letter.html.
53 Almut Rochowanski and Sopo Japaridze, 'Georgia's "Foreign Influence" Law Isn't What You Think', *Moscow Times*, 4 May 2024, https://www.themoscowtimes.com/2024/05/03/georgias-foreign-influence-law-isnt-what-you-think-a85029.
54 Baysha, *Miscommunicating Social Change*, p. xii.
55 Ladislav Zemanek, 'De-Russification and "Liberal Authoritarianism": The Czech Choice', *Valdai Discussion Club*, 19 April 2022, https://valdaiclub.com/a/highlights/de-russification-and-liberal-authoritarianism/.

security or political systems. The Kiev regime presents the war as one holding back the tide of barbarism flowing from the East and thus revived classic 'orientalist' tropes – the presentation of the 'other' as deficient in the attributes of what should constitute genuinely civilised behaviour. This is couched in the language of 'Europeanism', with Russia cast as an Asiatic outsider. Framing the conflict in these terms harks back to a Europe of the nineteenth century, in which liberals presented imperialism as a civilising mission, even though it led to the destruction of traditional societies. This is a Europeanism that repudiates what many had taken to be the essence of the new Europe born in the ruins of World War II, a Europe devoted to post-imperial peace and development. This was the spirit of 1945 that inspired the creation of the UN and the Charter International System as whole. It led to the creation of the Council of Europe and the framing of European integration as a peace project. This legacy is now repudiated. A 'geopolitical' Europe revives the hallowed European tradition of liberal imperialism.

The EU has turned out to be anything but devoted to peace. It has become an instrument – and one of the most aggressive – in conducting the struggle against Russia. The attempt to ensure the signing on the Association Agreement with Ukraine in 2013, and the brusque rejection of Moscow's appeals to conduct tripartite talks on the implications for trade between Russia and Ukraine, in large part provoked the conflict. Many factors explain this evolution, including the changed geopolitical profile of the EU since 2004 following the accession of postcommunist countries bitterly hostile to their former overlord. This factor is overlain by another structural feature, namely the change of generations. The boomer generation, those born in the immediate postwar years, may not have personal recollections of war, but they remember the fears that accompanied the onset of the nuclear age and the imminent threat of annihilation at the time of the Cuban missile crisis. We also recall seeing the bombed-out cities and the memories of suffering and savagery associated with the war.

The boomers built much that was important and enduring (including ramified national welfare systems), but their design of international politics in Europe, as with so much else that they achieved, was complacent and inward-looking.[56] When the Berlin Wall came down in 1989, the opportunity to move beyond the stale institutions of Atlanticism was missed. Instead, they cleaved even more tightly to the mother ship in Washington, encouraged by the influx of reinvigorated cold war warriors from Eastern Europe. These

---

56 For a critique, see Helen Andrews, *Boomers: The Men and Women Who Promised Freedom and Delivered Disaster* (New York, Sentinel, 2021).

represented a younger generation, but schooled in the self-indulgence and geopolitical irresponsibility of their boomer parents. Claiming to be fighting for a higher culture, they are ready to sacrifice the tenuous peace in Europe to redress historical grievances. Gone is the awareness of the supreme importance of maintaining peace through the dialogical application of ethical realism in international affairs. Instead, motivated by the spectre of democratic internationalism, the spirit of revenge and moral righteousness led Europe once again to war.

The Crisis of Representation and Populism

The erosion of pluralism in international politics feeds back into a growing intolerance of dissent at home. Space for critique, heterodox views and protest declines. In the United States, the 'infernal triangle' of 'ruthless Republicans, a mainstream media that accommodates their frames, and a Democratic Party whose timidity lets them both get away with it time and again' stifles debate. It fosters a polarised political culture intolerant of the views of others, with liberals too ready to weaken 'their institutions themselves'.[57] Repressive strategies are amplified by influential external actors, notably Israel and Ukraine.[58] Messianic neoconservatives are balanced by militant liberals. Everywhere, heterodox views are subject to a gamut of disciplining practises, and are close to vanishing in the leading 'Fifth International' states. The militancy of the participants in this cold war is striking. There is little scope for compromise. Dogmatic positions polarise society. Politics assumes the character of trench warfare. Countervailing forces are weak and divided.

During Obama's second term (2013–17), the terms of public policy debate underwent

> a radical and worrying transformation. In the space of a very short time, certain ideas and policy proposals were being ruled as out of bounds not on the grounds that they were unwise, impractical, or inefficient, but on

---

57 Rick Perlstein, 'First They Came for Harvard', *The American Prospect*, 10 January 2024, https://prospect.org/politics/2024-01-10-first-they-came-for-harvard/.

58 For a Ukrainian list of alleged pro-Russian propagandists (including me), see VoxCheck Team, 'The Network of Russian Propaganda: What Connects Western "Experts" Promoting Narratives Beneficial to Russia', *Vox Ukraine*, 9 February 2024, https://voxukraine.org/en/the-network-of-russian-propaganda-what-connects-western-experts-promoting-narratives-beneficial-to-russia.

the grounds that they were the products of 'disinformation' campaigns on the part of foreign intelligence services.

This affected in particular those who criticised Obama's policy towards Russia, who were labelled 'nefarious tools of a foreign disinformation campaign'. Obama's division of the world between 'democracies' and 'authoritarian regimes' generated a paranoia that had last been seen at the nadir of the original Cold War. The GEC, as we have seen, is under the auspices of the State Department and disbursed grants to 'disinformation' agencies such as NewsGuard. The effect was to stigmatise dissent while further taming the legacy media, such as the *Washington Post* and the *New York Times*. Alternative outlets, such as *Consortium News* (which sued the GEC for defamation), were condemned 'on grounds not that they are merely mistaken but on grounds they are treasonous, that they are Manchurian policies that ought to be dismissed out of hand, lest they play into the enemy's hands'.[59] Lenin's dreadful phrase 'useful idiots' is sprayed indiscriminately to slur critics.

The striving for global hegemony generates a commensurate endeavour in domestic politics. The demand for conformity in the public sphere ultimately forces a repudiation of the principles on which the Political West was established. Public opinion management destroys alternative sources of political mobilisation, including peace movements and other anti-war organisations. The acceptable spectrum of views has narrowed, reminiscent of Soviet-style informational management. What Antonio Gramsci called 'organic' intellectuals, those who serve the class interests of the dominant economic and political order, thrive in cold war conditions. They work in think tanks, institutes and even universities, promoted by a grant-giving establishment that nurtures conformity. Funds from the military–industrial complex by definition reward policy entrepreneurs that serve the establishment. The system of academic peer review, overlain today by a thick encrustation of equality, diversity and inclusivity standards, reduces the chances of heterodox projects being funded. The role of 'traditional' intellectuals, drawing on classical traditions of independent critical scholarship of high modernity, has been eclipsed. Critical commentary remains, but barely dents the hegemony of the ruling order. Identarian politics foster a 'cancel' culture, unable to tolerate genuine political diversity and dialogical reasoning.[60] Arguments are not

---

59 James W. Carden, 'The "Disinformation" Complex and US Foreign Policy', *ACURA*, 13 February 2024, https://usrussiaaccord.org/acura-viewpoint-james-w-carden-the-disinformation-complex-and-us-foreign-policy/.
60 See, for example, Greg Lukianoff and Rikki Schlott, *The Cancelling of the American Mind: How Cancel Culture Undermines Trust, Destroys Institutions, and Threatens Us All* (London, Allen Lane, 2023).

refuted but negated. Presented as a way of protecting democracy, society is insulated from democracy.

Nevertheless, a counter-movement is emerging. The crisis of conventional representation generates populist and other upsurges. The political stasis at the elite level is matched by the growth of insurgencies from below, a dynamic that threatens the Political West by pointing towards alternative geopolitical configurations and new domestic conjunctures. Insurgent elites and movements threaten the predominance of organic intellectuals and the whole network of power which they serve. Hungary's Viktor Orbán, for example, charges that the EU has become neo-Soviet. It is a common complaint, focused not only on the bureaucratism that dogs the work of EU agencies as well as the lack of political accountability, accompanied by the judicialization of power, but above all the dogmatic assertion of the superiority of the given political order. From this perspective, the ideological dogmatism of EU and national leaders is reminiscent of earlier authoritarian eras, repudiating the EU's peace-making origins. At a summit of 27 mostly European leaders in Paris in support of Ukraine on 26 February 2024, the prime minister of Slovakia, Robert Fico, noted the martial atmosphere and the total absence of a peace perspective. In its geopolitical manifestation, the EU is redolent of the Sovietism that it was established to counter.

Right-wing populists now position themselves not as opponents of the European project but as the defenders of the true Europe, loyal to the nation, the family and Christianity, and opposed to endless war with Russia. Proponents of a traditional West present it as liberated from US-style 'wokeness' and democratic messianism. In elections in two East German regions, Thuringia and Saxony, on 1 September 2024 the right-wing anti-immigrant Alternative for Germany (AfD) won a third of the vote, and for the first time gained the most seats in a regional parliament. The recently formed left-conservative Sahra Wagenknecht Bloc (BSW) won an astonishing 15.8 per cent of the vote in Thuringia and 11.8 in Saxony. In the Brandenburg regional election on 22 September the SPD came first with 30.7 per cent of the vote, but AfD came a close second with 29.4 per cent and BSW, astonishingly, came in third with 13.6 per cent. The latter two opposed open-ended military support for Ukraine. Their supporters argue that a 'better West' is struggling to emerge from the stifling and militaristic carapace of the Political West, although their solutions are ultimately very different.

In political economy, populists condemn the way that the benefits of globalisation have been appropriated by a narrow beneficiary class, leading to widening inequality. There is a growing demand for social justice and human dignity. The absence of a coherent ideology to express these aspirations encourages national populist movements. The Trumpian irruption and Brexit identified the problem, but provided inchoate and incoherent responses. The geoeconomic logic of Cold War II pushes the United States and the EU towards protectionism and revived industrial policies. Free trade has always been the privilege of the most powerful economies, and the shift towards neo-mercantilist strategies reflects the relative economic decline of the West. American imperialism has always 'fundamentally been about protecting the unequal structure of the capitalist world system and preventing the emergence of potential rivals to this system'.[61] The return to more inward-looking economies is geared not towards enhancing the public good but to strengthen military–industrial capabilities to thwart China and to contain Russia. We have been here before.

The Political West is beset by self-doubt, poor leadership and the absence of a coherent vision of the future. The 'diversionary' theory of international politics, usually applied to authoritarian regimes, is no less relevant for democracies as they strike out against recalcitrant others to buttress their rule at home. The contrast between the expansive geopolitical ambitions of the Political West and the paucity of its developmental agenda is increasingly stark. Deepening domestic contradictions and polarised domestic political orders have not tempered ambitious and universalist foreign policy agendas. Indeed, they have been intensified. Populist and leftist counter-movements threaten the accustomed hegemony.

---

61 Blakeley, *Vulture Capitalism*, p. 214.

Chapter 8

CONCLUSION

With the end of Cold War I in 1989, a new paradigm of international politics took shape. This was a world without the challenge of a communist superpower and its associated conception of world order. Instead, the world order associated with the Political West appeared to triumph, but the fruits of that putative victory contained some deadly toxins that would corrupt the triumphant order itself. It remains to be seen just how lethal this will be, but we can already see one of the outcomes in the form of Cold War II. As described in this book, a whole culture is associated with cold war as a form of international politics.

The inter-cold war paradigm, what we can call the postcommunist model, was characterised by a number of key features. First, the interpellation of the Political West, variously presented as the liberal international order, rules-based international order or Atlantic power system, between the Charter International System and the practices of international politics. The Political West effectively usurped the privileges and prerogatives that should properly belong to Charter institutions, above all the UN, its agencies and the whole body of international law that it has spawned. Second, this entailed the displacement of the fundamental Charter principle of sovereign internationalism, where states meet as normative equals and unite in various multilateral formats to resolve problems of mutual concern. Instead, the ideology of democratic internationalism was advanced, which introduces not only sovereign inequality but also an inherently didactic, if not outright interventionist, dynamic into international affairs. The allegedly more advanced societies bring enlightenment, by book or by crook, to the more backward. Third, the absence of a peer competitor encouraged neoconservatives to forge a grand strategy based on permanent US dominance, requiring the imposition of constraints on potential competitors. In the first instance, this applied to Russia and was then extended to China. At the same time, the rise of economic neoliberalism from the 1970s provoked the radical transformation of social orders into market states, with wrenching domestic consequences.

The culture of Cold War II permeates international politics and shapes the concepts and practices of international affairs. Even the language of international politics is affected. The balance of power, for example, is the core of the positivist tradition of international law. This was at the heart of peace-making at the Congress of Vienna in 1815, which established a new international system, the Concert of Europe, after the Napoleonic wars. The positivist tradition takes the anarchic character of international politics as a given, and on that basis seeks to manage antagonism between states. There is no attempt to use international law to change the character of states or societies, and instead it supports the practices of sovereign internationalism. This aligns with the pre-1898 American tradition of conservative internationalism, which survives today as a critique of the 'imperial' turn in US foreign policy. By contrast, as Wilsonian liberal internationalism gathered pace, it fostered a body of international law that evolved into 'a full-fledged legal order, including international tribunals, permanent interstate organizations and a greater number of rules limiting a state's autonomous behaviour'.[1] Liberal internationalism radicalised after 1989 to become democratic internationalism, increasingly unmoored from international law. The 'rules-based order' is by definition autonomous, drawing selectively on international law to usurp the prerogatives of the UN-based system.[2] Democratic internationalism draws on the liberal tradition's belief in progress in international politics. The resulting 'normativisation' elevates values over material interests in international affairs – although it goes without saying that when there is a clash, interests trump values. Double standards become systemic.

Cold war geopolitics are reinforced by the neoliberal revolution that has transformed societal expectations. There are few areas where this has been more marked that in higher education, now focused on creating the 'human capital' to service the rampant market economy. Training is focused on 'input capital' in post-industrial economies, with a burgeoning service sector characterised by labour precarity. Economies in the era of high globalisation were also transformed. Supply chains became ever longer and more 'just in time'. The Covid-19 pandemic in 2020 came as a shock, when supplies from the Far East were disrupted, and the Russo-Ukrainian war came as even more of a reality check. In a grinding war of attrition, Russia's old-style industrial economy (the subject of much criticism earlier) quickly shifted to the production of shells, munitions, artillery and tanks, whereas the Political West

---

1 A. B. Lorca, *Mestizo International Law: A Global Intellectual History 1842–1933* (Cambridge, Cambridge University Press, 2014), p. 143.
2 As argued by Dugard, 'The Choice Before Us'.

found itself denuded of the plants, workforce and even the skills to service a war economy. As one study notes, 'the modern American education system was built to defeat the Soviet Union, both in terms of science and technology leadership as well as moral authority'. The call now is to restore such a system.[3] According to Wolfgang Streeck, Western-style capitalism 'has been on a crisis trajectory since the 1970s', when the post-war social democratic settlement was abandoned and a neoliberal form of capitalism installed, punctuated by increasingly severe breakdowns.[4] Joseph Stiglitz concurs. He analyses the pathologies associated with the neoliberal form of capitalism and seeks to reclaim the language of freedom from neoconservatives.[5]

This book makes a similar argument. For the 'good life' to flourish, a shift in thinking is required from a model of internationalism designed to serve the imperial aspects of American power and of the Political West more broadly towards the strengthening of the commonwealth features. The Political West is far from monolithic, but the recasting of neoliberal capitalism and imperial globalism will require the combined efforts of domestic and international agents of change. The rise of the Political East and more assertive non-alignment strategies in World Majority countries demonstrates the emergence of countervailing forces at the global level. However, the revival of cold war practices at home is designed precisely to thwart their ability to reshape domestic discourse. The struggle is on, with geopolitical contestation in international politics reflected domestically in sharpening tensions between the old Atlanticist consensus and movements, typically derided as populist, challenging the militaristic and 'rogue' features of the postcommunist paradigm of world order. Just as in the first contest, cold war struggles abroad have profound domestic implications, many of which are only now becoming apparent.

Countries in Cold War II race to erect iron curtains at home and abroad. The practices of Cold War I have been revived, but this cold war is different in several important respects. First, the structuring principle is more diffuse although deeply entrenched, thus more difficult to overcome. The easily understood binary of capitalism versus communism has given way to vaguer formulations, such as democracy versus autocracy, liberalism versus illiberalism, Global North versus Global South and many more. Second, the context has changed. The postwar state system has matured, and decolonisation has

---

3 Julius Krein, 'The University Monopoly Must be Broken', *UnHerd*, 9 March 2024, https://unherd.com/2024/03/the-university-monopoly-must-be-broken/.
4 Wolfgang Streeck, *How Will Capitalism End?* (London, Verso, 2016), p. 15.
5 Joseph Stiglitz, *The Road to Freedom: Economics and the Good Society* (London, Allen Lane, 2024).

given way to a world populated by a plethora of fully fledged nation states, no longer tolerating neocolonial forms of exploitation and dominance. Few are willing to stake their sovereignty on the wars of the Global North and instead revive the principles of non-alignment. Third, the bipolarity of Cold War I has given way to multipolarity. The starkest expression of this is the presence of at least four major powers, China, India, Russia and the United States, with a host of important middle powers, including Brazil, Indonesia, Egypt and South Africa. The emergence of a Political East signals the radical repudiation of a unipolar world order. There is a nascent multipolarity at the level of states, but in terms of old-style bloc politics there is a fundamental asymmetry. The Political West prides itself on its cohesion and unity, under American tutelage, but the Political East precisely repudiates that form of hegemony and oppose bloc politics in all its manifestations.

Fourth, the economies of the major powers are far more deeply entwined than they were earlier, when the United States and the USSR stood at the head of largely separate economic systems. Today, the United States, the EU and China have deeply integrated supply chains and investments, but even here a grand decoupling is taking place. A fifth difference is in the field of technological development, with social media now an arena of contestation. This has generated a multifaceted 'disinformation industry', in which state and non-state actors seek to regulate and police the digital world of communications. This is accompanied by various cyberwars, in which the protagonists unleash cyber and ransomware attacks. A final difference is that Cold War II is global by its very essence. Cold War I was focused on Europe with global ramifications, whereas Cold War II is the reverse. In Cold War I, the conflict was static in Europe but dynamic in the rest of the world, but today the conflict is dynamic in Europe but relatively static elsewhere (although the United States is doing its best to introduce dynamism to the conflict in East Asia). War has come home to Europe. Overriding all these differences is a feature that determines the fundamental character of a cold war – the persistent threat of nuclear annihilation.

Two broad 'world orders' are contesting, based on contrasting approaches to international politics. The Political West was created and shaped by the logic of cold war and perpetuated this logic in a more expansive manner in the postcommunist era. In Europe, the logic of expansion ultimately provoked a return to interstate war. Democratic internationalism reflects a unilinear and teleological view of history, with ultimately a single model of modernity (derived from the civilisational West) as the end point. The logic of the Political East is very different. It asserts civilisational pluralism and multiple models of modernity. The proclaimed normative foundation of the Political East is sovereign internationalism and the body of international law and norms generated by the Charter system. Numerous resolutions and declarations assert UN principles, complemented by reference to the 10-point Bandung Declaration of 1955. These are based on Chinese foreign minister Zhou Enlai's Five Principles: respect for the sovereignty of others, respect for territorial integrity, non-interference in the internal affairs of others, a commitment to acting for mutual benefit and a commitment to peaceful coexistence. These clearly reflect the principles of the UN Charter. At the same time, the World Majority has revived the call for economic justice represented by the New International Economic Order, adopted without a vote by the UN General Assembly in May 1977. The 20 principles of the NIEO include the sovereign equality of states and their right to political and economic self-determination.

The emergence of a Political East does not threaten the Charter International System but strengthens it. In response, the Political West has opposed the elevation of representatives of the Political East to leadership positions in UN and other agencies, accompanied by boycotts and walkouts. It also misrepresents Russia and China as revisionist powers. In structural terms at least, they defend Charter principles, making them conservative status quo powers. As far as they are concerned, along with much of the Global South and critics within the West itself, an international politics based on Charter principles offer sounder prospects for peace and development than the self-referential and amorphous rules-based order.[6] While conservative with regard to the international system, at the level of international politics they refuse to accept the hegemony of the Political West. In that respect, they are revisionist. The combination renders them neo-revisionist: defending the Charter system, but repudiating the hegemonic practices of the Political West.

The shifting optics between system and order exacerbate cold war tensions. Adversaries are accused of violating Charter principles while ignoring one's own transgressions. The Charter system has itself become a bone of contestation. Double standards have become systemic. The positive peace spirit of 1945 has dissipated, and the New Political Thinking (NPT) hopes of reviving it at the end of Cold War I have been well and truly disappointed. Cold war is always a burden on humanity, but today it threatens its very existence. The world faces a number of increasingly sharp challenges. First, climate change is accelerating and eroding the physical foundations of existence for millions. Deserts are encroaching on ancestral pastures across the Sahel region and southern Eurasia, storms are increasing in intensity and frequency and floods and fires afflict the globe, while the melting of the polar ice caps

---

6 A point made by Dugard, 'The Choice before us'.

and glaciers are raising sea levels and threatening coastal cities.[7] The UN general secretary António Guterres warned that the war in Ukraine risked putting global climate targets, including the Paris 2015 goal of limiting global temperature rise to 1.5°C above pre-industrial levels, out of reach. Supplies of Russian gas were drastically cut back, increasing reliance in the short term on other fossil fuels, including coal.[8] The destruction of the Nord Stream pipelines in September 2022 released almost half a million tonnes of methane, a more damaging greenhouse gas than carbon dioxide.

Cultural diplomacy, artistic exchanges and educational links foster the trust without which a viable peace order is impossible. Instead, in Cold War II what were earlier taken as tokens of dialogue are painted with the brush of treachery. For example, the Scottish bagpipe player Jimi McRae insisted on continuing the long tradition of engagement between Scotland and Russia, in particular to honour the wartime alliance and the British sailors who perished on the convoys to Murmansk and Arkhangelsk. For his pains, McRae was labelled 'Putin's piper'.[9] In other countries, the tide of prohibition began to change. In January 2024, the Slovakian minister of culture Martina Sikmovicova revoked the March 2022 decree that suspended cultural cooperation with Russia and Belarus. She noted that 'There are dozens of military conflicts going on in the world, and in our opinion, artists and culture must not suffer because of them'.[10] In a commentary in the *Financial Times*, Martin Wolf took the opposite view:

> In the end, of course, there must be a peace. But it must be peace with honour. That will only come if Russia realises that this time might will not be allowed to be right. The west has the resources to ensure this. The question [...] is whether it believes enough in itself to show the will. If not, the price could prove to be beyond reckoning.[11]

---

7 Anatol Lieven, *Climate Change and the Nation State* (London, Penguin Books, 2021).
8 'War Puts 1.5C Goal at Risk, UN Secretary General Says', *The Guardian*, 22 March 2022, p. 3.
9 David Leask, 'Jimi McRae, the Scottish Piper Who Plays to Putin's Tune', *The Times*, 27 January 2024, https://www.thetimes.co.uk/article/jimi-mcrae-scottish-piper-vladimir-putin-russia-ukraine-hj2xjmqz9.
10 'Slovak Authorities Restore Cultural Cooperation with Russia, Belarus – Newspaper', *TASS*, 20 January 2024, https://tass.com/society/1735061.
11 Martin Wolf, '"Ukraine Fatigue" Is Unpardonable', *Financial Times*, 30 January 2024, https://www.ft.com/content/ca7fa865-97a1-4013-bde6-b69731b03232?emailId=2866caaf-e0ad-4386-994f-f0fc5bbebdf1&segmentId=22011ee7-896a-8c4c-22a0-7603348b7f22.

For him, the conflict shaped the very meaning of 'the West', and with the stakes so high, there could be no compromise.

Fighting a cold war erodes the values for which the cold war is ostensibly fought. In a paradoxical inversion, the Political West today has assumed increasingly delineated neo-Soviet features. The Marxist historicism chased out of the Soviet Union found a congenial home in the Political West. Historicism suggests that the meaning and purpose of history are knowable, and like Marxist–Leninists in the Soviet Union, democratic internationalists believe on that basis that history can be hurried along on its designated path. Those who stand in its way are not only misguided but ultimately evil. Unilinear and teleological views of history, in which society is presented as inexorably moving ever onwards and upwards, undermine the agonism essential to a pluralist democracy. Instead, democratism – the natural rights view that democratic procedures should be tailored to ensure correct outcomes – predominates. Liberal historicism was given expression at the dawn of the postcommunist era in the form of the ideology of the 'end of history', assuming that the riddle of human life and destiny had been resolved. This perverse application of the Hegelian dialectic, even when filtered through the work of the French philosopher Alexandre Kojève, gave a pseudo-philosophical grounding to the perilous transition from state socialism to capitalism. It reinforced the Political West's image of itself as the guardian of truth and justice and boosted its mission to reshape the world in its image. Neoconservatives in the United States rushed to embrace the idea, which was given material grounding in America's economic and military pre-eminence. Liberals may have had misgivings, but overwhelmingly endorsed an approach that reinforced their historicist view of the direction of human endeavour.

Historicism is reinforced by a dialectical view of history. The dialectic that was pushed out of the front door in the late Soviet Union entered the back door of the Political West. The dialectical approach stresses the clash of opposites rather than cooperative modes of conflict resolution. A dialectical view of history, whether derived from a materialist or theological foundation, generates a messianic approach to politics, accompanied by the Manichean division between the good and the evil. The former are licensed to advance their cause, even when the means subvert the ends, while the evil are not just mistaken but fundamentally illegitimate. It is hardly surprising that practices of diplomacy have been undermined and established institutions of cultural cooperation dismantled. The dialectical perspective to international politics repudiates the dialogical approach – one in which all sides change as a result of engagement and interaction. Citizen diplomacy is predicated on the idea that visits and cultural exchanges have a mutually beneficial effect – on the visitors and those visited. This applies equally to joint educational programmes, where knowledge is presumed to lead to enlightenment. This proposition inspired a thickening web of relationships that fostered trust, which in the final years of Cold War I helped transcend its divisions. It will be very hard if not impossible now to restore these sinews of trust.

Anthropologists have long abandoned the idea that human societies develop in successively higher stages, but this does not mean that the Traditionalist (the capital T denotes the philosophical school of that name) view of history as cyclical is justified. Cyclical theories of history were all the rage in the early twentieth century, notably in versions presented by René Guénon, Arnold Toynbee and Oswald Spengler. Their pessimistic perspectives on 'the decline of the West' were close to the mark, but encouraged fatalism and passivity. The alternative view suggests that determined action can change political outcomes. Engagement with alien societies and even antagonistic leaders can contain conflict and reduce tension. That certainly was the spirit in which Germany's *Ostpolitik* from the late 1960s was conducted, paving the way to the détente of the early 1970s. The dialogical approach does not necessarily evoke sympathy, but even where deep-seated differences remain, a degree of empathy is generated. Understanding the position, concerns and fears of the other is the beginning of effective diplomacy. All of this has been discarded in Cold War II. This not only makes the management of the conflict hazardous, but makes this cold war much harder to overcome than the first.

Democratism gives rise to a style of politics reminiscent of the dogmatic intolerance of the Soviet system. Orthodoxy is imposed, and heterodox ideas are persecuted. Critical thinkers in the West find themselves in the position of Soviet dissidents. The situation in some ways is worse. The Soviet project retained a residual sense of progress and belief in the betterment of humanity, while its opponents appealed either to some idealised neo-traditionalist past or some better Western-oriented future. Western 'dissidents' find themselves in multiple binds. Appeals to human rights generate double standards, the idea of 'progress' is associated with totalitarianism, and calls for peace are labelled appeasement and collusion with the enemy. Instead of coherent progressive ideologies and concern with the material development of society, identarian politics generates moral certainty and dogmatic absolutism of a new type. The 'wokeness' of what the Americans call the 'liberal-left' generates fragmented and divisive political practices, while the rejectionist politics of the right have become increasingly radicalised. Both seek to 'cancel' their opponents in the public sphere. The institutions and self-restraint essential for liberal democracy are eroding.

These elements have their counterparts in Russia, China and a number of other major states. A reviewer of Gary Saul Morson's *Wonder Confronts Certainty: Russian Writers on the Timeless Questions and Why Their Answers Matter* notes that once again the Commissars of Certainty rule triumphant. He argues 'More than any one ideology, it is access to unrestrained power that turns people into monsters'.[12] The intolerance practiced at home is reflected in international affairs. In the United States, communities are increasingly 'sorting': that is, drawing apart from antithetical groups and gathering in communities of like-minded people. A global process of 'sorting' is also taking shape, with nations aligning along ideological lines. The Political West has long been concerned with maintaining bloc unity, condemning Russian and now increasingly Chinese attempts to drive 'wedges' within Europe and between the United States and its European partners. Meanwhile, the Political East is becoming a community of anti-hegemonic states, devising alternatives to the presumptuous pre-eminence of the United States and the debilitated powerlessness of its allies. This is the culture of Cold War II. By analysing its features, this book may help transcend cold war as a way of conducting international affairs.

---

12 Vladimir Golstein, 'A Happy Guest in Russia's Pages', *Claremont Review of Books*, Fall 2023, https://claremontreviewofbooks.com/a-happy-guest-in-russias-pages/.

BIBLIOGRAPHY

Acharya, Amitav, 'After Liberal Hegemony: The Advent of a Multiplex World Order', *Ethics & International Affairs*, Vol. 31, No. 3, 2017, pp. 271–85.
Acharya, Amitav, *The End of American World Order*, 2nd edn (Cambridge, Polity, 2018).
Anderson, Perry, *The H-Word: The Peripeteia of Hegemony* (London, Verso, 2017).
Andrews, Helen, *Boomers: The Men and Women Who Promised Freedom and Delivered Disaster* (New York, Sentinel, 2021).
Arendt, Hannah, *The Origins of Totalitarianism* (San Diego, Harcourt, 1968).
Bacevich, Andrew, *The Age of Illusions: How America Squandered its Cold War Victory* (New York, Metropolitan Books, 2020).
Baud, Jacques, *Governing by Fake News: 30 Years of Fake News in the West* (Paris, Max Milo Editions, 2023).
Baudrillard, Jean, *Simulacra and Simulation* (Ann Arbor, University of Michigan Press, 1994).
Baudrillard, Jean, *The Intelligence of Evil* (New York, Berg, 2005).
Baysha, Olga, *Miscommunicating Social Change: Lessons from Russia and Ukraine* (Lanham, Lexington Books, 2019).
Baysha, Olga, *Democracy, Populism, and Neoliberalism in Ukraine* (London and New York, Routledge, 2022).
Baysha, Olga, *War, Peace and Populist Discourse in Ukraine* (London, Routledge, 2023).
Bergman, Ronen and Mark Mazzetti, 'The Unpunished: How Extremists Took Over Israel', *New York Times Magazine*, 16 May 2024, https://www.nytimes.com/2024/05/16/magazine/israel-west-bank-settler-violence-impunity.html.
Bergman, Tabe, 'Confronting Censorship: on Media Bias and the War in Ukraine', *Pearls and Irritations*, 4 September 2024, https://johnmenadue.com/confronting-censorship-on-media-bias-and-the-war-in-ukraine/.
Bergman, Tabe and Jesse Owen Hearns-Branaman (eds), *Media, Dissidence and the War in Ukraine* (London, Routledge, 2023).
Berletic, Brian, 'Georgia Fight against US Subversion and its Implications Worldwide', *New Eastern Outlook*, 22 April 2024, https://journal-neo.su/2024/04/22/georgia-fight-against-us-subversion-its-implications-worldwide/.
Bernays, Edward, *Crystallizing Public Opinion* (New York, Boni and Liveright, 1923).
Biden, Joe, 'State of the Union Address', *The White House*, 1 March 2022, https://www.whitehouse.gov/state-of-the-union-2022/.
Blakeley, Grace, *Vulture Capitalism: Corporate Crimes, Backdoor Bailouts and the Death of Freedom* (London, Bloomsbury, 2024).
Bordachev, Timofei, '"25 Years of the New Cold War', *Valdai Discussion Club*, 27 March 2024, https://valdaiclub.com/a/highlights/25-years-of-the-new-cold-war/.

Borosage, Robert L., 'The Empire Strikes Back', *The Nation*, 4 January 2024, https://www.thenation.com/article/world/the-empire-strikes-back/.

Borrell, Josep, 'Opening Remarks by High Representative Josep Borrell at the Inauguration of the Pilot Programme', European Diplomatic Academy, 13 October 2022, https://www.eeas.europa.eu/eeas/european-diplomatic-academy-opening-remarks-high-representative-josep-borrell-inauguration-pilot_en.

Bovard, Jim, 'Truth is the Biggest Threat to DC "Democracy"', *The Libertarian Institute*, 18 December 2023, https://libertarianinstitute.org/articles/truth-is-the-biggest-threat-to-dc-democracy/.

Boyd-Barrett, Oliver and Stephen Marmura (eds), *Russiagate Revisited: The Aftermath of a Hoax* (London, Palgrave Macmillan, 2023).

Brands, Hal, 'Ukraine is Now a World War: and Putin is Gaining Friends', *Bloomberg*, 12 May 2024, https://www.bloomberg.com/opinion/features/2024-05-12/china-russia-iran-have-made-ukraine-a-world-war-against-us-europe.

Browder, Bill, *Red Notice: How I became Putin's No. 1 Enemy* (London, Bantam Press, 2015).

Buranelli, Filippo Costa, 'Beyond the Pendulum: Situating Adam Watson in International Relations and the English School', *International Politics*, October 2023, online version.

Buzan, Barry, 'A New Cold War? The Case for a General Concept', *International Politics*, Vol. 61, No. 2, 2024, pp. 239–57.

Buzan, Barry, Ole Waever and Jaap de Wilde, *Security: A New Framework for Analysis* (Boulder, Lynne Rienner, 1998).

Carden, James, 'Biden and Co. Take Aim at Central Europe', *Antiwar.com*, 19 March 2024, https://original.antiwar.com/james-carden/2024/03/18/biden-and-co-take-aim-at-central-europe/.

Carden, James W., 'The "Disinformation" Complex and US Foreign Policy', *US Committee for US-Russia Accord*, 13 February 2024, https://usrussiaaccord.org/acura-viewpoint-james-w-carden-the-disinformation-complex-and-us-foreign-policy/.

Carden, James W., 'The Ukraine War Runs on Prevarication', *The American Conservative*, 17 February 2024, https://www.theamericanconservative.com/the-ukraine-war-runs-on-lies/.

Carden, James W., 'Where is Joe Biden's "Devil's Advocate"?', *The American Conservative*, 18 March 2024, https://www.theamericanconservative.com/where-is-bidens-devils-advocate/.

Caro, Carlo J. V., 'Is "The Chinese World" the Future? Confucianism and Xi Jinping', *The National Interest*, 19 March 2023, https://nationalinterest.org/feature/%E2%80%9C-chinese-world%E2%80%9D-future-confucianism-and-xi-jinping-206327.

Clark, Christopher, *The Sleepwalkers: How Europe Went to War in 1914* (London, Penguin, 2013).

Clinton, Hillary Rodham, *Hard Choices: A Memoir* (New York, Simon & Schuster, 2014).

Clinton, Hillary Rodham, *What Happened* (London, Simon & Schuster, 2017).

Connolly, Richard, *Russia's Response to Sanctions: How Western Statecraft is Reshaping Political Economy in Russia* (Cambridge, Cambridge University Press, 2018).

Connolly, Richard, *Russia's Responses to Sanctions: How Western Sanctions Reshaped Political Economy in Russia*, Valdai Paper No. 94, November 2018, http://valdaiclub.com/a/valdai-papers/russia-s-response-to-sanctions-how-western-sanctio/.

Cook, Jonathan, 'It was the Media, led by the Guardian, that Kept Julian Assange Behind Bars', 28 June 2024, https://www.jonathan-cook.net/2024-06-26/media-guardian-julian-assange/.

Cooper, Robert, 'The Post-Modern State', in Mark Leonard (ed.), *Re-Ordering the World: The Long-Term Implications of 11 September* (London, Foreign Policy Centre, 2002), https://www.esiweb.org/pdf/esi_europeanraj_debate_id_2.pdf.
Cooper, Robert, *The Breaking of Nations: Order and Chaos in the Twenty-First Century* (New York, Atlantic Press, 2003).
Cunliffe, Philip, *Cosmopolitan Dystopia: International Intervention and the Failure of the West* (Manchester, Manchester University Press, 2020).
Dal Santo, Matthew J., 'The Putin Interview', *Landmarks: A Journal of International Dialogue*, 13 February 2024, https://landmarksmag.substack.com/p/a-symposium-on-tucker-carlsons-controversial.
D'Anieri, Paul, *Ukraine and Russia: From Civilized Divorce to Uncivil War* (Cambridge, Cambridge University Press, 2019).
Dans, Thomas Emanuel, 'Why Was Tucker Carlson's Putin Interview the First Time Americans Heard the Russian Viewpoint?', *The American Conservative*, 13 February 2024, https://www.theamericanconservative.com/americans-most-dangerous-blind-spot/.
Debord, Guy, *Society of the Spectacle* (London, Rebel Press, 1994).
Devine, Miranda, *Laptop from Hell: Hunter Biden, Big Tech, and the Dirty Secrets the President tried to Hide* (New York and Nashville, Post Hill Press, 2021).
Diesen, Glenn, *Europe as the Western Peninsula of Greater Eurasia: Geoeconomic Regions in a Multipolar World* (London, Rowman & Littlefield, 2021).
Diesen, Glenn, *The Think Tank Racket: Managing the Information War with Russia* (Atlanta, Clarity Press, 2023).
Diesen, Glenn, *The Ukraine War & the Eurasian World Order* (Atlanta, Clarity Press, 2024).
Dilthey, Wilhelm, *Selected Works, Volume 4: Hermeneutics and the Study of History* (Princeton, Princeton University Press, 1996).
Dinsdale, Thom, 'Inside, Out of the Rain', *East-West Review*, Vol. 22, No. 3 (64), 2024, pp. 5–7.
Doshi, Rush, *The Long Game: China's Grand Strategy to Replace American Order* (New York, Oxford University Press, 2021).
Doyle, Michael, 'Kant, Liberal Legacies, and Foreign Affairs, Part 2', *Philosophy & Public Affairs*, Vol. 12, No. 4, 1983, pp. 323–53.
Dugard, John, 'The Choice Before Us: International Law or a "Rules-Based International Order"?', *Leiden Journal of International Law*, Vol. 36, 2023, pp. 223–32.
Eagleton, Terry, 'Where Does Culture Come From?', *London Review of Books*, 25 April 2024, pp. 5–7.
Economy, Elizabeth C., *The Third Revolution: Xi Jinping and the New Chinese State* (New York, Oxford University Press, 2018).
Economy, Elizabeth C., *The World According to China* (Cambridge, Polity, 2021).
Economy, Elizabeth C., 'Xi Jinping's New World Order: Can China Remake the International System?', *Foreign Affairs*, Vol. 101, No. 1, January–February 2022, pp. 52–67.
Emerson, Barbara, *The First Cold War: Anglo-Russian Relations in the 19th Century* (London, Hurst, 2024).
Falk, Richard, 'Exposing the Binding Chains of Discursive Bondage', *International Politics*, Vol. 60, No. 3, 2023, pp. 768–75.
Fazi, Thomas, 'Why Even Julian Assange's Critics Should Defend Him: The WikiLeaks Founder Must Not be Extradited', *UnHerd*, 20 February 2024, https://unherd.com

/2024/02/why-even-julian-assanges-critics-should-defend-him/#:~:text=If%20the%20British%20state%20allows,co%2Dauthored%20with%20Toby%20Green.

Fazi, Thomas, 'Inside the EU's War on Free Speech: Elon Musk Can't Win this Battle', *UnHerd*, 20 July 2024, https://unherd.com/2024/08/inside-the-eus-war-on-free-speech/.

Ferguson, Iain, 'Between New Spheres of Influence: Ukraine's Geopolitical Misfortune', *Geopolitics*, Vol. 23, No. 2, 2018, pp. 285–306.

Ferguson, Iain and Susanna Hast, 'Introduction: The Return of Spheres of Influence', *Geopolitics*, Vol. 23, No. 2, 2018, pp. 277–84.

Filatov, Sergey, 'The Roots of Russophobia', *International Affairs* (Moscow), 15 February 2024, https://en.interaffairs.ru/article/the-roots-of-russophobia/.

Finley, Emily B., *The Ideology of Democratism* (New York, Oxford University Press, 2022).

Freeman, Ben, 'The Lobbying Battle Before the War: Russian and Ukrainian Influence in the US', Quincy Brief No. 26, July 2022, https://quincyinst.org/wp-content/uploads/2022/07/QUINCY-BRIEF-NO.-26-July-2022-FREEMAN-5.pdf.

Freeman, Ben, 'The Ukraine Lobby Two Years into the War', *Responsible Statecraft*, 22 February 2024, https://responsiblestatecraft.org/ukraine-lobby/.

Freeman, Chas W. Jr., 'The Propaganda that Damned Ukraine', *UnHerd*, 4 January 2024, https://unherd.com/2024/01/the-propaganda-that-damned-ukraine/.

Freeman, Chas W., 'On Diplomatic Professionalism', July 2024, https://chasfreeman.net/on-diplomatic-professionalism/.

Fu Ying, *Facing You is Me* (Beijing, ACA Publishing, 2023).

Fukuyama, Francis, 'The End of History', *The National Interest*, No. 16, Summer 1989, pp. 3–17.

Fukuyama, Francis, *The End of History and the Last Man* (New York, Free Press, 1992).

Galtung, Johan, 'An Editorial', *Journal of Peace Research*, Vol. 1, No. 1, 1964, pp. 1–4.

Galtung, Johan, 'Violence, Peace, and Peace Research', *Journal of Peace Research*, Vol. 6, No. 3, 1969, pp. 167–91.

Galtung, Johan, 'Social Cosmology and the Concept of Peace', *Journal of Peace Research*, Vol. 17, No. 2, 1981, pp. 183–99.

Galtung, Johan, *Peace by Peaceful Means: Peace and Conflict, Development and Civilisation* (Oslo, PRIO, 1996).

Gerasimov, Valerii, 'Tsennost' nauki i predvidenii', *Voenno-promyshlennyi kur'er*, No. 8, 27 February 2013, http://vpk-news.ru/articles/14632.

Giles, Keir, *Moscow Rules: What Drives Russia to Confront the West* (Washington, DC, Brookings Institution Press, Chatham House, 2019).

Giles, Keir, *Russia's War on Everybody: And What it Means for You* (London, Bloomsbury Academic, 2023).

Glennon, Michael J., *National Security and Double Government* (Oxford, Oxford University Press, 2015).

Golstein, Vladimir, 'A Happy Guest in Russia's Pages', *Claremont Review of Books*, Fall 2023, https://claremontreviewofbooks.com/a-happy-guest-in-russias-pages/.

Gong, Gerrit W., *The Standard of 'Civilization' in International Society* (Oxford, Clarendon Press, 1984).

Goodman, Melvin, 'The New Cold War Could be Worse', *CounterPunch*, 6 January 2023, https://www.counterpunch.org/2023/01/06/the-new-cold-war-could-be-worse/.

Gray, John, 'These Times: Progressives are Using the Law to Attack Free Speech in a Bid for Unchecked Power', *New Statesman*, 26 April–2 May 2024, 27.

Greene, Samuel A. and Graeme B. Robertson, *Putin v. the People: The Perilous Politics of a Divided Russia* (New Haven, Yale University Press, 2019).

Gurri, Martin, 'Disinformation is the Word I Use When I Want you to Shut Up', *Discourse*, 30 March 2023, https://www.discoursemagazine.com/p/disinformation-is-the-word-i-use-when-i-want-you-to-shut-up.

Hale, Henry E., *Patronal Politics: Eurasian Regime Dynamics in Comparative Perspective* (New York, Cambridge University Press, 2015).

Hartung, William, 'The World Weeps While the Military Industrial Complex Keeps Winning', *Responsible Statecraft*, 19 January 2024, https://responsiblestatecraft.org/defense-industry-war-pentagon/.

Headley, James, 'Challenging the EU's Claim to Moral Authority: Russian Talk of "Double Standards"', *Asia Europe Journal*, Vol. 13, 2015, pp. 297–307.

Hersh, Seymour, 'How America Took Out the Nord Stream Pipeline', *Substack*, 8 February 2023, https://seymourhersh.substack.com/p/how-america-took-out-the-nord-stream.

Hill, William H., *No Place for Russia: European Security Institutions since 1989* (New York, Columbia University Press, 2018).

Hogan, Erica and Stewart Patrick, 'A Closer Look at the Global South', *Carnegie Endowment for International Peace*, 20 May 2024, https://carnegieeurope.eu/research/2024/05/global-south-colonialism-imperialism.

Holden, Paul, 'The "UK Files": A History of the Center for Countering Digital Hate', *Racket News*, 14 November 2023, https://www.racket.news/p/the-uk-files-a-history-of-the-center.

Hunter, James Davison, *Culture Wars: The Struggle to Define America* (New York, Basic Books, 1991).

Hunter, James Davison, *Before the Shooting Begins: Searching for Democracy in America's Culture War* (New York, Free Press, 1994).

Huntington, Samuel P., 'The Clash of Civilizations?', *Foreign Affairs*, Vol. 72, No. 3, Summer 1993, pp. 23–49.

Huntington, Samuel P., *The Clash of Civilizations and the Remaking of World Order* (New York, Simon & Schuster, 1996).

Hutchings, Stephen and Vera Tolz, 'Covid-19 Disinformation: Two Short Reports on the Russian Dimension', 6 April 2020, https://reframingrussia.com/2020/04/06/covid-19-disinformation-two-short-reports-on-the-russian-dimension/.

Ikenberry, G. John, 'The Rise of China and the Future of the West: Can the Liberal System Survive?', *Foreign Affairs*, Vol. 87, No. 1, January/February 2008, https://www.foreignaffairs.com/articles/asia/2008-01-01/rise-china-and-future-west.

Ikenberry, G. John, *Liberal Leviathan: The Origins, Crisis, and Transformation of the American World Order* (Princeton, Princeton University Press, 2011).

Ikenberry, G. John, *A World Safe for Democracy: Liberal Internationalism and the Crisis of Global Order* (New Haven and London, Yale University Press, 2020).

Ikenberry, G. John, 'Three Worlds: the West, East and South and the Competition to Shape Global Order', *International Affairs*, Vol. 100, No. 1, 2024, pp. 121–138.

Ishchenko, Volodymyr, *Towards the Abyss: Ukraine from Maidan to War* (London, Verso, 2024).

Jankowicz, Nina, *How to Lose the Information War: Russia, Fake News, and the Future of Conflict* (London, I. B. Tauris, 2020).

Jaspers, Karl, *The Question of German Guilt*, 2nd rev. edn. (New York, Fordham University Press, 2000).

Johnstone, Caitlin, 'The US Has a Standing Policy of Ignoring the Human Rights Violations of its Allies', 15 November 2023, https://caityjohnstone.medium.com/the-us-has-a-standing-policy-of-ignoring-the-human-rights-violations-of-its-allies-a2f90b851b76.

'Joint Statement of the People's Republic of China and the Russian Federation on Deepening the Comprehensive Strategic Partnership of Coordination in the New Era on the Occasion of the 75th Anniversary of the Establishment of Diplomatic Relations between the People's Republic of China and the Russian Federation', Xinhua, 17 May 2024, News.china.com.cn/2024-05/17/content_117193497.shtml.

'Joint Statement of the Russian Federation and the People's Republic of China on the International Relations Entering a New Era and the Global Sustainable Development', 4 February 2022, http://en.kremlin.ru/supplement/5770.

Kagarlitsky, Boris, 'Broken Windows and Broken Lives', *Canadian Dimension*, 16 April 2023, https://canadiandimension.com/articles/view/broken-windows-and-broken-lives.

Kalinovsky, Artemy, *Laboratory of Socialist Development: Cold War Politics and Decolonization in Tajikistan* (Ithaca, Cornell University Press, 2018).

Kedourie, Elie, *Nationalism* (London, Hutchinson, 1960).

Khalidi, Rashid, '"A New Abyss": Gaza and the Hundred Years' War on Palestine', *The Guardian*, The Long Read, 11 April 2024, https://www.theguardian.com/world/2024/apr/11/a-new-abyss-gaza-and-the-hundred-years-war-on-palestine.

Khudoley, Konstantin, 'Russia and the US: The Way Forward', *Russia in Global Affairs*, No. 4, 2017, http://eng.globalaffairs.ru/number/Russia-and-the-US-The-Way-Forward-19263.

Knight, Amy, *Orders to Kill: The Putin Regime and Political Murder* (New York, Thomas Dunne Books, 2017).

Korb, Lawrence J. and Stephen Cimbala, 'Putin's Tactical Nuclear Exercises: Old Wine in New Bottles?', *The National Interest*, 29 May 2024, https://nationalinterest.org/feature/putin%E2%80%99s-tactical-nuclear-exercises-old-wine-new-bottles-211211.

Kozyrev, Andrei, 'Partnership or Cold Peace?', *Foreign Policy*, No. 99, Summer 1995, pp. 3–14.

Kozyrev, Andrei, *The Firebird: A Memoir. The Elusive Fate of Russian Democracy* (Pittsburgh, University of Pittsburgh Press, 2019).

Krein, Julius, 'The University Monopoly Must be Broken', *UnHerd*, 9 March 2024, https://unherd.com/2024/03/the-university-monopoly-must-be-broken/.

Lauria, Joe, 'Russian Imperialism', *Consortium News*, 13 February 2024, https://consortiumnews.com/2024/02/13/russian-imperialism/.

Lavrov, Sergei, 'Speech by the Minister of Foreign Affairs of the Russian Federation S. V. Lavrov at the XXXII Assembly of the Council on Foreign and Defence Policy', Russian Foreign Ministry, 18 May 2024, https://mid.ru/ru/foreign_policy/news/1951435.

Lawson, Tom, 'Bloodlands: Europe Between Hitler and Stalin', *Reviews in History*, December 2016, https://reviews.history.ac.uk/review/2036.

Legvold, Robert, *Return to Cold War* (Cambridge, Polity, 2016).

Legvold, Robert, 'Ending the Cold War with Russia', *The National Interest*, 2 February 2022, https://nationalinterest.org/feature/ending-new-cold-war-russia-199997.

Leonhardt, David, *Ours Was the Shining Future: The Story of the American Dream* (New York, Random House, 2023).
Lesseraux, Mark, '"Noble Lies": How the Neocons Hijacked US Politics and Subsequently Altered America's Trajectory', *Pressenza*, 27 August 2024, https://www.pressenza.com/2024/08/noble-lies-how-the-neocons-hijacked-us-politics-and-subsequently-altered-americas-trajectory/.
Lewis, David G., 'Geopolitical Imaginaries in Russian Foreign Policy: The Evolution of "Greater Eurasia"', *Europe-Asia Studies*, Vol. 70, No. 10, 2018, pp. 1612–37.
Libman, Alexander and Evgeny Vinokurov (eds), *The Elgar Companion to the Eurasian Economic Union* (Cheltenham and Northampton, Edward Elgar, 2024).
Lieven, Anatol, *Climate Change and the Nation State* (London, Penguin Books, 2021).
Lieven, Anatol, 'To Seek Peace in Ukraine, Remember the End of the Cold War', *The Nation*, 22 February 2024, https://www.thenation.com/article/world/ukraine-us-russia-gorbachev/.
Lilla, Mark, *The Once and Future Liberal: After Identity Politics* (London, Hurst, 2017).
Lorca, A. B., *Mestizo International Law: A Global Intellectual History 1842-1933* (Cambridge, Cambridge University Press, 2014).
Lownie, Rob, 'Emmanuel Todd: World War Three has Already Begun', *UnHerd*, 16 January 2023, https://unherd.com/newsroom/emmanuel-todd-world-war-iii-has-already-begun/.
Lukianoff, Greg and Rikki Schlott, *The Cancelling of the American Mind: How Cancel Culture Undermines Trust, Destroys Institutions, and Threatens Us All* (London, Allen Lane, 2023).
Martin, James, *Hegemony* (Cambridge, Polity, 2022).
Martin, Terry, *The Affirmative Action Empire: Nations and Nationalism in the Soviet Union, 1923-1939* (Ithaca and London, Cornell University Press, 2001).
Maté, Aaron, 'FBI Helps Ukraine Censor Twitter', *Substack*, 7 June 2023, https://www.aaronmate.net/p/fbi-helps-ukraine-c.ensor-twitter.
Maté, Aaron, 'How 10 Years of US Meddling in Ukraine Undermined Democracy and Fueled War', 30 April 2024, https://www.aaronmate.net/p/how-10-years-of-us-meddling-in-ukraine.
Matlock, Jack F., *Reagan and Gorbachev: How the Cold War Ended* (New York, Random House, 2004).
Matthews, Owen, 'Sanctions against Russia Have Backfired', *The Spectator*, 25 November 2023, https://www.spectator.co.uk/article/sanctions-against-russia-have-backfired/.
McCain, John, 'Russia is a "Gas Station Masquerading as a Country"', *The Week*, 8 January 2015, https://theweek.com/speedreads/456437/john-mccain-russia-gas-station-masquerading-country.
McConnell, Scott, 'George Kennan's Internal Exile', *Modern Age*, 17 July 2023, https://modernagejournal.com/george-kennans-internal-exile/218597/.
Mearsheimer, John J. and Stephen M. Walt, *The Israel Lobby and US Foreign Policy* (London, Penguin, 2008).
Mehta, Krishan, 'Sanctions and Forever Wars', US Committee on US-Russia Accord, 4 May 2021, https://usrussiaaccord.com/acura-viewpoint-sanctions-and-forever-wars-by-krishen-mehta/.
Mettan, Guy, *Creating Russophobia: From the Great Religious Schism to Anti-Putin Hysteria* (Atlanta, Clarity Press, 2017).
Mitzen, Jennifer, 'Ontological Security in World Politics: State Identity and the Security Dilemma', *European Journal of International Relations*, Vol. 12, No. 3, 2006, pp. 373–93.

Moeini, Arta, 'Gaza, Ukraine and Our Quest for Catharsis', *UnHerd*, 4 November 2023, https://unherd.com/2023/11/gaza-ukraine-and-our-quest-for-catharsis/.
Morgenthau, Hans, *Politics Among Nations*, 1st edn (New York, Knopf, 1948).
Moyn, Samuel, *The Last Utopia: Human Rights in History* (Cambridge, Belknap Press, 2012).
Moyn, Samuel, *Liberalism against Itself: Cold War Intellectuals and the Making of our Times* (New Haven and London, Yale University Press, 2023).
NATO, 'Bucharest Summit Declaration', 3 April 1998, https://www.nato.int/cps/en/natolive/official_texts_8443.htm.
NATO 2022: Strategic Concept, Adopted by the Madrid NATO Summit, 29 June 2022, https://www.nato.int/nato_static_fl2014/assets/pdf/2022/6/pdf/290622-strategic-concept.pdf.
Neumann, Iver B., *Russia and the Idea of Europe: A Study in Identity and International Relations* (London, Routledge, 2016).
Niblett, Robin, *The New Cold War: How the Contest between the US and China Will Shape our Century* (New York, Atlantic Books, 2024).
Nikitin, Vadim, 'Georgia Dreaming: Is Another Colour Revolution about to Kick off', *The Nation*, 20 May 2024, https://www.thenation.com/article/world/georgia-dream-protests-ngo-color-revolution/.
Nitoiu, Cristian and Florin Pasatoiu, 'Hybrid Geopolitics in EU-Russia Relations: Understanding the Persistence of Conflict and Cooperation', *East European Politics*, Vol. 36, No. 4, October 2020, pp. 499–514.
Orenstein, Mitchell A., *The Lands in Between: Russia vs. the West and the New Politics of Hybrid War* (Cambridge, Cambridge University Press, 2019).
Orfalea, Matt and Matt Taibbi, 'Big Brother – War is Good', *Racket News*, 22 February 2024, https://www.racket.news/p/big-brother-war-is-good.
O'Rourke, Lindsey A., *Covert Regime Change: America's Secret Cold War* (Ithaca and London, Cornell University Press, 2018).
Owen, John M., 'Two Emerging International Orders? China and the United States', *International Affairs*, Vol. 97, No. 5, 2021, pp. 1415–31.
Palatskis, Al'girdas, *Naruchniki na mysl'* (Moscow, Komsomolskaya Pravda, 2022).
Pappe, Ilan, *Lobbying for Zionism on Both Sides of the Atlantic* (London, Oneworld, 2024).
Perlstein, Rick, 'First they Came for Harvard', *The American Prospect*, 10 January 2024, https://prospect.org/politics/2024-01-10-first-they-came-for-harvard/.
Peterson, Jeremy, 'Unpacking Show Trials: Situating the Trial of Saddam Hussein', *Harvard International Law Review*, Vol. 48, No. 1, Winter 2007, pp. 257–92.
Petro, Nicolai, *The Tragedy of Ukraine: What Classical Greek Tragedy can Teach us about Conflict Resolution* (Berlin, De Gruyter, 2022).
Pilger, John, 'Silencing the Lambs: How Propaganda Works', Trondheim World Festival, 7 September 2022, in *Consortium News*, 8 January 2024, https://consortiumnews.com/2024/01/08/john-pilger-silencing-the-lambs-how-propaganda-works-2/.
Platt, Kevin M. F., *Border Conditions: Russian-Speaking Latvians Between World Orders* (DeKalb, Northern Illinois University Press, 2024).
Plotnikov, Nikolai (ed.), *Pered Litsom Katastrofy* (Berlin, Hopf, 2023).
Pomerantsev, Peter, *Nothing is True and Everything is Possible: Adventures in Modern Russia* (London, Faber, 2015).
PRC Ministry of Foreign Affairs, *US Hegemony and its Perils*, 20 February 2023, https://www.fmprc.gov.cn/mfa_eng/wjbxw/202302/t20230220_11027664.html.

Proud, Ian, *A Misfit in Moscow: How British Diplomacy in Russia Failed 2014-2019* (Copyright Ian Proud, 2023).
Pullmann, Joy, 'State of Texas Joins The Federalist, Daily Wire in Suing the Federal Censorship-Industrial Complex', *The Federalist*, 6 December 2023, https://thefederalist.com/2023/12/06/state-of-texas-joins-the-federalist-daily-wire-in-suing-the-federal-censorship-industrial-complex/.
Putin, Vladimir, 'Presidential Address to the Federal Assembly', Kremlin.ru, 12 December 2013, http://eng.kremlin.ru/news/6402.
Putin, Vladimir, 'Interview with China Media Group', 5 June 2018, http://en.kremlin.ru/events/president/news/57684.
Putin, Vladimir, 'Valdai International Discussion Club Meeting', 5 October 2023, http://en.kremlin.ru/events/president/news/72444.
Putin, Vladimir, 'Plenary Session of the World Russian People's Council', *Kremlin.ru*, 28 November 2023, https://en.kremlin.ru/events/president/transcripts/72863.
Putin, Vladimir, 'Interview to Tucker Carlson', *Kremlin.ru*, 9 February 2024, http://en.kremlin.ru/events/president/transcripts/73411.
Ragozhin, Leonid, 'The Controversy of the Decolonization Discourse', *Russia.Post*, 17 January 2024, https://www.russiapost.info/society/decolonization.
Ramani, Samuel, *Russia in Africa: Resurgent Great Power or Bellicose Pretender?* (London, Hurst, 2023).
Rid, Thomas, *Active Measures: The Secret History of Disinformation and Political Warfare* (London, Profile Books, 2020).
Riker, William H., *The Art of Political Manipulation* (New Haven, Yale University Press, 1986).
Roberts, Geoffrey, 'A League of Their Own: The Soviet Origins of the United Nations', *Journal of Contemporary History*, Vol. 54, No. 2, 2019, pp. 303–27.
Robertson, Neil G., *Leo Strauss: An Introduction* (Cambridge, Polity, 2021).
Robinson, Paul, *Russian Conservatism* (DeKalb, Northern Illinois University Press, 2019).
Rochowanski, Almut and Sopiko Japaridze, 'Unrest in Georgia over the "Foreign Influence Transparency Law"', *LeftEast*, 3 May 2024, https://lefteast.org/unrest-georgia-foreign-influence-transparency-law/.
Roos, Jerome, 'Rewriting the Global Rulebook', *New Statesman*, 14–20 June 2024, pp. 26–29.
Rorty, Richard, *Achieving our Country: Leftist Thought in Twentieth Century America* (Cambridge, Harvard University Press, 1998).
Roussinos, Aris, 'The Post-America War Has Begun', *UnHerd*, 10 November 2023, https://unherd.com/2023/11/israel-could-collapse-the-american-empire/.
Sachs, Jeffrey D., *To Move the World: JFK's Quest for Peace* (London, The Bodley Head, 2013).
Sachs, Jeffrey D., 'How the CIA Destabilizes the World', *Common Dreams*, 12 February 2024, https://www.commondreams.org/opinion/cia-destablizes-the-world.
Sachs, Jeffrey D., 'Achieving Peace in the New Multipolar Age', 9 August 2024, https://www.jeffsachs.org/newspaper-articles/asfymsw3wydpfjlx4pbfz92mmcr4j5.
Sachs, Jeffrey D., 'How the Neocons Chose Hegemony over Peace Beginning in the Early 1990s', *IDN*, 4 September 2024, https://indepthnews.net/how-the-neocons-chose-hegemony-over-peace-beginning-in-the-early-1990s/.
Sakwa, Richard, 'The Regime System in Russia', *Contemporary Politics*, Vol. 3, No. 1, 1997, pp. 7–25.

Sakwa, Richard, *Postcommunism* (Buckingham and Philadelphia, Open University Press, 1999).

Sakwa, Richard, 'The Dual State in Russia', *Post-Soviet Affairs*, Vol. 26, No. 3, July–September 2010, pp. 185–206.

Sakwa, Richard, *Putin Redux: Power and Contradiction in Contemporary Russia* (London ānd New York, Routledge, 2014).

Sakwa, Richard, *Russia Against the Rest: The Post-Cold War Crisis of World Order* (Cambridge, Cambridge University Press, 2017).

Sakwa, Richard, 'Russian Neo-Revisionism', *Russian Politics*, Vol. 4, No. 1, 2019, pp. 1–21.

Sakwa, Richard, *The Putin Paradox* (London and New York, I. B. Tauris/Bloomsbury Publishing, 2020).

Sakwa, Richard, *Deception: Russiagate and the New Cold War* (Lanham, Lexington Books, 2022).

Sakwa, Richard, 'Is China Revisionist? China, The Political West, and the International System', in Nenad Stekić and Aleksandar Mitić (eds), *New Chinese Initiatives for a Changing Global Security*, The 3rd "Dialogues on China" International Academic Conference, Belgrade, 9–10 November 2023, Conference Proceedings (Belgrade, Institute of International Politics and Economics, 2023), pp. 33–46.

Sakwa, Richard, *The Lost Peace: How the West Failed to Prevent a Second Cold War* (New Haven and London, Yale University Press, 2023).

Sakwa, Richard, 'The Perils of Democratism', *Polis: Political Studies*, No. 2, 2023, pp. 88–102.

Sakwa, Richard, 'Realism, Ethics and the Ukraine War', in Anton Leist and Rolf Zimmermann (eds), *After the War? How the Ukraine War Challenges Political Theories* (Berlin, De Gruyter, 2023), pp. 55–88.

Sakwa, Richard, 'Living in the Void: The End of the Revolution and the Politics of *Krisis*', *International Political Anthropology*, Vol. 17, No. 1, 2024, pp. 63–80.

Sarotte, Mary Elise, *Not One Inch: America, Russia and the Making of Post-Cold War Stalemate* (New Haven, Yale University Press, 2022).

Sata, Robert and Ireneusz Pawel Karolewski, 'Caesarean Politics in Hungary and Poland', *East European Politics*, Vol. 6, No. 2, 2020, pp. 206–25.

Savranskaya, Svetlana and Tom Blanton, 'NATO Expansion: What Gorbachev Heard', National Security Archive, George Washington University, 12 December 2017, https://nsarchive.gwu.edu/briefing-book/russia-programs/2017-12-12/nato-expansion-what-gorbachev-heard-western-leaders-early.

Sayers, Freddie, 'Inside the Disinformation Industry: A government-Sponsored Agency is Censoring Journalism', *UnHerd*, 17 April 2024, https://unherd.com/2024/04/inside-the-disinformation-industry/.

Schmitt, Carl, *The Concept of the Political* (Chicago, University of Chicago Press, 1996).

Schwartz, Ian, 'Trump Strategist Brad Parscale vs. PBS "Frontline" on Campaign Use of Facebook: "A Gift"', *RealClearPolitics*, 3 December 2018, https://www.realclearpolitics.com/video/2018/12/03/trump_strategist_brad_parscale_vs_pbs_frontline_on_campaigns_use_of_facebook.html.

Schwarz, Benjamin and Christopher Layne, 'Why Are We in Ukraine?', *Harper's Magazine*, June 2023, https://harpers.org/archive/2023/06/why-are-we-in-ukraine/.

Scott, James C., *The Moral Economy of the Peasant* (New Haven, Yale University Press, 1976).

Shekhovtsov, Anton, 'Russian Malign Inspiration and How to Counter it', *EU Observer*, 9 January 2024, https://euobserver.com/opinion/157891.

Shellenberger, Michael, 'The Censorship-Industrial Complex, Part 2: Testimony to the House Select Subcommittee on the Weaponization of the Federal Government', 30 November 2023, https://judiciary.house.gov/sites/evo-subsites/republicans-judiciary.house.gov/files/evo-media-document/shellenberger_testimony.pdf.

Shellenberger, Michael, Alexandra Gutentag and Matt Taibbi, 'CTIL Files #1: 'US and UK Military Contractors Created Sweeping Plan for Global Censorship in 2018, New Documents Show', *Public*, 28 November 2023, https://public.substack.com/p/ctil-files.

Shifrinson, Joshua R. Itzkowitz, 'Put it in Writing: How the West Broke its Promises to Moscow', *Foreign Affairs*, 29 October 2014, https://www.foreignaffairs.com/articles/united-states/2014-10-29/put-it-writing.

Shifrinson, Joshua R. Itzkowitz, 'Deal or No Deal?: The End of the Cold War and the U.S. Offer to Limit NATO Expansion', *International Security*, Vol. 40, No. 4, 2016, pp. 7–44.

Shrayer, Maxim D., 'Punishing All Things Russian for Putin's Crimes: The Moral and Historical Illiteracy of Boycotting Russian Identity and Culture', *Tablet*, 4 April 2022, https://www.tabletmag.com/sections/news/articles/punishing-all-things-russian-for-putins-crimes.

Shullenberger, Geoff, 'How Cancel Culture Lost its Power: The Right Should be Wary of Norm Enforcement', *UnHerd*, 19 July 2024, https://unherd.com/2024/07/how-cancel-culture-lost-its-power/.

Simpson, Gerry, 'Two Liberalisms', *European Journal of International Law*, Vol. 12, No. 3, 2001, pp. 537–71.

Smith, William S., 'Jeane J. Kirkpatrick: 30 Years Unheeded', *The National Interest*, 13 June 2020, https://nationalinterest.org/feature/jeane-j-kirkpatrick-30-years-unheeded-162667.

Snyder, Timothy, *Bloodlands: Europe between Hitler and Stalin* (London, Vintage, 2011).

Snyder, Timothy, 'Hitler vs. Stalin: Who Was Worse?', *New York Review of Books*, 27 January 2011, https://www.nybooks.com/online/2011/01/27/hitler-vs-stalin-who-was-worse/.

Stiglitz, Joseph, *The Road to Freedom: Economics and the Good Society* (London, Allen Lane, 2024).

Streeck, Wolfgang, *How Will Capitalism End?* (London, Verso, 2016).

Stuenkel, Oliver, *The BRICS and the Future of Global Order* (London and Lanham, Lexington Books, 2015).

Stuenkel, Oliver, *Post-Western World: How Emerging Powers are Remaking Global Order* (Cambridge, Polity, 2016).

Stuenkel, Oliver, 'Why the Global South is Accusing America of Hypocrisy', *Foreign Policy*, 2 November 2023, https://foreignpolicy.com/2023/11/02/israel-palestine-hamas-gaza-war-russia-ukraine-occupation-west-hypocrisy/.

Suny, Ronald Grigor, *A State of Nations: Empire and Nation-Making in the Age of Lenin and Stalin* (Oxford, Oxford University Press, 2002).

Suslov, Mikhail, *Putinism: Post-Soviet Russian Regime Ideology* (London and New York, Routledge, 2024).

Taibbi, Matt, 'Report on the Censorship-Industrial Complex', *Racket News*, 25 April 2023, https://www.racket.news/p/report-on-the-censorship-industrial.

Taibbi, Matt, 'The Most Embarrassing "Facebook Files" Revelations? The Press, Exposed as Censors', *Racket News*, 28 July 2023, https://www.racket.news/p/the-most-embarrassing-facebook-files.

Taibbi, Matt, '"UK Files" Reports Show: Both Left and Right can be Targets of Censors', *Racket News*, 14 November 2023, https://www.racket.news/p/uk-files-reports-show-both-left-and.

Taibbi, Matt, 'Not a Nothingburger: My Statement to Congress on Censorship', *Racket News*, 2 December 2023, https://www.racket.news/p/not-a-nothingburger-my-statement.

Taibbi, Matt, 'Sue the Bastards: Federalist, Daily Wire Take the State Department to Court', *Scheerpost*, 6 December 2023, https://scheerpost.com/2023/12/06/matt-taibbi-sue-the-bastards-federalist-daily-wire-take-the-state-department-to-court/.

Taibbi, Matt, 'FOIA Exclusive: Did Pharma Companies Help Plan "Virality Project" Censorship Program?', *Racket News*, 11 December 2023, https://www.racket.news/p/foia-exclusive-did-pharma-companies.

Taibbi, Matt, 'Editor's Note: On "UK Files, Part 2"', *Racket News*, 31 January 2024, https://www.racket.news/p/editors-note-on-uk-files-part-2.

Talbott, Strobe, *The Russia Hand: A Memoir of Presidential Diplomacy* (New York, Random House, 2003).

Teitelbaum, Benjamin R., *War for Eternity: The Return of Traditionalism and the Rise of the Populist Right* (London, Penguin, 2021).

Timofeev, Ivan, 'Fighting Sanctions: From Legislation to Strategy', Valdai Club, 18 June 2018, http://valdaiclub.com/a/highlights/fighting-sanctions-strategy/.

Timofeev, Ivan, *Sanctions against Russia: A Look into 2021* (Moscow, RIAC Report No. 65. 2021), https://russiancouncil.ru/en/activity/publications/sanctions-against-russia-a-look-into-2021/.

Timofeev, Ivan, 'In 2022, the World as We Knew it Ended', *RT.com*, 5 January 2023, https://www.rt.com/russia/569440-the-end-of-the-end-of-the-history/.

Todd, Emmanuel, *After the Empire: The Breakdown of the American Order* (London, Constable, 2003).

Todd, Emmanuel, *La Défaite de l'Occident* (Paris, Gallimard, 2023).

Toosi, Nahal, 'Leaked Memo Schooled Tillerson on Human Rights', *Politico*, 19 December 2017, https://www.politico.com/story/2017/12/19/tillerson-state-human-rights-304118.

Tooze, Adam, *Crashed: How a Decade of Financial Crises Changed the World* (London, Penguin, 2019).

Torbakov, Igor, 'History, Memory and National Identity: Understanding the Politics of History and Memory Wars in Post-Soviet Lands', *Demokratizatsiya*, Vol. 19, No. 3, 2011, pp. 209–32.

Trump, Donald J., 'Transcript: Donald Trump's Foreign Policy Speech', *New York Times*, 27 April 2016, https://www.nytimes.com/2016/04/28/us/politics/transcript-trump-foreign-policy.html.

Tsygankov, Andrei P., *Russia and the West from Alexander to Putin: Honor in International Relations* (Cambridge, Cambridge University Press, 2012).

Tsygankov, Andrei P., 'Crafting the State-Civilization', *Problems of Post-Communism*, Vol. 63, No. 3, 2016, pp. 146–58.

Tsygankov, Andrei P., *Russia's Foreign Policy: Change and Continuity in National Identity*, 6th edn (Lanham, Rowman & Littlefield, 2019).

Tsygankov, Andrei P., *The 'Russian Idea' in International Relations: Civilization and National Distinctiveness* (London and New York, Routledge, 2023).

Valdai Discussion Club, *Towards the Great Ocean – 3: Creating Central Eurasia*, Valdai Report No. 3, June 2015.

Volkov, Denis and Andrei Kolesnikov, 'Alternate Reality: How Russian Society Learned to Stop Worrying About the War', *Carnegie Endowment for International Peace*, 28 November 2023, https://carnegieendowment.org/2023/11/28/alternate-reality-how-russian-society-learned-to-stop-worrying-about-war-pub-91118.

Von der Schulenberg, Michael and Ruth Firmenich, 'The EU Must Change Course on Ukraine, or Risk Breaking Itself Apart', *Brave New Europe*, 3 September 2024, https://braveneweurope.com/michael-von-der-schulenburg-ruth-firmenich-the-eu-must-change-course-on-ukraine-or-risk-breaking-itself-apart.

Walt, Stephen M., *The Hell of Good Intentions: America's Foreign Policy Elite and the Decline of US Primacy* (New York, Farrar, Straus, and Giroux, 2019).

Welch, David, *Propaganda: Power and Persuasion* (London, British Library Publishing Division, 2013).

Wertheim, Stephen, *Tomorrow the World: The Birth of US Global Supremacy* (Harvard, Belknap Press, 2020).

Wertheim, Stephen, 'Iraq and the Pathologies of Primacy', *Foreign Affairs*, 17 March 2023, https://www.foreignaffairs.com/united-states/iraq-and-pathologies-primacy.

Winstanley, Asa, *Weaponising Anti-Semitism: How the Israeli Lobby Brought Down Jeremy Corbyn* (New York, OR Books, 2023).

Wyatt, Tom, 'Counter-Disinformation: The New Snake Oil', *Racket News*, 19 May 2023, https://www.racket.news/p/counter-disinformation-the-new-snake.

Zakaria, Fareed, *The Post-American World* (New York, Norton, 2009).

Zemanek, Ladislav, 'De-Russification and "Liberal Authoritarianism": The Czech Choice', *Valdai Discussion Club*, 19 April 2022, https://valdaiclub.com/a/highlights/de-russification-and-liberal-authoritarianism/.

INDEX

11 September 2001 (9/11) 53
al-Assad, Bashar 73, 85, 99, 104
Al Qaeda 53
Alliance for Securing Democracy (ASD) 117
American Israel Public Action Committee (AIPAC) 125
Anglo-American invasion of Iraq in 2003, 141
Anglo-Russian rivalry 107
Anti-Ballistic Missile (ABM) treaty 1972, 60
Anti-Corruption Foundation (FPK) 66
anti-diplomacy: civilising mission 76; Cold War II attack 77; democratism 79–80; NATO enlargement 79; Obama's assault 77; pluralism 80; politicisation of international institutions 78; practice of boycotts 78; principles of self-determination 80; Russo-Ukrainian war 79; tit-for-tat expulsions 77; UN's 15 specialised agencies 78; values 79–80
anti-disinformation industry: adversarial narratives 113; bias towards Hillary Clinton's nomination 109; communicative struggles 110; EUvsDisinfo project in 2015, 111; Hunter Biden laptop story 109; Malign inspiration 111; monitoring agencies 113; National Security Act, UK 112; polices 145; 'Russiagate' allegations 108; Russian authoritarianism 112; Russophobia, dimensions 107–8; UK Files 114
anti-hegemonism 45; *see also* hegemony; alignments 48; Charter slogans 54; counter-movements 129; powers 20; resistance 48; world order 45

anti-immigrant violence 119
anti-Maidan insurgency 12
anti-populism 103
anti-understanding bias 136
Antiwar.com 126
anti-Zionism 125
Arendt, Hannah 128
Arms Control and Disarmament Agency 60
Artificial Intelligence 5
Asian Infrastructure Investment Bank (AIIB) 48–49
Assange, Julian 55–56
Association Agreement with Ukraine in 2013, 146
Association of Southeast Asian Nations (ASEAN) 46, 50–51
Atlantic alliance system 104
Atlanticism 70, 74, 87, 146
Australia, the UK and the United States, and potentially Japan (AUKUS) 51
Austrian State Treaty 1955, 64

Ball, George W., 131
Bandung Declaration of 1955, 155
Baud, Jacques 99
Baysha, Olga 13, 145
Belt and Road Initiative (BRI) 48–50
Bentham, Jeremy 91
Berger, Victor 102
Berlin Wall, fall of 4, 26, 146
Bernays, Edward 100
Biden, Joe 23, 42, 60, 62–63, 79, 84, 88, 108–10, 113, 117, 122–23, 135, 144
Blakeley, Grace 17
Blinken, Antony 64, 109
Borrell, Josep 57, 80
Brands, Hal 11
Brazil, Russia, India, China and South Africa (BRICS)+ association 42, 48–49, 51

Bretton Woods financial institutions 24
BRICS 49, 51
Bromwich, David 135
Buchanan, Patrick 100, 116
Bush doctrine 129
Bush, George H. W., 60, 105, 125, 129

cancel culture 1, 100–101, 148
capitalism 6, 9, 23, 153, 157
captive peoples 140
Carden, James 94, 115
Carré, John Le 99
Center for a New American Security (CNAS) 126
Center for American Progress 114
Central Bank of Russia (CBR) 88, 96
Central Intelligence Agency (CIA) 16, 56, 87, 104–6, 120
Cerella, Dr Antonio 1
Charter principle of sovereign internationalism 19–20, 24, 29, 32, 41, 46, 52, 57–58, 61, 70, 80, 108, 129, 151–52, 154
China (ese): bloc politics and military alliances 11; confrontational policy towards 145; *Global Civilization Initiative* 39; *Global Development Initiative* 39; *Global Security Initiative* 39; invasion of Taiwan 81; massive rearmament programme 63; multilateralism 39; 'one China' policy 81; part in Cold War I 10; programme of technological decoupling 42; and Russia, *Joint Statement* 50; state-owned enterprises (SOEs) 40; United States-China clash 41–42
CHIPS Act in 2022, 42
Christopher Steele dossier 109
citizen diplomacy 141, 157
Civilisational West 30, 103
Clark, Christopher 11
climate change 8, 28, 47, 53, 63, 155–56
Clinton, Bill 27, 60, 92, 114
Clinton, Hillary 92, 102, 109
Code of Practice on Disinformation, EU's 119
cognitive war, notion of 119, 133
Cold War: cyberwar 8; definition 11; democratic internationalist' bipartisan foreign policy 9; distinctive characteristics 8; hyper-normalisation 14; negative peace 12; neo-containment strategy 12; proxy wars 8; Russian hegemony in post-Soviet Eurasia 13

Cold war I 3; cultural and normative contestation 145; intelligence and media 130; revival of practices 153–54; static and defensive 9
Cold war II 3, 5, 6, 129; *see also* anti-diplomacy; acute diaphobia 76; battlefield weapons 60; binary of capitalism *versus* communism 153; business, tourism and educational exchanges 64; civilisational 145; closure of the Moscow Helsinki Group 67; coercion 75; communicative monopoly 73; cultural contacts 65; culture of 152; difference from earlier conflicts 10–11; emergence of a Political East 154; hegemony and hermeticism 69–75; Inflation Reduction Act 63; Intermediate Nuclear Forces treaty 60; intertwined economies of the major powers 154; media and public discourse 68; militarism 62–63; Military Keynesianism 62; multipolarity 154; nation states 154; national security 61; NATO 60–63; opposition to militarisation and securitisation 73–74; Political West, opposition to 68 (*see also* Political West); pro-Western and anti-Russian administration 66; relations with the West 66; shift in the balance of power 8; suppression of dissent 65–69; technological development 154; US defence appropriation for 2024, 63
colonialism 38–39, 46, 80, 103, 132, 140
communicative conflicts 115–26; Alliance for Securing Democracy (ASD) 117; anti-Ukraine narratives 120; censorship enterprises 122; geopolitical contestation and great power struggles 102; informational ecosystem 116; malinformation, concept of 124; media manipulation 120; Quiet Skies' programme 116; Russian narratives 121; Smith-Mundt Act 123; Twitter Files revelations 117–19; US security establishment 116
communism 6, 9, 13, 23, 76, 103, 127, 137, 139, 153; and capitalism 6, 9, 23, 103
Conference on Security and Cooperation in Europe (CSCE) 78
Connolly, Arthur 107
Conrad, Joseph 80
conservative internationalism 108, 116, 152

INDEX 177

Consortium News, website 121
context collapse 101
conventional representation, crisis of 149
Cooper, Robert 55
Corbyn, Jeremy 114, 125
counter-disinformation 107
Countering America's Adversaries through Sanctions Act (CAATSA) 84
Covid-19 pandemic 5, 66, 152
Cuban missile crisis 1962, 4, 8, 60, 77, 146
cultural diplomacy 156
cultural war 100
Culture and Society (Williams) 6
culture wars 37, 100, 102, 127
cybersecurity 117
Cyber-Threat Intelligence League (CTIL) 121

da Silva, Luiz Inácio Lula 57, 118
de Gaulle, Charles 3
Debs, Eugene 102
decolonial polarisation: collective punishment 137; complex interactions between the state and society 137; decoloniality 140; derussification' campaign in Ukraine 140; hybridity of the 'postcolonial' condition 142–43; NATO (*see* North Atlantic Treaty Organization (NATO)); political equivalence 139; polyculturalism 143; Russocentrism 140
deglobalisation 20, 83
Democratic internationalism 19–20, 23, 29, 32, 46, 52, 70–71, 75, 80, 106, 116, 129, 147, 151–52, 154
democratisation of international politics 43
democratism 33, 70–71, 75, 80, 113, 143, 144–45, 156, 157–58, 158
Deng Xiaoping 9, 38, 40
Department of Homeland Security (DHS) 117, 124
derussification campaign in Ukraine 140
Dialogue of Civilisations Research Institute 35
Diesen, Glenn 126, 140
Digital Forensic Laboratory 113
Digital Services Act (DSA), EU's 111, 118–19
Dilthey, Wilhelm 130
Disinformation Governance Board 113
disintegration of the Soviet Union (1989–91) 93, 97, 127, 143

diversionary theory of international politics 150
Dmitriev, Yury 66
Dobrynin, Anatoly 77
'domino' theory 131
double standards 21, 39, 46, 48, 54–55, 57, 75, 80, 87, 113, 141, 152, 155, 158
Doyle, Michael 76
Dozhd conundrum 95
Dugin, Alexander 132
Durov, Pavel 118

educational links 156
Eisenhower, Dwight D., 63, 104
Election Integrity Partnership 121
Enlightenment 16, 30–31, 80, 151, 158
Espionage Act 102
EU4FreeMedia 111
Eurasian Economic Union (EEU) 50
Eurocentrism 51
European Commission (EC) 88
European Day of Remembrance for Victims of Stalinism and Nazism 138
European Defence Community 70
European Parliament (EP) 6, 76, 138
EUvsDisinfo 111

Falk, Richard 71
Federal Security Service 7
Fico, Robert 149
Filatov, Sergey 107
Fleming, Ian 99
Flournoy, Michèle 126
Foreign Intelligence Service 7, 148
Freeman, Chas 75, 80, 106
free-speech absolutism 101
Freud, Sigmund 100

Gabbard, Tulsi 116
Gaddafi, Muammar 73, 126
genocide 4
Gerasimov, Valery 133–34
Gergiev, Valery 141
Girkin, Igor (Strelkov) 67
Glennon, Michael 16, 33
Global Disinformation Index (GDI) 113, 122
Global Engagement Centre (GEC) 122–23, 148
Global North 19, 47, 153–54
Global South 5, 8, 10, 19, 46–47, 49, 51, 57, 73, 83, 88, 128, 153, 155
globalisation 5, 9, 16, 19–20, 32, 37, 41, 51, 65, 71, 83, 89, 119, 149, 152

globalism 101, 153
gnosis 3, 31, 75, 130
Goodman, Melvin 61
Gorbachev, Mikhail 3, 8, 20, 25–26, 36, 60, 93
Gramsci, Antonio 148
Gray, John 2, 71
Guénon, René 158
Guterres, António 156

Hamilton, Booz Allen 117, 126
Hammond, Philip 81
Harris, Kamala 126
Heart of Darkness (Conrad) 80
hegemonitis 134
hegemony: Bloc unity 70; bombing of Yugoslavia 71; coercion 75; communicative monopoly 73, 75; global 62, 148; hermeticism 46, 69, 74–76; liberal hegemony 72; opposition to militarisation and securitisation 73–74; perpetual peace 70; *realpolitik* affairs 71; values 74
heresthetics 106
hermeticism 46, 74–75, 76
Higgins, Eliot 120
historicism 30, 157
Hitchens, Peter 72
Hitler, Adolf 63, 93, 139
Holy war 101
Hook, Brian 54
Hoover, J. Edgar 73
House Un-American Activities Committee (HUAC) 102
human rights 25, 31–32, 50, 55, 67–68, 71, 76, 78, 91, 112, 130, 138, 158
Hunter Biden laptop story 109, 113, 117, 123
hypocrisy 54–55, 80

Identarian politics 135, 148, 158
IELTS (international English language assessment system) 141
Ikenberry, G. John 40–41
imperialism 5, 25, 38, 46, 76, 79–80, 103, 146, 150
Inflation Reduction Act 16, 63
information management 127; Atlantic alliance system 104; categories of heresthetics 106; contemporary 100; global war on terror after 9/11, 105; manipulation 106; MICIMATT 106; security apparatus polices the Trumanite state 105; war scare of 1948, 105
information societies 115
Infrastructure Security Agency (CISA) 117, 121, 124
'input capital' in post-industrial economies 152
Institute for Policy Studies 116
inter-cold war paradigm 151
international affairs 2, 6, 15, 19, 23, 25, 31, 38, 48, 53–54, 57–58, 71, 74, 80, 102, 116, 127, 131, 134, 137, 147, 151–52, 157, 159
International Criminal Court (ICC) 15, 57
International Monetary Fund (IMF) 16, 24, 40
international order; hegemony (*see* antihegemonism): horror of the Hamas attack 20; multiple deaths., 20–21; NATO (*see* North Atlantic Treaty Organization (NATO)); proxy wars 19; rules-based order 21 (*see also* rules-based order); cold war in Kenya 19–20
international politics: Charter principles 24; cold war ideologisation 75; competitive system of 48; conduct of 7, 38–39; consequences on 108; contest for hegemony 9 (*see also* hegemony); contradictions 40; culture in 151; democratisation of 43; developments in 94; dialectical perspective to 157; diversionary, theory of 150; economic and ideological resources 25; Eurasia 50; in Europe 146; everyday practices of 18; expansive and illiberal view of 52; hegemonism in 46; liberal tradition's belief 152; logic of cold war 28; Manicheanism 15; morality 71; multipolar and plural 51; national interests of global actors 20; pattern of relationships 11; pluralism in 147; remoralisation of 53; strategic autonomy 62; sustainable framework 129; Westphalian plus approaches 53; world orders 154
international system 18, 25, 28, 32, 36, 40–41, 43, 152; Charter 3–4, 12, 20–21, 29, 39, 52, 61, 70, 79, 89, 133, 146, 151, 155; UN-based 15, 45, 47, 52
Internet Research Agency 109
Izborsky Club 35

INDEX

Jaspers, Karl 92
Johnstone, Caitlin 115, 136

Kagarlitsky, Boris 67
Kantian triptych of rationality 19
Kara-Murza, Vladimir 67
Kedourie, Elie 29
Kendall-Taylor, Andrea 124
Kennedy, John F., 77
Kennedy, Robert 77
Kerry, John 132–33
Khrushchev, Nikita 77
Kirillova, Irina 2
Kirpatrick, Jeane 116
Kislyak, Sergei 77
Kissinger, Henry 108, 144
Knight, Amy 110
Kojève, Alexandre 157
Korean War 9, 18
Korostelev, Alexei 95
Kristol, William 75

Lavrov, Sergei 59, 78
League of Nations 15, 25
Legvold, Robert 8
Leyen, Ursula von der 93
LGBT+ propaganda to minors, Russia 102
liberal democracy 30, 98, 145, 158
liberal international order (LIO) 16–17, 25, 30–31, 151
liberal internationalism 152
liberal-left 102, 158
Lieven, Anatol 115, 139
Los Angeles Olympics 1984, 64
The Lost Peace: How the West Failed to Prevent a Second Cold War (Sakwa) 3

Madisonian state 16, 17, 62, 65
Madrid summit 2022, 11, 37
Magnitsky Rule of Law Acts 91
Maidan 'coup' in Ukraine 32
Malofeev, Konstantin 35
Manchurian policies 148
Manichean logic of good *versus* evil 3, 23, 31, 71, 76, 144, 157
Manning, Chelsea 56
Mao Zedong 25, 40
Marx, Karl 30, 67, 72, 99, 102, 157
Maté, Aaron 2, 115
McCain, John 93
McCarthyite scare 102
McGovern, Ray 106, 116

McRae, Jimi 156
Medhurst, Richard 117
Medvedev, Dmitry 65–66, 85
Memorial Human Rights Centre 66
Memorial International 66
Menon, Shivshankar 47
Merkel, Angela 132
Mettan, Guy 107
Military-Industrial- Congressional-Intelligence-Media-Academia-Think-Tank complex (MICIMATT) 106
military Keynesianism 17, 62, 89
Minsk Accords 88
Missouri v. Biden 123
Mitterrand, François 3
Mitzen, Jennifer 129
Moeini, Arta 135
moral righteousness 5, 54, 147
Morgenthau, Hans 52
Morozov, Vyacheslav 69
Morson, Gary Saul 158
Moscow Carnegie Centre 86
Moscow-led Soviet bloc 24
Moscow Olympics 1980, 64
Musk, Elon 117–19
mutiny of Evgeny Prigozhin 's Wagner private military company 67

narrative management 72; clash of civilisations 103; communism and capitalist democracy, struggle 103; disinformation or 'conspiracy thinking', 103; geopolitical contestation 103; monological interactions 101; political contestation 102; power struggles 103; Russian propaganda 103; sources of 100–104
National Defence Authorisation Act 2020, 86
National Security Act, UK 112
Navalny, Alexei 66, 76, 110, 120
neoconservatives 31, 62, 116, 147, 151, 153, 157
neoliberal authoritarianism 134
neo-revisionism 33, 45
neutrality, concept of 63–64
New International Economic Order (NIEO) 155
New Political Thinking (NPT) 25, 155
New START agreement of 2011, 60
Non-Aligned Movement 10
non-alignment, principles of 47–48, 153–54

normativisation 152
North Atlantic Treaty Organization (NATO) 1, 7, 11, 13–14, 16, 18–20, 24, 26–27, 30, 37, 59–63, 65, 68, 70–71, 74–75, 77–79, 93–94, 99, 108, 119, 127, 133, 139; bombing campaign against the Federal Republic of Yugoslavia 13; enlargement 7, 20, 26, 50, 59, 61, 68, 75, 79, 93, 139; *Strategic Concept* 11
Nuremberg trials 138

Obama, Barack 62, 77, 83, 92, 102, 122, 126, 132, 147–48
oligarchs 14, 33, 84–85, 88, 126
On European Conscience and Totalitarianism 2009, EP resolution 138
Online Safety Act, Britain 118
ontological insecurities 131
ontological insecurity of civilian populations 136
ontological security, concept of 129
Open Society Foundation 113
Orbán, Viktor 149
Organisation for Security and Cooperation in Europe (OSCE) 59–60, 78, 138
Orlov, Oleg 68
Orthodoxy 31, 120, 158
Ostpolitik 42, 158

Paris Olympics 2024, 64
Parliamentary Assembly of the Council of Europe (PACE) 138
Parscale, Brad 109
Partnership for Peace programme, NATO 27, 59
Patriotic Union in Germany 111
Pearl Harbour, attack on 83
perestroika, Gorbachev's 25
Pilger, John 115
Pipes, Richard 105
pluralism 19, 36, 46, 51, 54, 80, 126, 137, 147, 154
Polish Economic Forum 2022, 95
Political East 42, 90; active non-alignment 47; AUKUS 51; autonomy of Charter international system 52; development and peace 46; dualism in conduct of international affairs 57; Eurasian Economic Union (EEU) 50; Eurasian powers with the Global South 47; features 47–48; International affairs in Cold War II 54; *Joint Statement* of Russia and China 50; pluralism and multipolarity 46; post-colonial state system 47; Quadrilateral Security Dialogue 51; sovereign internationalism 154; UN Charter 50; Universal Declaration of Human Rights 50
Political West 7, 10, 13–20, 24–30; Allies' victory in World War II 24; in Asia-Pacific region 51; Bucharest summit 27; characteristics 46; classical rationalism 31; democratic internationalism 23; European Economic Community or EU 24; hermeticism of 76; human rights and perpetual peace 31; Imperialism 25; intensified militarism 31; liberal international order 25; logic of expansion 154; Marxist-Leninist version of historicism 30; military-political institutions 74; NATO-Russia Founding Act on Mutual Relations 27–28; negative peace 28–29; neoconservative and liberal interventionist thinking, confluence of 29; Partnership for Peace programme of 1994, 27; post-Cold War reconciliation 26–27; radicalised in five main ways 30–31; rights and prerogatives of the international system 45; Russia as subaltern 28; Russia's inclusion 70; UN-based Charter International System 25; US hegemony and leadership 24, 31; Warsaw Treaty Organisation 26
polyculturalism 143
Pope Gregory XV 106
populism 13, 103, 147–50
post-colonial state system 47
postcommunism 127
post-Maidan Ukrainian leadership 13
post-Soviet decolonisation 143
'post-Western' organizational developments 49
prisca theologia, doctrine of 74
PropOrNot 126
Proud, Ian 81
public opinion management 72, 148
Putin, Vladimir 7, 20, 33–35, 39, 50, 57, 60, 63, 65–67, 73, 76, 83, 86–87, 89, 92–93, 95–97, 99, 109–10, 112, 122, 124, 130, 132–34, 136–37, 141–42, 156
Putinism 134

Putinversteher 130

Quadrilateral Security Dialogue (the Quad) 51
The Question of German Guilt (Jaspers) 92
Quincy Institute for Responsible Statecraft 115

rapid mob activation 101
Renaissance 30, 80
revisionist powers 78
Riefenstahl, Leni 115
Riker, William 106
Robinson, Paul 91
Ron Paul Institute 126
Roskomnadzor 68, 118
Rossotrudnichestvo organisation 35
rules-based order 21, 23–25, 36, 39, 45, 47, 52, 55, 57, 79, 129, 131, 152, 155; Charter International System 32; colour revolutions 32; definition 152; democratism 33; globalisation 32; liberal international order 31–32; Manichean inflexibility in foreign policy 31; postcommunist manifestation 30; rules 79; at stake in Ukraine 131
Russia(n): 2020 constitutional amendments 36; community of Russophone peoples 35; democracy 33; doctrine of military affairs 134; energy weapon 86; evil civilisation 37; intensification of cold war contestation 36; invasion of Ukraine 69; liberal democratic revolution 33; model of conservative nationalism 61; neo-revisionism 33–38; plural representation of national identity 12; power system 34; Putin as 'dictatorship of law,' 33; securitisation 65; self-evaluation 131; traditional values 35; transnational alignment of conservatives 37
Russian Institute for Strategic Research 35
Russian Orthodox Church (ROC) 35
Russkii Mir Foundation 35, 131
Russlandversteher 130
Russophobia 5, 85, 92, 107–8
Russophrenia 93
Russo-Chinese alignment 10
Russo-Ukrainian conflict /war 1, 5, 9–10, 79, 106, 109, 116, 131, 142, 152

Sachs, Jeffrey 93, 104–5
sanctions 10, 12, 51, 64, 81; adoption of Magnitsky sanctions 2012, 83; anti-Russian sanctions 85, 89; CAATSA 84; chemical weapons, alleged use of 84–85; containment strategies 90; counter-sanctions from Russia 87–88; description 89–90; EC measures against Russia 88; essentialisation of Russia 93; on Japan in 1941, 83; 'Protecting Europe's Energy Security Act,' 86; regional geopolitics 92–93; Skripal affair 84–85; UN, source of universal sanctions 90
Satanism 101
Sayers, Freddie 114
Schmitt, Carl 98
Scholz, Olaf 62
SCO members (China, Russia, Kazakhstan, Kyrgyzstan, Tajikistan and Uzbekistan) 49, 51
Scott, James C., 83
Sikmovicova, Martina 156
Silk Road Economic Belt 50
Simes, Dmitry K., 116
Sino-US war 5, 81
Smith-Mundt Act 122–23
Sochi Winter Olympics 64, 102
socialism 48, 52, 128, 145, 157
Soros, George 113
sorting, process of 10, 159
sovereign internationalism 19–20, 24, 29, 32, 41, 46, 52, 57–58, 61, 70, 80, 108, 129, 151–52, 154
Soviet-led communist system 25
Special Military Operation (SMO) 39, 66, 68, 94
Spengler, Oswald 158
Starmer, Keir 74
Stein, Jill 117
Stiglitz, Joseph 153
Stockholm International Peace Research Institute (SIPRI) 63
Stoltenberg, Jens 119
Strauss, Leo 31
Straussian neoconservative project 75
Streeck, Wolfgang 153
SWIFT 88

Taibbi, Matt 102, 114, 115, 119–20, 123–24
Telegram 118–19
Thatcher, Margaret 73

Third World 74
Thirty Years War 32, 53
threat inflation 105
Tillerson, Rex 54
Todd, Emmanuel 49, 53, 79
Tokyo Olympics 2022, 64
Toynbee, Arnold 158
Transatlanticism 69
Trenin, Dmitry 86
Trumanite state 16–17, 32, 55, 65, 105–6, 126–27
Trump, Donald J., 60, 62, 77, 84, 92, 103–4, 109, 123
Tucker Carlson 79, 112, 124
Twitter/X 111, 114–15, 117–19, 123

Ukraine War 3, 50, 84; 'cancellation' mania 95; and collective guilt 91–98; *Dozhd* conundrum 95; ethical dilemmas 96; justice through blacklists and sanctions 92; Moscow's security and other concerns 94; pragmatic realism 94; regional geopolitics 92–93; rise of an anti-Western policy 94; Russian economy 94; Russia's invasion of 18; sanctions, arbitrary and unjust 97–98 (*see also* sanctions); state disintegration in Russia 97–98; technocrats on money saving 96–97
UN-based international system 15, 45, 47
UN Security Council 12, 15, 20, 47, 57, 59, 89, 140
United States-based cloud-based storage systems 42
universalism of the Roman Catholic church 130
US Foreign Agents Registration Act (FARA) 112

Vatican's Congregation for the Propagation of Faith 106
Veteran Intelligence Professionals for Sanity group 116
Vienna, Congress of 1815, 152

Vietnam war 9, 72

wars in Ukraine and Palestine 135
Washington Treaty 16
Watson, Adam 78
Western-oriented progressive ideology 134
Westphalian settlement of 1648, 53
WikiLeaks 2006, 55–56, 126
Williams, Raymond 5
wokeness: Anglo-Saxon 140; 'liberal-left,' 158; US-style 149
Wonder Confronts Certainty: Russian Writers on the Timeless Questions and Why Their Answers Matter (Morson) 158
World Bank 16, 24, 40, 49
world orders: China's reframing (*see* China (ese)); clash of 15–19; cold war Manicheanism 15; empire 16; expansion of the Political West 24–30; 'hegemonic' peace order 18; Madisonian state 16–17; Military Keynesianism 17; neoliberal inflection of the commonwealth 17; Political West 19; post-1945 liberal international order 16; rules-based order 30–33; Russian Neo-revisionism 33–38; UN Charter 18; WTO's seven-member Appellate Court 17
World Trade Organization (WTO) 16–17, 40
World War I 11, 47
World War II 3, 4, 11, 24, 28, 47, 56, 105, 138, 146
World War III 11, 20, 79

Xi Jinping 40

Yakunin, Vladimir 35
Yanukovych, Viktor 12
Yeltsin, Boris 14, 27, 33, 93

Zeitenwende (Scholz) 62
Zelensky, Volodymyr 120, 134
Zyuganov, Gennady 33